EXCEPTIONAL

**Senior Student Affairs
Administrators'**

LEADERSHIP

NASPA
Student Affairs Administrators
in Higher Education

EXCEPTIONAL

Senior Student Affairs Administrators'

LEADERSHIP

*Strategies and Competencies
for Success*

EDITED BY

Gwendolyn Jordan Dungy and Shannon E. Ellis

NASPA
Student Affairs Administrators
in Higher Education

Exceptional Senior Student Affairs Administrators' Leadership: Strategies and Competencies for Success

Copyright © 2011 by the National Association of Student Personnel Administrators (NASPA), Inc. All rights reserved.

Published by
NASPA – Student Affairs
Administrators in Higher Education
111 K Street, NE
10th Floor
Washington, DC 20002
www.naspa.org

Additional copies may be purchased by contacting the NASPA publications department at 301-638-1749 or visiting http://bookstore.naspa.org.

NASPA does not discriminate on the basis of race, color, national origin, religion, sex, age, gender identity, gender expression, affectional or sexual orientation, or disability in any of its policies, programs, and services.

Library of Congress Cataloging-in-Publication Data

Exceptional senior student affairs administrators' leadership : strategies and competencies for success / edited by Gwendolyn Jordan Dungy and Shannon E. Ellis.
    p. cm.
Includes bibliographical references and index.
ISBN 978-0-931654-50-3
    1. Student affairs administrators—Professional relationships—United States. 2. Educational leadership—United States. I. Dungy, Gwendolyn Jordan. II. Ellis, Shannon E.
  LB2342.92.E93 2011
  378.1'97—dc22
               2010051287

Printed and bound in the United States of America

FIRST EDITION

CONTENTS

Foreword

I INVITE STUDENT affairs and higher education leaders and those aspiring to leadership positions to savor this book. Containing the collective experience and wisdom of many prominent higher education leaders, it provides specific strategies and competencies to guide us all in becoming more effective in leadership roles.

At some point in all of our administrative careers, we are faced with key questions: Do I seek more leadership responsibility and assume more risk? If I want such responsibility, how do I prepare? What distinguishes those who are successful in leadership roles from those who are not?

We all know that being competent in our assigned roles is a necessary condition for success. But it is not sufficient. Leadership requires seeing the larger landscape of the strategic goals of the entire institution, beyond divisional priorities. It also requires understanding how the requirements of modern society and the global economy set the context for our work. What are those requirements? I believe there are three. (1) Produce more degrees: The United States currently ranks 10th in the world in the percentage of our working people who possess postsecondary credentials, and we need to produce a million more degrees per year between now and 2025 to restore us to the number-one position (SHEEO, 2008, para. 7 & 14). (2) Challenge and support students to reach higher standards of academic performance, linked with modern workplace requirements. (3) Document that our institutions and students meet performance standards. This need to understand the larger landscape and modern context is reinforced by many of this book's authors.

This book also highlights the message that today's higher education leaders need a passionate commitment to student success and institutional effectiveness. The role of the student affairs leader as educator means engaging in systemic collaboration with academic affairs to create the conditions to ensure that our graduates possess the kinds of skills and knowledge needed to thrive in the modern world. The specific skills are often expressed as institutional general education outcomes, expected of all graduates. They often include such competencies as appreciation for diversity; ability to work in teams; ability to solve problems collaboratively; ability to think critically; and understanding how to innovate across disciplines, projects, and experiences. We also have important roles to play in fostering individual and social responsibility, self-management, integrity, creativity, enthusiasm, initiative, leadership, and global awareness.

We know that effective leaders must be able to move from problem identification to proposed solutions on their own initiative. Political awareness and competence are also important in understanding who our constituents are and how to serve them. For student affairs leaders, our obvious first constituency is students. But to be effective, we must understand that our colleagues in other major divisions of the college or university, such as the president and the board of trustees, as well as the expectations that flow from the needs of modern society are also key constituencies.

Most important of all is the understanding that leadership is ultimately about leading people and exerting positive influence and modeling the way toward achieving a common vision and purpose. Ultimately, people will follow leaders who possess the kinds of personal characteristics worthy of following. Many of these flow from intense self-awareness and insight into our own human relations skills and our personal strengths and weaknesses. Others require such personal attributes as integrity— the alignment of our behavior with the principles and values we espouse; courage in the face of setbacks; and determination to see our priorities through to completion. Stephen Covey (1992) reminds us that in order to build trust and teamwork, we must first be trustworthy. Enthusiasm and joy for the work are other essential conditions, since they will fuel the sustained high energy needed to perform leadership responsibilities.

There may be no greater role model for the importance of high personal standards related to leadership than Mahatma Gandhi. He practiced a single standard of conduct. The standard was derived from the absolute values of truth and nonviolence. His leadership was based on integrity and fidelity to those absolute values. The result of his work was the freedom and quality of life for his country during a time of tumultuous change. We higher education leaders also do our work in a time of a rapidly changing environment with rising expectations for continuous performance improvement. While we must understand that a sense of urgency is required to produce change, a commitment to nonviolence means that people need to be moved toward change gently, since the process of change is so difficult for so many.

So let us savor the lessons and wisdom contained in this volume. They will help guide us all to becoming more effective leaders in the complex context in which we find ourselves today.

Jack R. Warner

Executive Director and Chief Executive Officer

South Dakota Public Higher Education System

References

Covey, S. R. (1992). *Principle-centered leadership.* New York, NY: Fireside Press.

SHEEO (State Higher Education Executive Officers). (2008, September–October). Second to none in attainment, discovery, and innovation: The national agenda for higher education. *Change.* Retrieved from http://www.changemag.org/Archives/Back%20 Issues/September-October%202008/full-second-to-none.html

Preface

DIVERSE AND INSIGHTFUL perspectives on leadership are commonplace in the lexicon of books on business and education. However, few books focus on the competencies for exceptionally effective leadership in student affairs. Lest you think that coeditor Shannon Ellis and I began this book as a calm, deliberate musing on an instructional topic, I will share the impetus for the book and our first thinking about what we wanted the book to achieve.

I had read an article in one of the higher education dailies that quoted a college president explaining why there were not more people of color in the role of college presidents. The president said that most people of color who were administrators were in student affairs, and the route to the presidency was not through student affairs, but rather through academic affairs. I understood the probable reality of the comment, but my emotional reaction was that this pattern needed to be changed.

Soon after reading the article, Shannon and I discussed the need for a book that would focus on exceptional leadership among senior student affairs officers (SSAOs). We envisioned a book that would challenge the assumption that the academic route was the only path to a presidency and would reveal the competencies required of an exceptionally effective SSAO in a new world. Finally, we wanted to urge SSAOs to break out of their self-imposed boundaries and demonstrate that they are collegewide and community leaders.

Student affairs work has changed dramatically, and we welcome the responsibility. We are business people; architects; contract readers; negotiators; landlords; landscapers; and proposal writers soliciting funds and seeking high-quality in low-cost software packages, athletic equipment, food court vendors, and after-hours health and counseling services. We see this book as both a how-to and an inspirational guide to all who want to explore the expectations, competencies, and strategies of exceptionally effective SSAOs in today's context and, more important, in the future tense.

Thinking in the future tense was particularly important to us. We see this book as a prelude to the new job requirements and expectations of SSAOs from this day forward. The SSAO of the 21st century will be shaped less by the practices of leaders who came before and more by the wisdom of forward-thinking leaders who are attuned to the evolving nature and demands of students in a larger and more complex environment that knows no boundaries.

Upon soliciting the contributing authors, we were struck by the eagerness with which these busy professionals accepted our request. In this book, 28 higher education leaders—ranging from presidents to SSAOs to leadership experts—share the wisdom that comes with the experience of changing leadership roles, either by choice or circumstance. We thank these revolutionary leaders who so generously contributed their time and knowledge to this text.

We recognize that new times, roles, and responsibilities demand new competencies, and we hope that you find this work to be not just another book about leadership, but an opportunity to open up, recreate, and amend the work of student affairs as you explore being the most effective leader possible.

Gwendolyn Jordan Dungy

Executive Director

NASPA–Student Affairs Administrators in Higher Education

The Authors

Kathleen E. Allen is the principal of Allen and Associates, a consulting practice that specializes in leadership coaching and organizational change in human service organizations, foundations, higher educational institutions, and collaborative networks. Allen has written and presented widely on topics related to leadership, human development, and organizational development. She has coauthored (with Cynthia Cherrey) *Systemic Leadership: Enriching the Meaning of Our Work,* and is a contributing author to *Leadership Reconsidered: Engaging Higher Education in Social Change.*

James R. Appleton served as the eighth president of the University of Redlands from 1987 to 2005, and has commenced his two-year term as tenth president in May 2010. Since 2005, he served as the university's chancellor and then was appointed president emeritus. Under his leadership, the University of Redlands saw significant enhancements in campus facilities and technology, strong enrollments, balanced budgets, and record-breaking private fundraising. Prior to joining the Redlands team, he served for 15 years at the University of Southern California as a member of the faculty, as vice president for student affairs, and then as vice president for development. He received his undergraduate degree from Wheaton College in Wheaton, Illinois. He earned a master's degree and a doctorate from Michigan State University.

Dean L. Bresciani is the 14th president of North Dakota State University, a student-focused land-grant research university. He has served in a variety of academic, administrative, and student affairs roles at selective liberal arts and comprehensive master's-level universities, as well as three Association of American Universities research universities, two of which were distinctive land-grant institutions. He holds a doctorate in higher education finance with a doctoral minor in economics from the University of Arizona, complemented by a master of education in college student personnel from Bowling Green State University.

Jesus "Jess" Carreon is the interim vice president of academic affairs and student services at Truckee Meadows Community College in Reno, Nevada. He is the owner of Jess Carreon and Associates, a consulting firm that provides services in areas such as leadership coaching and training, strategic planning and implementation, assessment and enhancement in organizational development, coordination and implementation of capital campaign planning, and foundation visioning and planning. Prior to running his own business, he served as a community college president and chancellor at four institutions in three states, as well as a variety of senior-level management positions in community colleges for nearly 35 years. His degrees include an associate in arts from Grossmont College in California; a bachelor of arts from San Diego State University; a master of science in management from the University of California, Irvine; and a doctor of education in higher education with a specialization in legal issues from the University of Southern California.

Cynthia Cherrey is the vice president for campus life and a lecturer in the Woodrow Wilson School of Public and International Affairs at Princeton University. She is the president of the International Leadership Association, a global network of leadership scholars, educators, and practitioners. Prior to working at Princeton, she held administrative and academic appointments at Tulane University and the University of Southern California. She has published in the areas of leadership, organizational development, and higher education, and is a fellow of the World Business Academy and a recipient of a J.W. Fulbright Scholarship.

Marguerite McGann Culp, a former faculty member and senior student affairs officer in Florida, Texas, and Virginia, is a nationally recognized leader in student affairs, student retention, and creating cultures of evidence that include student learning outcomes. Coeditor of *Community College Student Affairs: What Really Matters, Life at the Edge of the Wave: Lessons from the Community College*, and *Promoting Student Success in the Two-Year College*, she also has written book chapters and journal articles on a variety of topics from assessment to team building, held offices in state and national associations, and received numerous state and national awards. She is currently assisting more than 50 colleges to reengineer student services, build cultures of evidence, design learning-centered programs and services, increase partnerships between academic and student affairs, and improve student success and graduation rates.

Charlene M. Dukes is the president of Prince George's Community College in Largo, Maryland. More than 40,000 students are enrolled in transfer and career programs, workforce development training, and continuing education courses. Under her leadership, the administration has embarked on major initiatives to broaden the scope of programmatic offerings and service delivery that supports student success and completion, attracting and retaining highly qualified employees, and transforming the infrastructure and physical landscape of the college. With more than 30 years of experience in higher education, she has served as vice president for student services, dean of students, director of minority affairs, and director of admissions in the community college sector.

Gwendolyn Jordan Dungy has been executive director of NASPA–Student Affairs Administrators in Higher Education since 1995. In her capacity as a national advocate for students and a primary spokesperson for student affairs administrators and practitioners, she draws on more than 30 years of experience in higher education. An accomplished speaker, leader, and educator, she has pursued a number of initiatives designed to enhance the association's role in public policy, research, professional development, and student learning and assessment. She initiated and convened the authors for the well-received publication *Learning Reconsidered: A Campus-wide Focus on the Student Experience.* She consults regularly for colleges, universities, corporations, and government agencies on strategic planning and leadership, and presents frequently at national association meetings, institutes, conferences, and professional development events.

Shannon E. Ellis has been the vice president for student services at the University of Nevada, Reno, since 1998. During this time, the dramatic changes in Nevada's population and economy along with multiple changes in institutional leadership and shifts in the role of higher education and student affairs required new found capabilities in visionary leadership, administrative practice, and decisiveness in uncertain times. She has worked in the field of higher education for more than 30 years as both a faculty member and administrator. Her contributions to the field include serving as NASPA President in 2000–2001 and the book *Dreams, Nightmares, and Pursuing the Passion,* which chronicled her first year as a new vice president of student services. She continues to impart wisdom for success through her writing, speaking, mentoring, and teaching. She received a doctorate in higher education and the law from the University of Southern California, a master's in public administration from the University of Massachusetts Amherst, and a bachelor's degree in journalism from the University of Illinois at Urbana-Champaign. Her interests lie at the intersection of transformational leadership and strategic planning.

Ellen T. Heffernan is a partner with SJG–The Spelman and Johnson Group, a retained executive search firm that, in partnership with client institutions, recruits the talent and leadership that defines the future of higher education.

Kathleen Hetherington's commitment to student success, community service, and performance excellence helped her move from vice president of student services, to executive vice president and then to president of Howard Community College in Maryland. During her student affairs career at the Community College of Philadelphia and at Howard, she promoted student-centered goals, assessment of student learning and success rates, and community involvement. As vice president for student affairs, she also assumed leadership responsibility for a major capital campaign that ended in March 2007 after Howard raised $14 million, $2 million above the campaign's stated goal. Under her leadership, Howard Community College received the U.S. Senate Productivity Award for Performance Excellence in 2007 and was recognized by the *Chronicle of Higher Education* as a "Great College to Work For" in 2009 and 2010.

Eileen Hulme, PhD, is the executive director of the Noel Academy for Strengths-Based Leadership and Education and an associate professor in the doctoral program in higher education at Azusa Pacific University. She possesses more than 25 years of experience in higher education administration. Prior to joining Azusa Pacific University in 2005, she served as the chief student affairs officer at Baylor University, George Fox University, and the University of Houston–Clear Lake. Currently, she consults with more than 20 institutions a year on topics related to positive student development and a strengths-oriented approach to higher education.

Joanna M. Iwata is the chief executive officer and founder of Paragon Management Solutions, an educational and nonprofit leadership and consulting organization based in Southern California. As a former chief student affairs officer on several different campuses, her experience in higher education spans more than 20 years and includes working on eight different campuses (both private and public institutions) with student populations ranging from 1,500 to 33,000. An active NASPA member, she has published several articles focusing on leadership, change management, and assessment. She has been featured in *Student Affairs Today* and *Deans and Provosts* for her innovative work as a senior student affairs officer.

Michael L. Jackson has worked in the field of higher education for more than 35 years. He is vice president for student affairs at the University of Southern California, and served previously as dean of students at Stanford University. He was president of NASPA in 2002–2003 and received the Scott Goodnight Award for outstanding service as a dean in 2008. He is a commissioner for the Western Association of Schools and Colleges, the accreditation body for California, Hawaii, and the Pacific Basin. He holds a master's and doctorate in higher education administration from the University of Massachusetts at Amherst and a bachelor's in anthropology, with distinction, from Stanford University.

Walter M. Kimbrough is the 12th president of Philander Smith College in Little Rock, Arkansas. As the first college president from the hip-hop generation, he is one of the youngest college presidents in the nation. Prior to Philander Smith College, he served in administrative capacities at Albany State University, Old Dominion University, Georgia State University, and Emory University.

John R. Laws has been the vice chancellor for student affairs at Ivy Tech Community College in Lafayette, Indiana, for 11 years. Prior to joining Ivy Tech, he worked at Hampden-Sydney College in Virginia, Hendrix College in Arkansas, Wichita State University in Kansas, and Indiana State University. He earned his doctorate in higher education administration at Indiana University in 1986.

Larry Moneta, EdD, has served as vice president for student affairs at Duke University since 2001. His responsibilities include oversight for student and university services, including student health and counseling, career services, housing and dining, student activities, cultural and religious centers, and auxiliary functions. Prior to working at Duke, he served in related roles at the University of Pennsylvania, the University of Massachusetts Amherst, the University of Michigan, and the University of Rochester.

James M. Montoya, vice president of higher education relationship development at the College Board, joined the organization in 2001 after a decade of service with his alma mater, Stanford University, where he was dean of admissions and financial aid, and then vice provost for student affairs, the university's chief student affairs officer. He serves as a lecturer in the Center for Comparative Studies in Race and Ethnicity at Stanford University. Though best known for his work in the college admissions process, he has a deep and abiding interest in public policy as it relates to education and global education. He currently serves on the advisory board of the Stanford School of Education.

Karen L. Pennington was appointed vice president for student development and campus life at Montclair State University in 1998. She received a master's in education from Gannon University, a master's in history from the University of Scranton, and a doctorate in educational administration from the State University of New York at Albany. She served as president of NASPA in 2003–2004. Her current appointments include chair of the NASPA Stevens Institute; member of the Board of Directors of the American Conference on Diversity; consultant for the National Higher Education Center for Alcohol, Other Drug and Violence Prevention; and member of the Board of Trustees of the University of Scranton in Pennsylvania.

Larry D. Roper has served as vice provost for student affairs and professor of ethnic studies at Oregon State University since 1995. He is coeditor of the book *Teaching for Change: The Difference, Power and Discrimination Model.* From May 2007 to September 2008, he served as interim dean of the College of Liberal Arts. He has chaired more than 25 successful doctoral dissertation committees. He has served on the NASPA Board of Directors and as editor of the *NASPA Journal.*

Laurence N. Smith is cofounder and senior partner of New Campus Dynamics, a consulting company for higher education that provides breakthrough solutions to solve the graduation crisis in America's public universities and colleges. He is emeritus vice president for university marketing and student affairs at Eastern Michigan University, founder and first chair of NASPA's James E. Scott Academy for Leadership and Executive Effectiveness, and recipient of NASPA's Fred Turner Award in recognition of his outstanding service. Smith's innovative approaches to change management, organizational revitalization, and executive development, as well as his lecture series on "Understanding Changing America," keep him in high demand as a keynote speaker, workshop presenter, and consultant in both the public and private sectors.

Barbara Hancock Snyder is the vice president for student affairs at the University of Utah, a position she has held since 1999. Previously, she served as vice chancellor for student affairs at the University of Nebraska at Kearney. She led the initiative to strengthen graduate programs in educational leadership and policy at the University of Utah and holds an adjunct appointment in the department where she teaches regularly. She has chaired the NASPA Public Policy division, served as Region V vice president for NASPA, and serves as president of the NASPA Foundation Board of Directors. She has been recognized as a NASPA Pillar of the Profession and has received the Scott Goodnight Award for outstanding service as a dean.

Brian Sullivan is the vice president for students at The University of British Columbia where he is responsible for shaping the student experience and broad learning environment at the university's Vancouver and Okanagan campuses. He oversees enrollment management, classroom services, student development and services, international student recruitment, residences, food services, athletics, and student government liaisons. He was associate vice president of student affairs at the University of Guelph from 1988 to 1999. He received his AB (biology) from Harvard College in 1968 and a master's of public health (hospital administration) from Yale University in 1970. His professional interests include approaches to increasing student involvement and leadership development; the preparation of students as global citizens; and new organizational arrangements for planning, funding, and delivering student services.

Marc Wais is the vice president for student affairs at New York University. Under his leadership, the university has won 14 NASPA Excellence Awards—recognizing excellence and innovation in student affairs programs and initiatives—in the past five years. Previously, he served as dean of students, resident fellow, and university fellow at Stanford University. He received his doctorate in administration, planning, and social policy from Harvard University.

Jack R. Warner is the executive director and chief executive officer of the South Dakota Public Higher Education System. Prior to this position, he spent seven years as commissioner of the Rhode Island Board of Governors for Higher Education. He spent 32 years in the Massachusetts public higher education system, five as vice chancellor of the Massachusetts Board of Higher Education, two as associate chancellor at the University of Massachusetts Dartmouth, and 17 as dean of student affairs at Bristol Community College. He is a past president of NASPA and is currently chair of the Executive Committee of the State Higher Education Executive Officers.

Sarah B. Westfall has served as the vice president for student development and dean of students at Kalamazoo College. She edited and contributed to *The Small College Dean*, a monograph in the *New Directions* *for Student Services* series. She has been very involved in the Small College Division of NASPA, including chairing the biennial Small Colleges and Universities Institute in 2008. She serves as a consultant-evaluator for the Higher Learning Commission and as a peer reviewer for the Fulbright Senior Specialists Program.

Karen M. Whitney became the 16th president of Clarion University on July 1, 2010. To the presidency, she brings nearly 30 years experience in public higher education and a deep commitment to student success and civic engagement. She served for 11 years as vice chancellor for student life and dean of students at Indiana University Purdue University Indianapolis. Previously, she served as associate vice president for student life at the University of Texas at San Antonio, where she also held positions as assistant vice president of student life and director of residence life; and held a number of positions in residence life at the University of Houston.

Cliff L. Wood has dedicated his career to community college leadership, serving in senior management over four decades at five institutions. He has served as president of the State University of New York Rockland since 2004, overseeing major growth in the college's physical plant and enrollment. Educated at Texas A&M University at Commerce, he serves as president of the New York Community Colleges Association of Presidents, and provides volunteer leadership to numerous organizations, including Big Brothers Big Sisters, Holocaust Museum & Study Center, and the Rockland Economic Development Corporation.

CHAPTER 1

The New World of Student Affairs

LARRY MONETA AND MICHAEL L. JACKSON

IN THIS CHAPTER we will present a fresh look at the leadership of the student affairs organization in higher education and challenge some conventional assumptions about the work of senior student affairs officers (SSAOs) in American colleges and universities. This discussion is offered in the context of rapid changes occurring in higher education: the emergence of distance education programs; the establishment of for-profit colleges and universities; and budget realities that are forcing cuts in student affairs on many campuses. Student affairs operations are being drastically reduced on some campuses; while we do not see this as a trend, it is a cautionary tale.

These challenges force us to consider the question, "What is student affairs worth?" Currently the vast majority of campuses value the contribution of student affairs to the education of students. That said, some dilemmas are inherent in our work, particularly during difficult economic times and in the face of rapid changes.

We hope that by sharing our thinking on the ever-changing role of

1

the student affairs leader we will encourage readers—those currently in senior roles and those on the verge of leadership—to examine the competencies they need for continued success and what they need to do to prepare younger colleagues for leadership roles in the future.

Our Experience

The authors are student affairs veterans with more than 60 years of combined leadership in higher education at large institutions: University of Massachusetts Amherst, Stanford University, University of Pennsylvania, University of Southern California, and Duke University. We have consulted at smaller institutions and collaborated with friends from these schools, but our experience has been at large universities.

Each of us was trained and mentored by some of the most renowned student affairs leaders of the past half-century. In our careers, we have overseen thousands of employees and dozens of programs in academic affairs, student services, auxiliary enterprises, admissions, financial aid, property management, housing, parking, food services, bookstores, and affiliated business enterprises, including hotels and retail shopping outlets owned by the university. We are professors of higher education who serve on regional accreditation teams for colleges and universities, teach master's students how to lead and manage student affairs organizations, and supervise students earning doctorates in education.

The Student Affairs Role

Both of us are dedicated to the national dialogue about the role of student affairs and its leaders at the beginning of the 21st century. We know that the faculty are the foundation for our institutions. They ensure the institutional raison d'être through curricula, courses, research, departments, institutes, and recruitment of faculty peers. That said, SSAOs and their staffs make significant contributions to enhancing the quality of the overall educational experience on campuses. In some respects, we are like the deputy mayors of small to medium-sized cities, responsible for the services and programs that create and maintain communities of common purpose based on shared vision, values, and commitment to excellence.

We are part of a cadre of educated and experienced professionals and specialists who handle numerous and complex administrative and experiential matters, including the affairs of students outside the classroom that faculty used to handle. The most highly ranked and dynamic colleges and universities have vibrant student affairs programs staffed by senior officers who help lead the academic enterprise beyond the classroom in a way that complements and reinforces overall institutional academic expectations and excellence. The evolving partnership between faculty and student affairs should allow institutions to adapt more readily to the changing external environment of government regulation, societal demands for accountability, increased competition for students, new modes of educational content delivery, and new technologies .

However, we would be naïve to suggest that a smooth partnership is universally the case. The roles, responsibilities, and effectiveness of student affairs programs are under continuous scrutiny, particularly in these tight financial times.

A RADICAL VIEW

Student affairs programs in the United States are not indispensable in colleges and universities. We wish they were, and we believe that our society needs the educational, social, and cultural programs we oversee to produce productive citizens and societal leaders. Pascarella and Terenzini (2005) and others have enumerated our contributions, but if student affairs programs were to disappear, students would still graduate and succeed, although surely in smaller numbers and with narrower perspectives. But life would go on.

Schools might once again organize activities for students around the faculty. This would require major adjustments to faculty work life, but it could be done. One need only look at universities in Europe, the Middle East, and Asia to see that higher education models exist that have no or very streamlined support for students outside the classroom (Ludeman, Osfield, Hidalgo, Oste, & Wang, 2009). Yet these institutions produce leaders and productive citizens. A country can develop an educated citizenry and a government and business leadership class in a variety of ways. We are not saying that student affairs will disappear from campuses any time soon (nor should it), but the rapid expansion of online degree programs and virtual universities that provide low cost and increasingly good quality educational programs puts pressure on traditional campuses with resource-draining physical plants. We cannot forecast how this will evolve in the coming decades and how schools will adapt.

If you are an SSAO today, you should be aware of these dynamics and constantly ask yourself if your efforts are helping your institution do all it can to provide excellent, cost-effective programs and services for your educational community. What would you and your student affairs colleagues do if your institution took the radical approach of recentering institutional activities around the faculty—providing resources only for activities that support faculty teaching and student learning? What would you do if your institution's online programs became so successful that it began shifting money toward virtual teaching and learning and de-emphasizing the campus experience; began selling buildings and let it be known, for example, that campus-based programs for residential education, fraternities and sororities, ethnic and socially focused community centers, counseling programs, residential education, intramural activities, and community service activities were going to be phased out or outsourced? What if your institution decided that a student could earn a degree by combining more online courses, professionally supervised internships, courses from any regionally or nationally accredited college in the United States, and study abroad travel programs that included enrollment at foreign universities? What is the role for student affairs in this model?

This brave new world of assembling college credits is emerging.

Students are seeking ways to certify that they have "advanced level education" and should be accorded the same respect and rights as students who earned their degrees on traditional campuses. In the next 5 to 10 years, online college degrees will probably be more commonplace and more readily accepted by employers and graduate schools (Ewell, 2009). The Western Governors University and the University of Phoenix are examples of higher education models that attract students who seek to earn a degree without attending a traditional school.

COMPETENCIES NEEDED TO KEEP CURRENT

As we think about the broad portfolio of the modern student affairs leader, we realize how much we need to stay in continuous learning mode. Many of us lead organizations that include important and complex subfields, including health care; counseling; housing and dining; career services; diversity and multicultural support and programming; transportation and parking systems; police and security services; and technology and information systems. We function in the context of the globalization of higher education, which demands that we prepare our students to compete with their peers from around the world for the best postbaccalaureate benefits—that is, jobs and graduate and professional school admission.

Although some campuses might significantly reduce student affairs programs or do away with them entirely, many more will continue to offer these programs. In the face of shifts in higher education and the issues new generations of students are bringing to campuses, Van Der Werf and Sabatier (2009) described the competencies SSAOs need to have. Both of us agree that it is paramount that SSAOs have a deep understanding of the educational and developmental needs of students, as many of our colleagues report working more with troubling and troubled students who are in need of medication and therapy to keep them stable and functioning. We also need to have a working knowledge of the legal, regulatory, and compliance expertise required by the Health Insurance Portability and Accountability Act of 1996 (HIPAA) and the Family Educational Rights and Privacy Act of 1974 (FERPA), and of the myriad related obligations in the mental health field.

We must respond to the preprofessional drive of students and their parents, along with societal demands for accountability. We must create environments that allow students to gain experiences that will give them more confidence to navigate in a turbulent economic environment that requires one to be even more flexible and adaptive. The career centers of the future will have far more complex and comprehensive roles in career "intelligence," pregraduation experiential sampling, integration with course and major selection, gap experiences, global opportunities, industry, nongovernment organizations, government agencies, and every other locus of employment. The demand for these services will grow among graduate and professional students.

Advocates for Our Institutions

The political dimension of our work has become increasingly important. Advocacy for institutions and programs must be undertaken with legislators at the local, state, and national levels, and with trustees of both public and private institutions. We must develop relationships that will lead to enhanced support. We should have a keen understanding of the factors influencing decisions that affect our work. Advocacy could include working more closely with institutional lobbyists at the local, state, and federal levels; testifying in front of state government committees that oversee budget allocations for our schools; or working directly with legislators on the development of bills that will benefit our institutions. We must have the wisdom and strength to know when and how to advocate for programs that can make a difference in students' lives.

Working With Parents

Over the past 15 years, institutional relationships with parents and families have changed dramatically (Merriman, 2007). Parents are now considered partners with the institution. We must become more effective at communicating with them through specially designed websites, newsletters, personal correspondence, phone calls, and other emerging media, responding to their inquiries and addressing their concerns. It is as if they are the clients of an investment firm and we are managing their portfolios: their children. Parents increasingly tend to see institutional rules as simply the starting point for negotiation, so we must make clear that we support the judgment of our faculty and staff colleagues to evaluate students and determine whether they have met the academic and behavioral standards of our institutions.

Managing and Leading in Tough Economic Times

Tough economic times mean restricted budgets and, in many cases, budget cutting and the shifting of funds from nonacademic programs to academic priorities. One response has been the recognition that the SSAO who oversees programs and services that affect almost every student must become a fundraiser—someone who can create an environment that encourages charitable giving for student affairs programs and facilities. It also means becoming entrepreneurs—starting or expanding business enterprises that can replace or supplement dollars from the college or university. These skill sets were not part of our graduate school training, but they are required on the job. We must recognize our own particular strengths and weaknesses—if we do not have or cannot learn the skills for this work, we must hire staff with such skills and expertise.

Both authors of this chapter manage large and complex organizations with hundreds of employees and budgets approaching $100 million. We oversee facilities worth many times that amount. Our preparation for these roles included years of incremental growth in functions and responsibilities, periods of role deflection and experimentation, and expanding perspectives on the roles and responsibilities of student affairs. Because of the contraction of higher education and the expansion of alternative ways to earn college degrees, our successors may have considerably fewer opportunities for incremental skill development and will need "just in time" skill sets to handle the revolutionary changes under way in American and international higher education. By "just in time," we mean that our contemporaries and successors will need both attitude and resources to adjust to immediate needs. Are we equipped, for example, to respond immediately to a trademark violation by a social networking site posing as institutionally authorized to deliver roommate matching services? As legislation and rules regarding student health insurance shift seemingly on a daily basis, are we equipped to deliver essential and legally binding reforms? Are we prepared to deliver services to students all the time and everywhere in the world? "Just in time" has real meaning to a group of students studying abroad in a country subject to an unexpected political coup.

The array of explicit skills needed for the new world of student affairs has widened and deepened along with the expanding universe of our areas of responsibility. Many of the skills essential for the next generation of student affairs practitioners have yet to be identified, but in the immediate future, we believe SSAOs will have to be better trained to oversee large and diverse staffs, better prepared to manage complex fiscal responsibilities, and far more literate in technology in all its forms and functions. This model requires more training in management, business, and technology than was offered in the traditional student affairs models of the past.

FINDING THE RIGHT STAFF IS KEY

One factor will not change: The future of student affairs, like the past, will depend primarily on our ability to recruit and retain talented people. Historically, we have turned to traditional student affairs graduate programs to provide our workforce. Student affairs career paths were relatively stable, often with entry positions in residence life and student activities. Related graduate programs focused on counseling, individual and community development, and familiarity with identity distinctions, multiculturalism, and other "people skills." Over time, as student affairs has diversified in terms of roles and functions, these areas of focus have become far too limited.

Increasingly, the unique needs of health care delivery, dining services, facilities management, recreation and athletics enterprises, media and communications applications, and the myriad other components of our operations require alternatively and more broadly prepared staff. The wide technical diversification of our staffing challenges us to develop new forms of connective tissue between and among functional areas to encourage and support a common vision and mission, cross-functional collaboration, and collective measures of success and achievement. The staff required for the "new student affairs" will be trained in graduate programs across a far wider range of disciplines and skill sets. Traditional student affairs graduate programs will become anachronistic if they do not adjust to these emerging needs.

FINANCIAL ACUMEN

Our financial responsibilities have evolved, and each of us now "touches" every form of institutional currency. We allocate tuition dollars; charge various auxiliary fees; receive and manage public and private grant dollars; raise funds from individual, foundation, and corporate donors; charge back to institutional service users; and manage and spend investment dollars. Our portfolios include oversight for considerable real estate with significant operations and facilities management requirements. We are expected to know how to debt-finance new construction and renovations; how to decide when to self-operate a function and when to outsource; how to rank capital priorities; and how to make compelling arguments for essential investments in academic support functions and facilities.

TECHNOLOGY

Everything we do today and in the future will depend on technology. The extraordinary and rapid progression of online education has changed higher education and will continue to do so in as yet unrecognized ways. Every physical campus will integrate e-learning into its educational model in some fashion; in fact, many are already leading the way with hybrid forms of teaching and learning. We can hardly imagine what technological skill set will be essential in the new student affairs, but it is absolutely clear that to be technologically illiterate is to be obsolete.

We imagine that nearly every student affairs functional area will adopt unique technological approaches. Career support expectations for students have grown, and increasingly more information will be online, with personal contact reserved for counseling and planning, perhaps provided by faculty, generalist academic advisors, or, as now, specialty career guidance mentors. Technology is already abundantly visible throughout our organizations: student organization management applications, medical records and scheduling systems, housing assignments, facilities condition and utility auditing applications, dedicated physical and virtual servers, and assorted communications devices.

Are we ready for cloud technologies; for the further convergence of voice, video, and data applications; for on-demand, handheld, ubiquitously accessible, and encrypted systems? Our financial and human resource challenges will be daunting and exciting in the new world of student affairs, but they will pale in comparison with the opportunities and requirements of the technological advancements.

The effect on student affairs is obvious. The development of the student affairs workforce of the future will require dramatic redesign of our points of entry and our ongoing professional development programs. Formal training and preparation of student affairs practitioners will continue in schools of education and related programs, with terminal degree preparation increasingly shifted to "executive education" formats. But these programs will be challenged by new online models and other nontraditional degree-attainment options. For those who will be engaged directly in student development, a background in the psychosocial development of young adults will remain essential; however, for many others, a rudimentary familiarity with this area will suffice. For everyone, in-depth understanding of the political, managerial, financial, administrative, and technological landscape of student affairs will be required.

We hesitate to draw conclusions, because doing so suggests reliable forecasting competencies. Rather, we have described movements and trends that seem to be offering clues about the emerging world and work of student affairs. The increasing regulatory climate, both state and federal, coupled with current economic and political conditions, guarantee further pressures to adapt. The globalization of education and the worldwide competition for students guarantee further pressures to adapt. The continued polarization of socio-economic capacity; blending of racial, ethnic, and religious identity; and student bodies that reflect the diversity of physical abilities, sexual orientation, veteran status, countries of origin, and legal documentation guarantee further pressures to adapt. Factors that we can't yet see over the horizon will guarantee further pressures to adapt. The new world of student affairs will require unparalleled flexibility and agility.

We have been explicit about the widening and deepening of certain skill sets that will be necessary for the future, but SSAOs should also be prepared in a general way to be experts in whatever is needed. Our careers and those of many of our contemporaries have been marked by unanticipated, often opportunistic, and occasionally directed role shifts—shifts that have required the immediate development of new skills and competencies. The new entrepreneurial and technologically sophisticated student affairs practitioner will embrace such opportunities and welcome broad diversification of roles and responsibilities.

Our success in the future also requires a bit of an attitude adjustment. The persistent and tedious debate about our roles and importance relative to the faculty must end. Students do not enroll in our institutions to engage with us and our programs and services. The essential nature of cocurricular complementarity is undeniable, but claims of equivalence with academics engender discomfort and distrust among faculty and deans. Student affairs—today and in the future—integrates institutional practices to provide an experiential overlay to classroom education and deliver essential auxiliary, academically supportive, and consumer-expected services.

"Student Affairs Profession?"

You may have noticed that we have avoided using the term "student affairs profession." Our aversion to the phrase reflects our discomfort with this concept. Are we a profession? Are we a collection of professions? Why are these questions pertinent?

We believe, in the broadest sense, that student affairs is as much a profession as medicine or health care is for those who engage in those functions. We presume that phlebotomists, X-ray technicians, nurses, cardiovascular surgeons, and hospital administrators have distinctive professional characteristics, associations, and certifications but coexist somewhat peacefully under the umbrella of health care. Student affairs, too, offers a large tent under which numerous professional practices gather, share, and collaborate. But the unnecessary and distracting focus on some distinctive view of a student affairs profession, with corresponding detailed competencies and accreditation requirements, serves only to trivialize our genuine efforts and achievements. That we are and will be essential will come from what we do, not what we call ourselves.

Conclusion

We hope this chapter will stimulate fresh thinking about our current roles as student affairs leaders and what the future holds. If, as the old saying goes, "what is past is prologue," we must be nimble and ready to adapt as our institutional circumstances and higher education delivery models change and evolve. This should not lessen our passion for what we do. It should inspire us to keep current and thoughtfully adjust our strategies of working with leaders of our institutions, finding new staff, and developing staff teams that are effective with each new generation of students.

Experience has shown us that the student affairs leader who refuses to adapt and embrace change will be bypassed by those who do. It has also shown us that we if keep students and their needs at the forefront of our thinking and are open to taking on tasks with which we have no direct experience, we will succeed and thrive.

REFERENCES

Ewell, P. T. (2009). *Into the future, U.S. accreditation and the future of quality assurance.* Council for Higher Education Accreditation, A Tenth Anniversary Report, Chapter 6.

Ludeman, R. B., Osfield, K. J., Hidalgo, E. I., Oste, D., & Wang, H. S. (2009). *Student affairs and services in higher education: Global foundations, issues and best practices.* United Nations Educational, Scientific and Cultural Organisation (UNESCO).

Merriman, L. S. (2007, Spring). Managing parents 101: Minimizing interference while maximizing good will. *Leadership Exchange, 5*(1), 14–18.

Pascarella, E. T., & Terenzini, P. T. (2005). *How college affects students: A third decade of research* (Vol. 2). San Francisco, CA: Jossey-Bass.

Van Der Werf, M., & Sabatier, G. (2009). *The college of 2020: Students.* Washington, DC: Chronicle Research Services.

CHAPTER 2

Don't Fence Me In: The Senior Student Affairs Officer in the 21st-Century Community College

MARGUERITE McGANN CULP

SENIOR STUDENT AFFAIRS officers (SSAOs) in the 21st-century community college must respect and build on their profession's legacy, while recognizing the need to expand traditional boundaries, develop new skills and competencies, and challenge their colleagues in academic and student affairs to reconceptualize how student support services are designed, delivered, and assessed. This chapter identifies the skill sets that SSAOs must bring to the table. It also describes their role in helping colleges become learning-centered institutions committed to student success. Finally, it outlines strategies SSAOs can use to help institutions understand the importance of expanding student affairs, empowering SSAOs, and stopping efforts to downsize and outsource.

The student affairs profession that emerged early in the 20th century

15

and expanded significantly from 1945 to 1985 could face an uncertain future in today's challenging economic climate. The profession whose members helped shape higher education by advocating for the development of the whole student, championing diversity, teaching that access without success is meaningless, designing programs to help each wave of new students succeed in and reshape higher education, serving as translators (and at times mediators) between students and the college community, and helping students apply what they learned in the classroom to the real world is being asked to outsource some of its functions to third-party vendors (Lipka, 2010). For the sake of students, faculty, and the higher education community, SSAOs cannot allow colleges to reduce their role or diminish the importance of the programs and services they provide. Now, more than ever, student affairs must be led by highly effective SSAOs.

HIGHER EDUCATION CHALLENGES

The college completion rate for American 25- to 34-year-olds, once first in the world, now ranks 10th and continues to fall; yet economists predict that 63% of future jobs will require some type of education beyond high school. Between now and 2050, America's K–12 population will grow by 19 million, and 17 million of all U.S. students will be Hispanic, but college entrance and completion rates for Hispanic students are low. In fact, college entrance, attendance, and completion rates for many groups historically served by community colleges (first generation in college, low-income, students of color, returning or retooling adults) are significantly lower than the rates for more traditional students (Merisotis, 2010).

In an attempt to address this challenge, President Barack Obama recently announced the American Graduation Initiative: Strong Skills through Community Colleges, which asks community colleges to graduate 5 million additional students by 2020 and creates the Community College Challenge Fund to finance innovative strategies that promote college completion, modernize community college facilities, and create innovative online software (Obama, 2010). However, efforts to respond to the president's challenge are being undertaken in colleges already struggling to cope with increased enrollments, flat or decreasing state funding, demands for increased transparency and accountability, and the challenges associated with shifting from a teaching-centered to a learning-centered approach to education.

While working with more than 40 community colleges in the past seven years, I have had the opportunity to assess the impact of these challenges on student affairs professionals and SSAOs. I observed many SSAOs who were skilled at solving day-to-day problems and keeping current systems functioning; some who excelled at inspiring and motivating but fell short when it came to implementing and managing; and a few highly effective leaders who were pushing traditional boundaries, helping their institutions reconceptualize student affairs, and challenging staff members to update their skills, refocus their efforts, and reinvent their roles. As I asked presidents, faculty, and staff to compare the skill sets of highly effective versus competent SSAOs, five significant differences emerged. Highly effective SSAOs share the following traits:

1. They are leaders as well as managers and realize that no one-size-fits-all student affairs model exists.

2. They connect student affairs to learning and the college to its students.

3. They understand the competencies and knowledge of skilled student affairs professionals and leverage these capabilities into collegewide partnerships with academic affairs.

4. They know how to build trust, create teams, communicate effectively, motivate and inspire, and influence the college community.

5. They do not allow themselves to be fenced in; they view themselves as leaders in the college and the community, not just in student affairs.

Exploring the Characteristics of Highly Effective SSAOs

Table 1 shows the significant difference between managing and leading. Highly effective leaders need both sets of skills: managing keeps the current system functional; leadership produces useful change. Strong leadership without strong management leads to chaos; strong management without strong leadership produces stifling bureaucracies (Kotter, 1999, p. 11). Learning how to lead and when to manage is an essential skill for highly effective SSAOs. Effective leaders also must understand that there is no one perfect approach to student affairs, especially in the community college, and that the student affairs model must be congruent with the institution's mission (Manning, 2006).

The more isolated student affairs professionals are from their academic colleagues, the less effective and more vulnerable they are (Culp, 2008). Conversely, partnerships between academic and student affairs tend to increase student engagement (McClenney, 2004); student involvement and success (Kinzie & Kuh, 2004); and student agency, success, and graduation rates (Kuh, Kinzie, Schuh, Whitt, & Associates, 2005). The student affairs division benefits when staff members view programs and services from a learning-centered perspective; the college benefits when faculty, staff, and administrators build and use a student-centered yardstick, asking, "How does what we are proposing to do increase the chances that students will be able to access, succeed in, and graduate from our institution?" One of the first tasks of a highly effective SSAO is to help student affairs and the college become more learning-centered and more student-focused.

One of the reasons student affairs professionals can become isolated is that few of their colleagues understand their skill sets and competencies. As Table 2 illustrates, student affairs professionals have the knowledge and tools to help students, faculty members, and the institution. Effective SSAOs have an accurate picture of their staff members' skill sets and the skills each needs to reach the next level; they understand the importance of helping staff members design and follow professional development plans that relate to the mission and goals of the division. They also take the time to educate the college community about the skills and knowledge within the student affairs team, to share research results about the effect of academic–student affairs partnerships on student success and graduation rates, and to advocate for student affairs. Highly effective SSAOs encourage student affairs professionals to see themselves through faculty eyes and to avoid the seven deadly sins of their faculty colleagues:

1. Offering the same laundry list of seminars or workshops term after term, even though participation is low.
2. Believing that student satisfaction survey results demonstrate effectiveness.
3. Using the "counting heads" approach to accountability.
4. Viewing students but not faculty as clients.
5. Not offering faculty the opportunity to evaluate student affairs programs and services or identify new services that might be needed.
6. Lacking a collegewide focus and sense of shared purpose.
7. Failing to demonstrate in a concrete manner the effectiveness of the programs and services offered by student affairs (Culp, 2008).

The ability to earn respect and influence the college community is a hallmark of highly effective SSAOs. How new SSAOs spend their first year often determines whether they can earn the respect and develop the influence they need to become highly effective. Many new SSAOs are tempted to request additional resources as soon as they understand the challenges they face, but they would be better served if they spent six to nine months doing their homework, building credibility, and forging alliances. Figure 1 suggests goals for the first-year SSAO. Figure 2 provides a checklist to help SSAOs monitor progress toward these goals and quick tips to help them save time and resources. Figure 3 lists the traps that new SSAOs must avoid.

Table 1

Managing and Leading in Student Affairs

Major Functions	A Manager's Primary Focus	A Leader's Primary Focus
Budgeting	Creates strategies and timelines for developing and managing the budget. Monitors compliance with procedures and timelines.	Sets a direction for allocating resources and managing the budget that is consistent with the mission of the college and the vision, values, and goals of student affairs.
Communication	Uses the need-to-know approach to sharing information. Prefers to operate through an orderly chain of command.	Uses communication to teach, build trust, inspire, and motivate. Employs a variety of communication strategies driven by a need-to-share philosophy.
Change	Has a low tolerance for change. If change is needed, prefers incremental change (evolution, not revolution).	Realizes that change is a fact of life. Works with the student affairs team and the college community to create a vision, and then empowers people to translate that vision into reality.
Morale and motivation	Believes that morale follows from job accomplishment. Prefers self-motivated staff members.	Believes in building a culture that emphasizes recognition, motivation, morale, and in helping staff members acquire the skills they need to function in the new culture. Skilled at keeping staff members committed to the vision and moving in the right direction.
Organizational structure	Prefers a well-organized hierarchy that produces orderly results for student affairs and the college. Prefers to lead within student affairs, with occasional side trips to communicate with academic affairs or to assist, when requested, with a community-based initiative.	Prefers to blur the lines between student affairs, academic affairs, and the college to align everyone with the college's mission, vision, and goals. Prefers to lead within the college and the community, not just within student affairs.

Table 1 *(continued)*

Managing and Leading in Student Affairs

Major Functions	A Manager's Primary Focus	A Leader's Primary Focus
Outcomes/ results	Focuses on operational outcomes that are negotiated with the college, translated into detailed plans, and monitored until desired results are achieved.	Focuses on strategic outcomes that support the college's evolving mission, vision, and values. Helps student affairs professionals and the college learn by consistently exposing them to assessment data.
Planning	Commits to long-range planning, timetables, and step-by-step implementation procedures. In implementing the plan, prefers to control variables, develop policies and procedures, and solve problems.	Prefers to gather and analyze data, spot trends, develop a vision, and move people toward that vision. Views planning as important but not as important as setting a direction and empowering staff to move in that direction. In implementing a plan, prefers to inspire, motivate, and remove barriers.
Resources	Organizes resources (people, equipment, space, and budgets) to get the job done. Believes in creating systems to help staff members do their jobs efficiently and effectively.	Allocates or reallocates resources to support vision and values. Believes it is a function of the SSAO to make people feel that they matter and that their work is important.

Table 2

A Sampling of the Skill Sets of Student Affairs Professionals

To Help Students	To Help Faculty	To Help the Institution
Orient students to learning. Connect students to the college. Help students manage the many transitions associated with college life and make sense of what is happening.	Provide faculty with an accurate picture of their students. Orient faculty to the diverse student populations served by the college. Help faculty understand and connect with these populations.	Provide the college with accurate pictures of its current and future students. Help the college develop and assess the effectiveness of strategies to meet the needs of these students.
Help students to understand and apply cognitive, adult development, and learning theories to their academic and personal lives.	Help faculty understand cognitive and adult development theories and apply them to the different student populations they teach.	Use team-building skills to help the college build and train cross-functional teams.
Help students assess their interests, abilities, and values; understand and use career choice theories; and identify and test career choices.	Help faculty understand the impact of learning and teaching styles on student success, and incorporate this knowledge into their instructional approaches.	Help the college translate theory and research into practices, programs, and support services that increase student success, program completion, and graduation rates.
Understand the role culture plays in the adult development and career choice processes, and translate this knowledge into programs and services for students who have been historically underrepresented in higher education.	Collaborate with faculty to design and implement strategies to improve classroom management, classroom assessment, student motivation, and student engagement.	Leverage cocurricular activities to help connect students to the college, reinforce general education goals and learning outcomes, and create a positive learning environment.
Design and implement learning-centered out-of-classroom experiences that contribute to the achievement of collegewide learning outcomes.	Collaborate with faculty to differentiate between and respond to stage-appropriate student behavior, behavior that requires further analysis, and inappropriate behavior.	Use knowledge of national databases to help the college identify best practices, obtain comparative data, and identify institutional strengths and weaknesses.
Help students apply what they learn in the classroom to real-life situations in the residence hall, at home, or in the community.	Collaborate with faculty to design and implement intrusive advising models, and help faculty and staff work effectively within the models.	Draw on experiences with authentic assessment strategies to help the college design innovative ways to gather data and document effectiveness.
Help students learn how to study, prepare for tests, manage their time, solve problems, make decisions, take responsibility for their learning and their lives, and acquire the skills they need to survive in college.	Identify risk factors and work with faculty to design interventions for academically at-risk students.	Use knowledge of research methods and measurement tools to build cultures of evidence within student affairs and across the college.

Figure 1. Goals for a First-year Senior Student Affairs Officer

- Evaluate your strengths, identify the skill sets you need to acquire, and design a plan to maximize your strengths and, if necessary, fill in the gaps.
- Assess the college's existing culture and the CEO's expectations.
- Create an effective working relationship with the CEO, college leaders (cabinet, faculty senate, student government association, etc.), and the student affairs team.
- Evaluate and strengthen the student affairs team.
- Engage the student affairs team and the college community in building a vision, adopting values, and outlining goals for student affairs.
- Identify the major challenges facing student affairs and the plans in place to address these challenges.
- Forge partnerships with academic affairs based on collaboration and cooperation, not just information sharing. Use these partnerships to increase the likelihood of success for students and the faculty who teach them.
- Design or update the existing collegewide student success model to increase student access, student success, and faculty support.
- Make sure the student success model is transparent, data-based, and outcomes-driven.

Figure 2. Checklist for Goal Achievement

Goal 1. Review existing data

- Sections of accrediting association reports, institutional self-studies, or quality enhancement plans that focus on student affairs (if less than five years old)
- Current student affairs model (if available)
- Program evaluations (if available) completed by students, faculty, and staff
- Organization charts
- Job descriptions, staff evaluation models, and goal-setting procedures
- Procedures manuals
- Forms and reports (including minutes of major committee and council meetings, if available)
- Community College Survey of Student Engagement, National Study of School Evaluation, or Inventory of Student Engagement and Success results
- Technology (websites, portals, applications to day-to-day functions, best practice applications)
- Other (data unique to your institution)

Quick tips:

- Enlist the vice president for technology and the vice president for institutional effectiveness/institutional research in your data-gathering and analysis quest. This will help you focus your energies, borrow technology and research skills, and forge working relationships with two influential areas in the college.
- Remember, there is no one-size-fits-all model for student affairs.

Figure 2. Checklist for Goal Achievement *(continued)*

Goal 2. Conduct informal data-gathering sessions

- The team at the top (CEO, cabinet, and faculty senate leaders)
- Student leaders (including club and association officers)
- Random sample of faculty, staff, students, and administrators
- Student affairs leaders and staff by area of responsibility
- Community leaders with a stake in the college (e.g., businesses and government agencies)
- Educational leaders with a stake in the college (e.g., K–12 systems and local colleges)
- Other (constituencies unique to your institution)

Quick tips:

- Develop a set of standard questions that you can use to jump-start the data-gathering sessions. This makes it easier to compare results and identify patterns.
- Schedule time after each meeting to record the highlights, identify what you learned, and list action items.
- In group meetings, bring your administrative assistant or a trusted colleague to take notes. This leaves you free to facilitate the session and to listen.

Goal 3. Gather additional data from internal (student affairs staff) and external (faculty, students, staff, administrators, community members) clients

- Design or purchase a needs analysis instrument to help you identify programs and services that various client groups consider essential to student success.
- Design or purchase a program evaluation/satisfaction with services instrument that allows faculty, students, staff, and

Figure 2. Checklist for Goal Achievement (continued)

administrators to assess the effectiveness of the major programs and services offered by student affairs.

- Conduct focus groups to identify strengths, weaknesses, and gaps in the programs and services currently provided by student affairs.
- Ask members of the student affairs team and the college community to identify best practice programs in colleges across the country that have potential to increase student access and success at your institution.
- Invite members of the student affairs team (all, or a stratified random sample if the college is exceptionally large or is a multicollege/multicampus institution) to participate in a strengths, weaknesses, opportunities, and threats (SWOT) exercise to identify the strengths and weaknesses of the current student affairs model, identify opportunities available to student affairs now and in the future, and define the challenges with which student affairs must deal. Combine the SWOT exercise with a modified Delphi approach to help staff members reach consensus.
- Visit each area, campus, or college to meet with staff and observe day-to-day activities.
- Conduct open forums on each campus that offer everyone the opportunity to review and react to data and share their vision for student affairs.
- Schedule vice president work days in various student affairs areas throughout the college.
- Use secret shoppers to test the various systems in place throughout student affairs.

Figure 2. Checklist for Goal Achievement *(continued)*

Quick tips:

- Help the college community understand the importance and purpose of the data-gathering phase. Emphasize the need to build on (or strengthen) the student affairs foundation already established at the college.
- Be visible. Communicate directly with the student affairs staff via weekly e-mails or updates on your web page. Reduce the chance that others will speak for you or misinterpret your motives.
- Consider inviting an external consultant to conduct the SWOT exercise to maximize participation and give the SSAO a neutral perspective.
- Look beyond higher education for organizational approaches, assessment strategies, and models that may work in student affairs.

Goal 4. Establish a baseline

- Identify collegewide patterns, followed by patterns that differ from campus to campus or college to college (if you are in a multicampus or multicollege institution).
- Identify student patterns based on subgroup analysis (e.g., ethnicity, gender, campus/college, age, or major).
- Invite consultants to evaluate selected functions: Are student affairs professionals using technology effectively? Are they creating an outcomes-based culture of evidence? Are they incorporating best practices into their areas of responsibility?
- Identify gaps that matter.
- Develop a clear working definition of the existing organizational culture (not what you hope or want, but what is).
- Review the literature (e.g., research results and best

Figure 2. Checklist for Goal Achievement (continued)

practices) to identify new programs and services that might work within your college's culture, strengthen student affairs, and increase student access and success.

Quick tips:

- College cultures are not identical. This means that ideas will transfer more easily than exact duplications of implementation procedures.
- Not all gaps matter, at least in the beginning. Identify and address the most important gaps first.

Goal 5. Keep the current system functional while collaborating with faculty and staff to create useful change

Keep the current system functional

- Build or strengthen the student affairs leadership team.
- Develop strategies to keep everyone informed about what is happening in student affairs and committed to supporting the changes. Inform the student affairs team, the CEO, the cabinet, faculty members, and student leaders.
- Appoint process improvement teams to analyze, evaluate, and recommend changes to major processes within student affairs (e.g., recruitment, registration, use of technology).
- Standardize student affairs processes and procedures across the institution (particularly important in multicollege or multicampus operations).
- Create one *Procedures Manual* for major functions within student affairs that is followed throughout the institution.
- Design and implement an ongoing program review process for major student affairs functions.

Figure 2. Checklist for Goal Achievement *(continued)*

- Design and implement a program evaluation schedule for major functions within student affairs.
- Design and implement research studies to measure the contributions of major programs and services to student access and success.
- Appoint a collegewide committee to develop (or update) the technology plan for student affairs.
- Develop strategies to share assessment results (needs analysis, satisfaction with services, program evaluations, and research studies) with the college community; to analyze and evaluate the information generated by the various assessment tools; and to modify programs and services based on assessment data.

Collaborate with the student affairs team and the college community to create meaningful change

- Develop a vision for student affairs that fits the data you have collected as well as the institution's mission and goals.
- Identify major obstacles to achieving the vision. Remove or neutralize these obstacles.
- Develop a one-to-three-year plan to implement the vision. Include strategies to assess and learn from the implementation process.
- Build and empower teams within student affairs and across the college community to help share, shape, and carry out the vision.
    - o Use communication to build trust, commitment, and a culture of change.
    - o Help team members acquire the skills needed to function in the "new" student affairs.

Figure 2. Checklist for Goal Achievement *(continued)*

    o   Create a culture within student affairs in which people feel that their work is important, is valued by the college community, and makes a difference.

    o   Keep people moving in the right direction, even when the unexpected happens.

    o   Celebrate successes. Learn from failures.

- Allocate or reallocate resources to support the vision and the plans for implementing the vision.

    o   Tie the new student affairs model to the planning, evaluation, and budgeting processes.

    o   Eliminate positions and programs that do not fit the new student affairs model.

    o   Reassign staff to balance interests and skills, update job descriptions, and revise annual evaluation procedures.

    o   Create annual plans for each area and each staff member within student affairs. Link the plans to the vision, values, mission, and goals of student affairs.

- Provide the college community with periodic, focused, easy-to-read progress reports on how the vision, values, and goals of student affairs are evolving.
- Highlight the contributions of student affairs to student access and success.

Quick tips:

- New programs and behaviors must be anchored in and respectful of the existing college culture. Do not assume that nothing significant happened in student affairs before your arrival.
- Effective SSAOs must function as both leaders and managers. It is not an either-or situation.

Figure 2. Checklist for Goal Achievement *(continued)*

- Change is messy, and there will be failures, but it is important that team members enjoy some successes, however small, in the first few months of the change process.
- Consider adapting some of the change strategies pioneered by business and industry (e.g., one of the variations of the Kaizen process).
- Remember, staff training, learning, and competence are the three pillars of success for student affairs divisions.

Goal 6. Create partnerships between academic affairs and student affairs

- Identify and take steps to close the gaps (culture, information, and perception) between academic affairs and student affairs.
- Work with the senior academic affairs officer and the CEO to appoint a joint academic affairs–student affairs committee to tackle one or more major challenges that the college faces, such as the following:
  o Design and implement an effective advising model.
  o Design and implement a model that increases student retention and graduation rates.
  o Design and implement a model to create learning communities across the college, especially in the residence halls.
  o Identify strategies to create partnerships with the K–12 systems in the college's service area to better prepare students for college.
- Pilot test partnerships between academic and student affairs that have worked at other institutions:
  o Course syllabi that include targeted information about support services

Figure 2. Checklist for Goal Achievement *(continued)*

o   Faculty teaching students in all entry-level courses how to study as well as what to study

o   Cocurricular experiences that reinforce collegewide learning outcomes

o   College Success or Freshman Year Experience courses

o   Early academic alert systems

o   Intrusive advising model

o   Service–learning

o   Student success centers/student success models

o   Workshops for student affairs professionals conducted by faculty (e.g., assessment strategies, writing rubrics, developing learning outcomes)

o   Workshops for academic affairs professionals conducted by student affairs professionals (e.g., classroom management techniques, motivating students, mediation and conflict resolution techniques)

Figure 3. Top 10 Traps for New Senior Student Affairs Officers

1. Failing to understand the existing college culture and factor it into the leadership equation
2. Failing to understand and shape the CEO's expectations for student affairs and the SSAO
3. Not taking the time to listen to, build relationships with, and then educate the CEO, college leaders (formal and informal), and members of the student affairs team about how student affairs can help the college fulfill its mission and achieve its goals
4. Moving too quickly or too slowly
5. Pursuing change for its own sake, or gathering data for the sake of gathering data
6. Assuming that the change process will meet with little or no resistance, and that all student affairs team members have the skills to implement new programs and services
7. Expecting the change process to be linear
8. Failing to communicate effectively and in a timely manner with student affairs team members and the college community
9. Accepting partnerships that are merely periodic information exchanges rather than pushing for true partnerships that address collegewide challenges and involve collaboration and cooperation
10. Requesting new resources before evaluating and reallocating existing resources

During that first year, SSAOs should remember that being visible and forging alliances in the community are almost as important as being visible and forging partnerships within the college. Because the mission and goals of community colleges are rooted in the communities they serve, SSAOs must understand, interact with, and influence these communities. It is equally important for SSAOs searching for organizational alternatives and change strategies to look beyond traditional higher education approaches and investigate what is happening in business and industry, not only in the United States but around the globe. Once again, "don't fence me in" is the guiding principle.

HIGHLY EFFECTIVE SSAOs IN ACTION

Martha Smith, currently completing her 16th year as president of award-winning Anne Arundel Community College in Maryland, is the classic example of a highly effective SSAO. As dean of students and later president of Dundalk Community College in Maryland, Smith helped craft a collegewide diversity plan that increased minority student enrollment, led a comprehensive study of learning, and set in motion a planning process that focused on both learning and student success. In her inaugural address at Anne Arundel, Smith challenged everyone to put students first. She worked with faculty, staff, students, and the community to develop a strategic plan that met community needs, built internal and external partnerships, focused on student success, and did, indeed, put students first.

Student success was an important concept for Kenneth Atwater, recently appointed president of Hillsborough Community College in Florida, when he became president of South Mountain Community College in Arizona. Using strategies he had learned as vice president for student services at Kellogg Community College in Michigan and Midlands Technical College in South Carolina, Atwater focused on creating partnerships within the college and the community. These partnerships paid off in increased enrollment, improved graduation and program completion rates, shared facilities (a library on campus built in partnership with the city of Phoenix), and improved fund-raising capabilities for a college in one of the most economically challenging areas of Maricopa County.

Kathleen Hetherington's commitment to student success, community service, and performance excellence helped her move from vice president of student services to executive vice president and then president of Howard Community College in Maryland. During her student affairs career at the Community College of Philadelphia and at Howard, Hetherington promoted student-centered goals, assessment of student learning and success rates, and community involvement. While serving as vice president for student affairs, she assumed leadership responsibility for a major capital campaign that raised $14 million, $2 million above its stated goal. Under her leadership, Howard Community College received the U.S. Senate Productivity Award for Performance Excellence in 2007 and was recognized by the *Chronicle of Higher Education* as a "Great College to Work For" in 2009 and 2010.

Hank Dunn, president of Asheville–Buncombe Technical Community College in North Carolina, was an early proponent of focusing on student success rather than student retention. While serving as vice president of student services at Sinclair Community College in Ohio, Dunn was part of a team that developed the Student Success Plan, a comprehensive model designed to identify and increase the success, retention, and graduation rates of at-risk students. The model featured web-based support and monitoring systems that won the 2004 EDUCAUSE Excellence in Information Technology Solutions award. His commitment to students, partnerships, and the effective use of technology served him well in his role as chancellor of Ivy Tech Community College–Central Indiana, where he built strong ties with local school systems and the business community, created college readiness centers to prepare students to enter college, and dramatically increased enrollment.

Beginning as an admissions and financial aid officer at the University of Pittsburgh at Johnstown, Charlene Dukes became intrigued by the potential of community colleges, accepted a position as assistant director of admissions at the Community College of Alleghany County in Pennsylvania, and never looked back. After a short time as dean of students at the Community College of Allegheny, Dukes became vice president of student services at Prince George's Community College in Maryland, where she earned accolades for her commitment to implementing and assessing outcomes in student affairs, creating partnerships between academic and student affairs, and connecting the college and its students to the community. One of the founders of the Community College Student Development Leadership Institute, Dukes also served on dozens of national, state, and local committees. In 2007, she became the first female president of Prince George's Community College.

As associate dean of student development and then vice president of learning support services at Paradise Valley Community College in Arizona, Paul Dale championed partnerships between academic and student affairs, pioneered the use of student learning outcomes in student affairs, and assembled cross-functional teams to develop strategies to improve student success. These teams produced innovative programs such as iGoal, a web-based program to help students set and monitor progress toward goal achievement; iStartSmart, to increase the chances that new students will succeed, and Get a GRIP (Goals, Relationships, Information, and Participation), to help all students succeed. In March 2010, Dale became the fifth president of Paradise Valley Community College.

Walter Bumphus, the new chief executive officer (CEO) of the American Association of Community Colleges and former chair of the Department of Educational Administration at the University of Texas at Austin, served as dean of students at East Arkansas Community College and vice president and dean of students at Howard Community College in Maryland before becoming president of Brookhaven College in Texas and then chancellor of Baton Rouge Community College in Louisiana. As president of the Louisiana Community and Technical College System, Bumphus used the skills he developed as a highly effective SSAO to focus on student success, build partnerships, champion diversity, design and implement a systemwide leadership development program, lead statewide efforts to create transfer articulation agreements, and organize post-Hurricane Katrina initiatives in affected areas.

Many highly successful SSAOs choose to remain in student affairs. Debbie Kushibab, currently vice president at Estrella Mountain Community College and previously vice president at Phoenix College, both in Arizona, established the Student Services Institute to provide a shared introduction to student affairs for all staff across the Maricopa County Community College District, championed partnerships between student and academic affairs, and co-founded the Women's Philanthropy Circle to support women pursuing higher education to change their lives. Kushibab also developed the student services knowledge and skills assessment that the National Association of Student Personnel Administrators uses to determine the training and development needs of a student services area.

Since 1995, Joyce Romano has presided over systematic changes at Valencia Community College in Florida designed to help student affairs become more learning-centered and outcomes-oriented. Changes include a realignment of student affairs, a focus on measurable results, an emphasis on faculty alliances, the development of a student handbook based on developmental theories and research, and the creation of LIFEMAP (http://valenciacc.edu/lifemap), which links all the components of Valencia's developmental advising system (publications, programs, services, and activities) to enable students, faculty, and staff to see the big picture and understand what to do—and what to expect—at each point in the process. Romano, a believer in the importance of crossing boundaries, worked with K–12 schools to develop School to Work, Dual Enrollment, and Tech Prep initiatives; with academic affairs to redesign developmental education, and write and implement Title III, Title V, and Achieving the Dream grants; and with universities to develop transfer plans and implement Direct Connect to the University of Central Florida.

Like many highly effective SSAOs, Tina Hoxie, dean of student affairs at Grand Rapids Community College in Michigan, used business theories and models as well as higher education research and best practices to guide the redesign of student affairs. Employing the Kaizen event process pioneered by Japanese businesses, Hoxie and her team designed and implemented an integrated student affairs model that supports student access, learning, and success, and created a culture of shared responsibility between the student and the college. The model includes redesigning existing programs and services (the application process, orientation, testing, and online services), aligning policies and procedures to support student learning and success, and creating new programs (an Enrollment Center, a First-Year Experience course, and IDEA [**I**magine, **D**evelop, **E**xplore, and **A**chieve], a learning-centered advising model).

CONCLUSION

Just as there is no one model for student affairs in the community college, there is no one approach to becoming a highly effective SSAO. However, these people share many traits. They are skilled at leading and managing, linking student affairs to student learning and to the mission of the college, creating powerful partnerships across the institution and within the community, and building high-performing teams that are data based and outcomes driven. Most subscribe to the "don't fence me in" philosophy, welcoming collegewide leadership roles and building support and respect for the college in the community, the state, and the country.

How many highly skilled SSAOs are there in community colleges? More than you think and fewer than we need. If higher education is to respond to the challenges it faces, that number must increase dramatically. Highly effective SSAOs and the teams they lead bring unique perspectives, skills, and knowledge to the table, dramatically increasing an institution's capacity to respond to the challenges it will face in the 21st century.

REFERENCES

Culp, M. M. (2008, March). *Creating and sustaining partnerships between academic affairs and student affairs.* Paper presented at the annual conference of the National Association of Student Personnel Administrators.

Kinzie, J., & Kuh, G. D. (2004, November–December). Learning from campuses that share responsibility for student success. *About Campus*, 2–8.

Kotter, J. P. (1999). *John P. Kotter on what leaders really do.* Cambridge, MA: Harvard Business School Press.

Kuh, G. D., Kinzie, J., Schuh, J., Whitt, E. J., & Associates. (2005). *Student success in college: Creating conditions that matter.* San Francisco, CA: Jossey-Bass.

Lipka, S. (2010, June 13). Student services, in outside hands. *The Chronicle of Higher Education.* Retrieved from http://chronicle.com

Manning, K. (2006, February). Student engagement, project DEEP, and models of student affairs practice. *NetResults.* Retrieved from http://www.naspa.org/pubs/mags/nr/default.cfm

McClenney, K. M. (2004). Keeping America's promise: Challenges for community colleges. In K. Boswell & C. D. Wilson (Eds.), *Keeping America's promise: A report on the future of the community college.* Denver, CO: Education Commission of the States and the League for Innovation in the Community College. Retrieved from http://www.league.org/league/projects/promise/download.html

Merisotis, J. P. (2010). *Challenges and opportunities: Future pathways toward immigration and higher education.* Retrieved from http://www.luminafoundation.org/about_us/president/speeches/2010-04-27.html

Obama, B. H. (2010). *Excerpts from the president's remarks in Warren, Michigan, and the fact sheet on the American Graduation Initiative.* Retrieved from http://www.whitehouse.gov/the_press_office/ Excerpts-of-the-Presidents-remarks-in-Warren-Michigan-and-fact-sheet-on-the-American-Graduation-Initiative

CHAPTER 3

Student Affairs Leadership
in a Networked Knowledge Era

CYNTHIA CHERREY AND KATHLEEN E. ALLEN

HAVE YOU OBSERVED that the traditional strategies of creating change in your organization trigger more problems than they used to? Are decisions made outside the institution complicating your work more than in the past? Do you and your peers struggle to synthesize an overwhelming amount of data into practical knowledge?

These are all symptoms of living in a world of increased connectivity and the resulting challenges of working in a world of geometrically multiplying data. Two major shifts are having a significant effect on how we work together, influence change, and lead our organizations. The first shift is from a world of fragmentation to one of connectivity and integrated networks. The second is from an industrial to a knowledge era. Both shifts are fueled by the trend toward a global economy and by the increased use of information technology and social media. In this chapter, we will—

- reflect on some of the implications of these outside forces for student affairs and higher education,
- describe the significance of the new, networked knowledge era, and
- examine the reality of our work in relationship to the traditional expectations our organizations hold of student affairs leaders.

FROM A HIERARCHICAL WORLD TO A NETWORKED WORLD

A hierarchical world view has its roots in Newtonian science, which describes a mechanistic worldview. As people began to harness the power of machines,they started to think of organizations as machinelike. Even human dynamics and individual behavior were measured against a machinelike efficiency. This kind of thinking has developed to such a point that we do not even realize how ingrained it is in our thoughts and actions. Hierarchies became a model for organizational structure because they allowed a few individuals to control and direct many unskilled laborers (Capra, 1992; Kuh, Whitt, & Shedd, 1987; Wheatley, 1992).

Most hierarchical organizations create departments or divisions (independent parts) that are responsible for specific tasks. The position managers are expected to control the speed and direction of the organization. The organization has distinct boundaries from its outside environment, yet it is designed to access resources from the environment as well as contribute to it.

The Shift to Networks

A networked world operates differently than a hierarchical world. The Internet is a wonderful example of a network. It represents the paradoxes of networks, as well as some of the ways networks maintain order. The Internet has a basic structure within which individuals and organizations can operate. Its structure consists of nodes and links. Each node is a center for a web of connections, and each of those nodes has web-like connections with other nodes. This structure is simple and yet allows for great flexibility and evolution in the design and content of the World Wide Web. Social media sites such as Facebook, MySpace, YouTube, Wikipedia, and individual blogs are examples of how many different actors continually contribute to and change the content. Within basic structures, the opportunities for individual initiative are endless. In fact, the locus of engagement and intelligence in a network shifts to its participants (Negroponte, 1995). They shape the system on the basis of their own knowledge and interests.

Characteristics of a Networked Worldview

Shared purpose, agreement on the organizing principles, and active collaboration are assumed in network designs. Many student affairs staff members have been called upon to influence residence hall cultures or do crowd control at a major event. We know from experience that influencing works much better than force or control. The more people who are intentionally nudging a networked system (such as a campus culture, retention strategies, or student development) in the same direction, the more we can influence the direction of the network and the outcome.

Table 1 summarizes the characteristics of fragmented hierarchies and connected networks.

Table I

Characteristics of Hierarchies and Networks

Fragmented/Hierarchical Orientation	Networked Orientation
Parts perspective	Whole system perspective
Distinct boundaries	Blurred boundaries
Linear causality	Nonlinear causality
Incremental change	Dynamic flux
Simple complexity	Complex complexity
Can be controlled	Can be influenced

These characteristics of networks have become increasingly familiar to student affairs professionals. Over the past decade, we have felt the increasing speed of change and the lessening effectiveness of control strategies. We have encountered more people who have opinions about how we do our jobs. In addition, we are affected by the blurred boundaries between our divisions and the community. Global, economic, political, and societal issues affect our campus and our students. Effective divisions of student affairs are adapting their practice to networked dynamics. Effectiveness used to be measured in part by the ability to be autonomous and protect one's boundaries. Now, effectiveness depends on the ability to develop and maintain cross-boundary relationships and see the whole system, not just one's own part.

Over time, higher educational institutions have been adjusting to the incorporation of networked dynamics into our traditional hierarchies. However, because we have not named the differences in dynamics between hierarchies and connected networks, we often find ourselves caught between old and new practices. Student affairs leaders can offer our institutions advice and leadership on how to adapt to networked dynamics because we have practice influencing student cultures, which operate more like networks than hierarchies.

FROM AN INDUSTRIAL TO A KNOWLEDGE ERA

At the same time our world has become more interconnected, it has been moving from the industrial age to the postindustrial age—also called the knowledge era. The shift in value from capital to knowledge began in the 1950s (de Geus, 1997). As the external environment became more turbulent and less controllable, an organization's ability to cope with a changing world became more important. Therefore, the capability to shift and change became more critical, as did new skills and attitudes toward organizational learning (Senge, Kleiner, Rovarts, Ross, & Simon, 1994).

Characteristics of an Industrial Worldview

In an industrial world, capital assets, mass production, and economies of scale form the basis for how an organization does things. In higher education, labor and capital in the form of quality faculty, tuition revenue, and endowments are considered our primary resources. The production of knowledge is one of our products, measured in part by the number of publications our faculty produces. The prerequisites, general curriculum, and major requirements set up for our students resemble an assembly line. This should not surprise us; many institutions were created and designed during the industrial era. *But what if we are challenged to change the basic assumptions of operation from an industrial model to a knowledge worldview?*

There are two good reasons to consider this possibility. First, we are experiencing greater outside turbulence, which is creating more need for higher education to embrace the challenge of change (Ikenberry, 1996). The following are some indications that higher education is responding to the challenges:

- growing tensions around learning versus instruction paradigms;
- experimentation in the way we structure our organizations (e.g., distance learning versus residential colleges);
- discussions of how we develop and sustain teaching and research-bounded disciplines versus blurred boundaries between traditional disciplines, and collaborative versus individual research; and
- debates about our role in society—for example, production of knowledge versus the need to develop citizen leaders, liberal arts versus vocational preparation, "diversity" versus "excellence."

Second, our students will be knowledge workers. To prepare them for the 21st century, we need to develop their capacity to learn individually and organizationally as well as their ability to think systematically. This will require a shift in how we structure our organizations and the pedagogy we use to facilitate learning.

The Shift to a Knowledge-based World

Increasing connectivity and networking mark the advent of the knowledge era. As social media, mass communications, the global economy, and information technology create ever-expanding webs of connections, a series of second-, third-, and fourth-order implications results. This is called the spiral effect of connectivity. As connectivity increases, it feeds dynamic movement within a system. This accelerating movement is the result of the radically increasing number of variables that can affect the dynamics of the system. This movement in turn increases the amount of complex complexity within the system. As connectivity increases the number of variables and movements within a system, it becomes more difficult to fully understand the system. This in turn increases the need for continual learning on both individual and organizational levels. Individual intelligence must be leveraged into organizational intelligence for the organization to adapt and thrive in this turbulent environment (Dixon, 2000). The organization that can learn faster and apply this learning to the way it operates will maintain a competitive advantage (de Geus, 1997).

Figure 1. The Spiral of Connectivity

- Connectivity feeds dynamic movement,
- which feeds complexity,
- which feeds the need for learning on both an individual and organizational level,
- which is necessary for the organization to continually evolve and thrive in a turbulent environment, and
- which requires greater connectivity.

The knowledge era is driven by the explosion of information and knowledge, accelerating advancements in information technology, new modes of social media, extension of our cognitive powers, and a resulting new worldview that includes systems thinking and leveraging intellectual capital within an organization (Banathy, 1993).

Characteristics of a Knowledge-based Worldview

Five characteristics capture the shift in the value and use of information in the knowledge era. The main resource is knowledge. Knowledge is infinite and the amount of information in our organizations is increasing exponentially. There are expanding mediums by which information flows through and into organizations. Social media and information technology have increased the ways in which information can be generated and spread throughout an organization. Student affairs professionals also need to think systemically and holistically rather than compartmentally about the information that permeates our organizations. In a knowledge-driven world, ongoing learning is critical at both the individual and organizational levels in order to transform information into knowledge and learning.

Table 2 summarizes the characteristics of an industrial era and a knowledge era.

Table 2

Characteristics of an Industrial Era and a Knowledge Era

Industrial Era	Knowledge Era
The primary resources are labor, capital, and material, which are finite.	The primary resource is knowledge, which is infinite.
Needed information is knowable.	Accelerating amounts of information lead to information overload and misinformation.
The flow and direction of information is controllable, leading to withholding information.	Expanding vehicles spread information, leading to sharing information.
Contained application of information.	Systematic knowledge.
Learning is sequential and task-specific.	Ongoing learning and integration of knowledge are needed on both individual and organizational levels.

These knowledge-era ideas and behaviors are not modeled widely in institutions of higher education. Much of the pedagogy in use reinforces individual generation of knowledge based on a competitive model. It teaches students to withhold information rather than learn cooperatively.

There are signs of hope, however. Many cocurricular and residential environments are designed to support the development of community learning, not just individual learning. When student affairs practitioners help a student organization learn to function more effectively as a group, they are teaching the skill of shared learning that students will need in the future.

Living in Both Worlds

The paradigm of a hierarchical world is one truth, one single answer, one best way. Taylor (1915), in his scientific management theory, wrote that there is always one best strategy. It is a paradigm of either-or logic. Its roots are in Aristotelian logic, which argues that a statement is either true or false, and in Newtonian science, which argues that physical systems are linear. Either-or logic is part of our traditional paradigm.

There are times when the traditional mind-set is advantageous. Yet, in this networked knowledge era, there is a significant downside to using only this method. These two paradigms are not mutually exclusive. Instead, our resources should include competencies for both. Leading in a networked knowledge organization requires different ways of thinking and doing.

IMPLICATIONS FOR HIGHER EDUCATION— CHANGE TO THRIVE

It is clear that institutions are adapting to the networked knowledge era. However, that behavior is often hindered by their design and hierarchical structure. Teaching is structured on industrial-age principles, putting us increasingly out of sync with the world around us. As the world becomes ever more connected and knowledge-based, higher education and student affairs will be challenged to develop students who can contribute to this world. This will be difficult to do unless we are willing to transform organizations and ourselves in a way that supports interdependence and facilitates learning. In this section, we will describe a primary traditional assumption and juxtapose it with the underlying assumptions needed for each new way of working. Then we will identify a new role for student affairs professionals to help their institutions adapt to these external forces.

New Ways of Relating

A networked world operates on links and connections. To work in a networked world, we need to optimize these connections. One way for student affairs practitioners to do this is to prioritize their time to build relationships. Effective SSAOs take time to nurture and maintain their network of relationships within an organization. Intentionally building relationships is key to new ways of relating.

Traditional assumptions. Relationships in hierarchical organizations are predetermined according to one's position and location in the organization. Autonomy is highly valued, which results in a narrow task orientation toward relationships. A few independent variables can predict many dependent variables. Knowledge and information flow through supervised channels within an organization.

New assumptions. The following underlying assumptions support new ways of relating:

- *Never underestimate the interrelatedness that exists within a system.* The traditional view minimizes the number of connections to which we need to pay attention. As networks and connections increase, underestimating interrelatedness becomes a liability. Ignoring connections hinders our capacity to anticipate organizational dynamics.
- *Variables in a system shape each other.* The number of variables in play radically increases owing to the openness of a networked system and the multiple networks that keep affecting each other. When these variables interact, they shape one another, causing

circles (rather than single chains) of causality. Networks are too dynamic for linear causality. Because variables shape each other, we need to think relationally.

- *Networks facilitate the flow of emotions as well as information.* Networks amplify everything—misinformation, powerful emotions, deep wisdom, and data with no differentiation as to their quality or veracity. The receivers in the network will determine the reliability and validity of these messages. These multiple receivers will construct their own reality regarding the messages. Therefore, we need to increase our emotional stability and trust in our relationships and ourselves to avoid misinformation and amplification of negative emotions.

The new role for student affairs practitioners is to influence the organization to practice new ways of relating. This entails optimizing relationships and connections in the organization and the external environment, thinking and acting relationally, and fostering emotional intelligence.

New Ways of Influencing Change

Change occurs differently in networks than in traditional hierarchies. Because networks are highly dynamic, change is a constant. Because networks are open systems, the number of variables in play increases, in turn increasing the level of complexity. Therefore, organic strategies can be more effective in influencing change in a network.

Traditional assumptions. Change is a controlled, incremental event accomplished by applying positional power and organizational resources. This belief implies that the timing and direction of change can be controlled. The person at the top of the network often initiates change. Change is a step-by-step process that builds toward a specific goal in a rational and linear way. Change can only be initiated from key positions within an organization and must be backed by organizational resources.

New assumptions. Networks respond to intentional influencing but not to direct applications of force. Nor are they controllable—there are too many variables. The following underlying assumptions support new ways of influencing change:

- *To create change, multiple persons must intentionally influence in the same direction.* Collaboration is both a prerequisite and a requirement for influencing change. These change collaborators must be strategically placed throughout the network and must work in concert with each other to nudge the system in a common direction.
- *Nonlinear logic is necessary to understand the change dynamics in a network.* The dynamics of a network are influenced by factors occurring at a distance, which can result in nonlinear jumps in the local context. The network is paradoxical in that it can both accelerate and delay change.
- *Change can be triggered from anywhere.* Change can be initiated from anywhere, because the resources that can be used to influence the system are available to everyone in the network. The resources needed to influence change in a networked system are relationships, powerful ideas, shared commitment to a common intent, and access to a communication vehicle.

The new role for student affairs practitioners is to influence change organically in the organization. Individually, this entails an engaged, active mind-set and a systemic perspective that targets the points of leverage within a network. Organizationally, it requires active collaboration directed toward a shared intent. Having others to collaborate with to influence change implies the capacity to build trusting and intentional relationships.

New Ways of Learning

In a networked world, learning is constant. Ongoing learning is how organizations adapt to changing conditions in the external environment.

On an individual level, learning integrates knowledge with capacities and practice. Being able to learn from day-to-day practice or to feed insights from skill acquisition into knowledge are ways of increasing "learning access points" to a networked world. For an integrated learner, practice, capacities, and knowledge build on each other to accelerate and reinforce changes in thinking and perceiving. On an organizational level, shared learning leverages the integrated learning of many persons into a collective organizational intelligence.

Traditional assumptions. Traditional assumptions suggest that effective leaders can fully understand their organization and the external environment. These assumption imply that not knowing is a liability for leaders.

New assumptions. In a networked world, the following assumptions support new ways of learning:

- *What is important to know changes—sometimes drastically.* Because networks are dynamic, they are never stable long enough for anyone to completely know the system. This means we will never know all we think we need to know to make a decision. Our understanding of what information is important will change as the network evolves.
- *We can never learn enough or unlearn enough—therefore continual learning and unlearning are critical.* Sometimes network dynamics cause nonlinear jumps in the direction or functioning of the network. When this occurs, one of the challenges is to forget the things we have learned that no longer help explain the dynamics of the system.
- *Learning is social—it occurs in concert with others.* Traditionally, our school systems have structured learning as an individual activity. In a networked world, individual learning will be, by its nature, limiting. Therefore, learning with others and sharing differences actually facilitates a more holistic understanding of the networked world.

The new role for student affairs practitioners is to introduce shared learning processes into organizational decision making and planning. This entails bringing our skills of facilitating shared learning in student organizations and residence halls to an institutional level.

New Ways of Leading

A networked world needs new ways of leading. Networks function like an infinite game; they operate continually, and the playing field constantly changes. Therefore, leadership in a networked world continually seeks better ways to adapt to changing conditions. Short-term effectiveness is valued in finite games, because if we just put in an extra effort and win the game, the organization will have a breathing space before the next game. Networks operate over the long term, and their survival depends on how well people can pace themselves for endurance rather than a sprint. Leadership in a networked world concerns itself with developing human resources that can provide continued leadership over time.

Traditional assumptions. The hierarchical assumption is that leaders are individuals who hold positions of authority. Traditional leadership assumptions focus on vision and direction of leadership and sometimes suggest that the means justify the ends. Policies, procedures, goals, power, and supervisors have control within an organization. Leadership in a networked world can only be understood through a systemic set of actions, not the actions of a lone individual.

New assumptions. In a networked world, the following underlying assumptions support new ways of relating:

- *Leadership facilitates the process.* In a networked organization, both the process and product are taken into consideration. Due to the connectivity of a network, the way we do things becomes as important as what we do. How we communicate, involve others, build community, and integrate our work are all important aspects of leadership in a networked world.

- *Networked leadership pays attention to meaning and forces of cohesion.* Networks do not respond to control strategies; therefore, we need to seek new ways of reinforcing organizational cohesion. Seeking and creating meaning in our work is one good example. Other intangibles such as values and purpose also help sustain organizational cohesion.
- *There are many agents of leadership dispersed throughout a networked organization.* Leadership within a networked world can be practiced from anywhere. In this sense, leadership has the potential to be abundant, especially if we think of it as nonpositional: not attached to position and rank. If leadership capacities are encouraged and developed, anyone in the network can become a leader.

The new role for student affairs practitioners is the development of systemic leadership. Systemic leadership goes beyond new ways of leading to encompass all four new ways of working. This kind of leadership weaves together the assumptions and practices of new ways of relating, new ways of influencing change, new ways of learning, and new ways of leading into a whole cloth.

Table 3 summarizes the relationship between the driving forces of change, new ways of working, underlying assumptions, and the new role for student affairs.

Table 3

New Assumptions and New Roles for Student Affairs

Forces of Change	Resulting Underlying Assumptions for New Ways of Working	Student Affairs Role in the Organization
Networked	**Relating:** • Never underestimate the interrelatedness that exists in a system. • Variables in a system mutually shape each other. • Networks facilitate the flow of emotions as well as information.	Influence the organization to think and practice new ways of relating.
Networked	**Influencing change:** • Multiple people intentionally influencing in the same direction are needed to activate or create change. • Nonlinear logic is necessary to understand change dynamics in a network. • Change can be triggered from anywhere.	Influence change organically.
Knowledge	**Learning:** • What is important to know changes—sometimes drastically. • We can never learn enough or unlearn enough. • Learning is social—it occurs in concert with others.	Introduce shared learning processes into organizational decision making.
Networked and knowledge	**Leading:** • Leadership facilitates the process. • Networked leadership pays attention to meaning and cohesion. • There are many agents of leadership dispersed throughout a networked organization.	Develop systemic leadership.

A NEW ROLE FOR STUDENT AFFAIRS LEADERS

Student affairs leaders have many capacities and insights to help organizations transform themselves into networked knowledge-era organizations (Allen & Cherrey, 1994, 2000). Relating is a key strength of our profession, because we have so many opportunities to practice bringing people together. We are skilled at influencing change. For example, our experience in planting seeds in the student culture to facilitate individual development is an organic change strategy. We also have experience helping students integrate their learning experiences, especially in relation to developing the whole person. While these are good starting places, student affairs leaders will have to let go of their constraining beliefs about their capacity to influence institutional change. In the world of academe, we often see ourselves as being on the margin, as being powerless. We need to recognize that we can no longer fail to influence the needed change in our institutions. Given the shift to a networked and knowledge-based world, our capacities are critical to the institution's ability to meet the demands for change (Cherrey & Isgar, 1998). Student affairs professionals must bring their talents to the table, make changes in their practice, develop new capacities, challenge traditional ways of working, and develop new relationships to influence institutional leadership and transformation. To do so, we need to develop new ways of relating, influencing change, learning, and leading.

Higher education can and must make a difference in our society. Student affairs practitioners have a responsibility to help institutions respond to the challenges facing higher education. Our students will affect the world in greater proportion than their numbers. Higher education needs to fulfill its promise to these students and society, and prepare students to live and work in a networked, knowledge-based world. Our students learn in part by watching what we do as individuals and institutions. To prepare students for the 21st century, we must transform our institutions and ourselves. The time for student affairs to take a significant role in institutional leadership is now.

REFERENCES

Allen, K. E., & Cherrey, C. (1994). Shifting paradigms and practices in student affairs. In J. Fried (Ed.), *Different voices: Gender and perspective in student affairs administration* (Monograph 16) Washington, DC: National Association of Student Personnel Administrators, 1–29.

Allen, K. E., & Cherrey, C. (2000). *Systemic leadership enriching the meaning of our work*. Lanham, MD: University Press of America.

Banathy, B. H. (1993). The cognitive mapping of societal systems: Implications for education. In E. Laszlo & I. Masulli (Eds.), *The evolution of cognitive maps: New paradigms for the twenty-first century*. Amsterdam, Netherlands: Gordon and Breach Science Publishers S.A.

Capra, F. (1992). Changes in management–management of change: The systematic approach. *World Business Academy Perspectives, 6*(3), 7–17.

Cherrey, C., & Isgar, R. (1998). Leadership education in the context of the new millennium. *Concepts and connections—The future of leadership education*. College Park, MD: National Clearinghouse for Leadership Programs.

de Geus, A. (1997). *The living company: Habits for survival in a turbulent business environment*. Boston, MA: Harvard Business School Press.

Dixon, N. (2000). *Common knowledge: How companies thrive by sharing what they know*. Boston, MA: Harvard Business School Press.

Ikenberry, S. O. (1996). ACE's new president: The challenge is change. *Education Record, 77*(4), 7–13.

Kuh, G., Whitt, E., & Shedd, J. (1987). *Student affairs work, 2001: A paradigmatic odyssey* (American College Personnel Association Media Publication No. 42). Washington, DC: American College Personnel Association.

Negroponte, N. (1995). *Being digital.* New York, NY: Knopf.

Senge, P., Kleiner, A., Rovarts, C., Ross, R., & Smith, B. (1994). *The fifth discipline fieldbook: Strategies and tools for building a learning organization.* New York, NY: Doubleday.

Taylor, F. (1915). *The principles of scientific management.* New York: Harper Brothers.

Wheatley, M. (1992). *Leadership in the new science: Learning about organization from an orderly universe.* San Francisco, CA: Berrett-Koehler.

CHAPTER 4

Type of Institution *May* Matter: The Senior Student Affairs Officer As Leader in Different Settings and Under Different Circumstances

A Big Place Requires a Big Picture

BARBARA HANCOCK SNYDER

I STARTED MY higher education career at a large public research university and will likely end my career at the same type of institution. Even as an undergraduate, I enjoyed the energy of a large campus with the many opportunities it had to offer, and I appreciated the sense of anonymity that came from walking across campus and not seeing a soul I knew. I have worked on a wonderful smaller campus, with close connections among students and faculty, but have learned that a large university better suits my interests and passions.

Many student affairs professionals aspire to be the senior student affairs officer (SSAO) at a large public research university—and who wouldn't?

Think about the opportunities you would have to influence the lives of students, to interact with incredible colleagues, to shape institutional policy development and sometimes even state law. Your colleagues would include you in important decisions and welcome your input because of the exceptional experience you bring to the job. You would be able to sleep soundly every night, knowing that you had accomplished a great deal and had a profound impact on your university. A job like that would be the crowning achievement in terms of professional and personal recognition and career attainment. Right? Not so fast.

Much of the work done by the SSAO at a large university can be anything but satisfying. You are often functioning in a highly decentralized environment, where silos of administration don't communicate well, where the faculty are more interested in their department and their individual research than in working with undergraduates, where state politics influence campus resources and practices, where athletics can control a disproportionate share of attention and alumni support . . . the list goes on. It's often difficult to measure your success, because the metrics constantly change, student leaders turn over every year, and much of our work is never really done. But fortunately, the SSAO is in a unique position to have an effect on all these challenges by keeping a few important core understandings and values close to heart.

First, any success we are able to have involves at its very heart the care and nurturing of positive relationships with those around us—students, colleagues, donors, the president, and other members of the cabinet. Having good relationships often enables you to smooth over small differences that could become major hurdles in your path to success. At one point in my career, I made the difficult decision to turn down a wonderful opportunity on another campus at about the same time that our director of athletics turned down a similar opportunity at another university. Until then, we had never had a very close or collegial relationship, but I took him to lunch and said, "You've committed to being here and so have I; what are we going to do *together* to make this a better place?" Since that day, we have been visible and collegial partners in countless enterprises to improve campus life. We have quietly set an example of reaching out to another area on campus to partner on initiatives that have been seen as widely successful.

Second, being the SSAO at a large university means you often have to leave behind the very things that led you into the profession, like spending lots of quality time with students, serving as a close advisor to a student organization, or serving as a judge for a student competition. These activities are replaced by representing students and the student affairs division to the rest of the university and the community. That means sitting in the president's box with donors at football games rather than yelling your head off in the stands; representing the university at countless on- and off-campus dinners, with nary a student in sight; and being involved in regional and national professional associations that take you away from your family far more often than you might like. These tasks and dozens more make you and your division successful, but you accomplish many of them by spending time *away* from student affairs. At a large university, we are usually blessed with a large staff who fill the roles we once filled and keep us up-to-date on what is happening on campus. This is absolutely critical—the SSAO is expected to know *everything* that is going on with students but will often need to learn about it from other sources. On the other side of that coin, your staff must understand that it is often more important for you to focus your energy outside the division, so you can enhance their resources, their influence, and their ultimate success.

Third, the SSAO must be at the table when important institutional decisions are being discussed. Every president has an inner circle of cabinet members upon whom he or she relies when tough decisions have to be made and implemented. It's human instinct to draw close your best allies, your most inquisitive thinkers, your most politically astute planners, and your most trusted leaders to look out for the best interests of the university. Whether it's a significant budget reduction, a campus crisis, a national event with strong local impact, or simply a complex issue that requires careful analysis, the SSAO *must* be in the conversation as it occurs to affect the outcome. SSAOs are uniquely qualified to serve in this capacity, as we have been problem solvers throughout our professional lives. Your colleagues and your staff will know whether you are one of the president's trusted allies; if you are not, you need to have candid conversations about how to make yourself a more valuable member of the institutional leadership team. As one of my colleagues says, "If you want to be an equal player, you have to act like you belong on the team!"

Fourth, BIG PICTURE, BIG PICTURE, BIG PICTURE! You are, of course, ultimately responsible for your own areas, but it is essential that you prove to others *daily* that you know and care about their share of the university as well. Take time to understand the issues confronting faculty at various points in their careers; to listen to the facilities staff when they want to close an access road to campus on the first day of fall classes; to appreciate the needs of the dean of fine arts when he asks you to help increase student funding; to make sure an athletic coach knows you really care about a student athlete even though you have to discipline her. You must also look beyond the daily issues that scream for your attention in favor of addressing the sometimes quieter but more important items that can enrich the life of the institution in the long run. It is often easier to be caught up in the moment of a crucial administrative response than to look for and solve the underlying cause of a problem. Your value as an administrative leader will be directly correlated with your ability to see the big picture.

Fifth, you can serve your students, staff, and university community by keeping yourself informed about state, regional, and national trends and best practices. New developments in the field (e.g., campus safety, student mental health, advances in technology and assessment) are almost always followed by a reaction. This might be the passage of new laws, calls for accountability from the public and our governing boards, changes in staffing needs, or responsiveness to media inquiries. The SSAO is often expected to be the public face of the university—you should be well informed not only about what is happening on your own campus but about what is occurring at other institutions. For example, my university is currently being greatly affected by the actions taken by a sister institution in response to a student death. Information is a powerful tool to increase your effectiveness and influence.

My career has not involved significant geographic changes. I have worked at three great universities—for 13 years, 11 years, and 11 years, respectively—and have been an SSAO for 24 years. Serving as a senior campus leader means being directly accountable to the president, and thus subject to the president's expectations. I have worked with and for chief executive officers whom I respected greatly and a few with whom I had very difficult relationships. My advice is to always make sure that you are professionally prepared to leave if you feel you must. If you cannot trust and respect your boss, your own integrity and self-worth will diminish. Life is too short to stay in a position in which you are uncomfortable and unhappy. Your supervisor deserves your loyalty, and only you can determine if it has been earned.

One of the great joys of being the SSAO at a research university is the opportunity to teach the student affairs administration class in our graduate school of education. I am immediately refreshed and energized when I leave my administrative office and return to the place that is the soul of a great university: the classroom. A favorite book that I use in the class is *The Art and Practical Wisdom of Student Affairs Leadership* (Dalton & McClinton, 2002). In it, Jon Dalton describes "practical wisdom which combines sound knowledge and good judgment, and is the art of effective student affairs practice" (p. 3). The statement resonates, because serving as an SSAO allows us to develop cumulative skills and competencies that are the result of practicing our professional craft and knowing how to respond effectively to most issues that confront us. After 35 years of practice, I still encounter situations that are new and decisions that require a different perspective, but I can rely on the experience and wisdom that I have developed over a lifetime of professional commitment. There is no finer calling than a career in student affairs—what a blessing to have made it my professional and personal home.

REFERENCE

Dalton, J. C., and McClinton, M. (Eds.). (2002). *The art and practical wisdom of student affairs leadership.* San Francisco, CA: Jossey-Bass.

Success As a Small College Senior Student Affairs Officer

Sarah B. Westfall

MANY OF THE competencies necessary for success as a small college or university SSAO (senior student affairs officer) are universal. A strong work ethic, professionalism, and integrity are three characteristics that will serve any SSAO well. However, in this section I focus on the competencies necessary for success at a small college or university. I define "small" as a college or university with an enrollment of 5,000 students or fewer and "SSAO" as the senior student affairs officer, regardless of title.

Small colleges are terrifically diverse—some serve fewer than 100 students, some are tightly connected to religious denominations or native/tribal nations, some are richly endowed, some are single-sex, some serve traditional-aged students exclusively, some are in urban areas, some are publicly funded, some have a strong history of advocacy and social justice, some are extremely progressive, some are homogenous, some have open admissions, and many are just the opposite of each of these characteristics. This variation leads to a central competency requirement for small college SSAOs: understanding of and commitment to institutional mission.

While many institutional missions have similar characteristics (inspirational and aspirational language that invokes the highest ideals of education, for example), small institutions are often tangibly mission-driven. To be effective internally and externally, a tribal college SSAO must understand and be committed to the mission of the institution. The SSAO of a small public liberal arts campus that is part of a state system must understand and be committed to its mission. Small college SSAOs are officers of the institution, legally and in terms of ethical and moral leadership. Small institutions require that leaders perform their work with the mission as the ultimate guide and arbiter for institutional decision making. The uniquely strong and historically important identities, missions, and work of small institutions (sometimes referred to as "distinctiveness") require fidelity on the part of leaders. If you cannot support the mission of your small college, you are doing yourself and the institution a disservice by working there. The match between institutional mission and personal and professional values is essential at small colleges.

Small college campuses are highly relational, and relationship skills are a key competency for SSAOs. The "intensely personal and communal nature" (Colwell, 2006, p. 56) of many small college environments requires that SSAOs have strong interpersonal skills, build and maintain relationships across and off campus, and manage the inevitable conflicts of interest that will arise in a small environment. The size of the college means that there are few administrative and staff layers between the SSAO and everyone else: students, staff, parents, faculty, institutional colleagues, trustees, community members, media, civil authorities, and others. Burning bridges is a real risk in small college environments and is a luxury that SSAOs can rarely afford. Excellent relationship skills are necessary to manage the range and quality of these relationships. SSAOs must be prepared for a great deal of contact with a wide range of constituents. A key competency is to understand the importance of these relationships, have the requisite skills to maintain them, and, if possible, enjoy them.

Small colleges are "human scale" in many important ways—you will probably know the custodian and know, for example, that he has suffered a death in his family—so you must have a well-informed institutional perspective. A well-informed institutional perspective is different from understanding the mission in that it focuses on functional and operational matters. The *work* of the whole must be in view at every step—you must care as much about what happens with admissions and academic affairs, for example, as you care about your own division. While small colleges differ in their degree of internal competition, hierarchy, collaboration, and so on, good SSAOs focus on the elements that support and advance the work of the institution as a whole. An understaffed financial aid office or poor academic advising are as important to a competent small college SSAO as a lack of resources in his or her own division. In other words, you need to know as much horizontally across the divisions of the institution as vertically within your own division, and you must make decisions that are driven by a commitment to the effectiveness of the whole.

SSAOs must be competent as generalists, and they must be able to "change the channel" quickly, depending upon the work before them. Small college SSAOs are often closely tied into the day-to-day operational matters in the division while at the same time involved in institutional planning, work with the trustees or legislature, and budget processes. Several years ago, a senior student at the small college campus where I worked committed suicide early in the academic year. In the midst of dealing with the local authorities, our legal counsel, the press, the campus community, roommates and their parents, and other sad matters related to that event, I was approached by a student who was unhappy with his meal plan. This illustrates the range of very high-level work that occurs in close proximity to mundane efforts for many small college SSAOs. Their work is broad. An essential competency is appreciating the range of the work, seeing it as one of the advantages of a small place, and being patient with this reality.

Obviously, liking students is a key competency. Since many small college SSAOs stay fairly close to the student experience, it is especially important that they continue to enjoy students. This requires an ongoing level of interest and investment in perennial issues that can become less novel over time: alcohol, parking, sexual misconduct, crisis response, dining, and the like. It is important to remember that although you may have dealt with a particular issue numerous times, it may be the first time an individual student has experienced it. Liking students a lot will sustain you during the repetitious moments.

The historic role of the SSAO as a student advocate is particularly important at the small college. Scale alone often militates against the development of a critical mass of certain student populations (e.g., veterans, transgender folks, children of migrant workers). It is imperative that small college SSAOs view students with an advocate's lens so that all students have the best chance of having a robust college experience. At small colleges, cost-benefit and return-on-investment analyses must be framed at the level of the individual student. Students who are singular or part of very small populations on campus require that SSAOs see, hear, and act for them.

Good small college SSAOs are comfortable working with and learning from their senior colleagues. The best way to learn about budgeting, fundraising, admissions, and academic affairs is to take advantage of the expertise of senior colleagues at the same institution. The common frame of reference (one's employing institution) provides a good way to understand a variety of issues in a real-world context. Small colleges may offer a higher level of collaboration and deliberation in decision making than larger ones, and the opportunity to learn about the work of other divisions (how problems are approached, basic assumptions, best practices, and so on) is invaluable. The opportunity for SSAOs to inform the perspective of senior colleagues is also significant at a small college. Finding opportunities to inform colleagues and institutional decision making is as important as willingness to learn. This discourse is what enables real institutional change.

Competent staff recruitment and supervision can make the difference between success and failure for a small college SSAO. Many small colleges are located in rural areas, many have young staff members, and many have limited opportunities for upward mobility within the institution. As a result, SSAOs may work frequently and hard at recruiting entry-level staff members, who then require much supervision (as most of us did early in our careers). Recruiting and interviewing freshly minted master's graduates or "green deans" (new bachelor's graduates) is a fact of life for many small college SSAOs. Concurrently, there are typically at least a few long-serving staff members who may require a very different supervisory approach. Ongoing contact with early-career professionals as well as more seasoned colleagues is one of the best and most challenging things about a small college. The ability to see this reality as an advantage (it keeps one grounded and in touch with the frontline work in very helpful ways) is important. The challenges of recruiting staff at all levels (especially to rural areas) and the knowledge that many good staff members will have to "move out to move up" adds to the need for competent staff recruitment and supervision.

Most small college SSAOs do not have an assistant or chief of staff to whom daily operations and special projects can be delegated. The ability to do a lot of work with a small staff and limited resources is another key competency. The increasing complexity of student life—legal and regulatory mandates, ever more involved parents, "new" diversity (e.g., learning differences, neuro status, physical abilities, mental health status), campus security expectations, technology-related behavioral concerns, and increased academic misconduct, to name a few—affects every SSAO. Small college SSAOs and their staffs are required to meet all the demands and changes in the environment, typically with no increase in resources and limited access to experts. To do this, SSAOs need to be effective at prioritizing their own time and at understanding and cultivating the ability of their staff to respond to new demands. This situation requires the SSAO to stay reasonably abreast of professional developments, student trends, and external requirements.

A final competency for small college SSAOs is to fully understand the financial resource context for their institution and their work. Some small colleges are extraordinarily wealthy, while others depend almost entirely on enrollment. Good SSAOs understand how resources flow through the institution, how to collaborate with other entities to leverage resources, and how to secure additional resources when they are needed. Understanding the institutional budget process, the recent history of fiscal decisions (e.g., staffing increases or decreases, employee benefits, capital projects, grants), and identified needs across campus is necessary to engage fully and appropriately in resource-related decisions. Small college SSAOs can have a great deal of influence in these decisions if they are informed and prepared. Good small college SSAOs invest time in learning and understanding campus financial resources.

While competent SSAOs share many characteristics regardless of institution type, small college SSAOs are best served by a particular set of general competencies. They must understand and be committed to the institution's mission, must have excellent relationship skills, must understand the functional and operational work of the institution as a whole, must attend to a wide range of day-to-day operational and high-level institutional responsibilities, must like students and enjoy spending time with them, must advocate for all students all the time, must effectively recruit and supervise staff at all levels and stages of their careers, must be able to do a lot of work in an increasingly complex and staff-limited environment, and must fully understand and engage in the institution's financial processes. The proximity of a small college SSAO to all parts of the institution and its constituents, and the scale of the environment, require a unique skill set and temperament. When the appropriate competencies are in place, there is no better setting for student affairs work.

Reference

Colwell, B. W. (2006). "Partners in a community of learners: Student and academic affairs at small colleges." In S. B. Westfall (Ed.), *The small college dean* (New directions for student services, no.116). San Francisco, CA: Jossey-Bass, 53–66.

Competencies for the Community College Senior Student Affairs Officer

JOHN R. LAWS

THE ROLE OF community colleges in the development of students is recognized as an important component in the economic growth of the local area and the nation. Students must be able to progress through coursework and college experiences on a variety of pathways, while dealing with complex life issues. Essential to students' success is the learned ability to cope, progress, and successfully complete their educational journey.

Community college administrators and institutional practices play a vital role in supporting these students. The work is challenging but also exciting and rewarding. Compared with their peers, student affairs units at community colleges are more likely to include enrollment management structures such as admissions, registration, and financial aid, in addition to the typical student life, disability support, wellness, and judicial affairs. The size of the community college and of the surrounding community has a major influence on programming and services, which, in turn, affect the organizational structure of the institution. In more rural areas, more services are often necessary to meet the needs and expectations of the student body. These services may include institutional identification of community based programming and volunteer opportunities, service–learning choices, career employment assistance, child care options, and more. The large percentage of part-time students and lower number of community resources combine to make providing cocurricular learning options and support services for rural students more challenging.

The traditional-aged college student population will decline in the next decade, but as older, well-educated adults retire from the workforce, community colleges will be called upon to improve educational attainment among undereducated adults to meet the knowledge and skills gap (Galagan, 2010). At the same time, the skills and knowledge required of student affairs administrators is also changing. For example, the increasing complexity of global economies and issues, rapidly changing priorities and initiatives, the ever-shifting resource base, and security issues make the administrator's role different than it was in the past. Senior student affairs officers (SSAOs) must learn to think and act entrepreneurially, instilling the vision and providing the leadership for activities, programs, policies, and services that will enhance student success.

THINKING AND ACTING AS ENTREPRENEURS

Entrepreneurial leadership is the directed application of innovation, using risk and uncertainty as opportunities for creativity. Student affairs professionals, especially in the community college setting, must be able to think in these terms and apply principles differently than their predecessors. The decision-making processes of the past are outdated and no longer respond to the demands of today's world.

Effective communication is equally critical to successful leadership. If employees are unclear about the vision of the college or the SSAO, or receive mixed messages, they will be unable to focus on achieving goals. Conversely, if the SSAO clarifies the vision and goals, and reinforces them over time with a consistent message, the information will become ingrained in the employees. In addition, leaders in the community college should be more in touch with and responsive to the needs of the local area by cooperating on issues such as local economic development, community problem solving, and shared resources.

The most effective entrepreneurial leader will be skilled in aligning the goals of staff members and administrators, the college, and the community by providing a vision that is easy to understand and is similar to those of other stakeholders. Keys to entrepreneurial leadership include:

- Ongoing self-improvement. A great leader always seeks to become even better, taking advantage of webinars, conferences, and workshops, and staying up-to-date with professional journals.

Regular evaluations and other forms of feedback should also be considered as opportunities for improvement.

- Creating opportunities for change, leadership, and creative thinking. Student affairs professionals should be at the leadership table of the college and eager to take on challenges. Initiatives and restructuring can be opportunities for the future. Consider nontraditional approaches such as sharing faculty and financial aid staff or having student affairs staff oversee event planning and the information center. Volunteer to facilitate meetings, take minutes, or do other tasks to ensure your involvement.

DECISION-MAKING SKILLS

Student affairs professionals need problem-solving and decision-making skills suited to dealing with a wide variety of challenges. In just the past decade, the rate of change has increased and the complexity of issues has multiplied. Decision makers must review risk-benefit outcomes in a world of volatility, uncertainty, complexity, and ambiguity. They must see the big picture and the connections. They will have to embrace shared assets and opportunities as never before, and work through the chaos to influence the future.

Today's students are more complex and diverse than those of previous generations. Often, their issues and biases are not known until they surface and must be handled in some way, often with limited state funding and few private dollars (Traynor, 2009; Gallagher, 2007). For example, community colleges are seeing more students with mental illness. They are entering community colleges in record numbers—this is a socially acceptable alternative to being unemployed, but it often taxes resources and introduces unknown quantities to the campuses. Campuses are not usually equipped to help troubled students even when they are identified, and often such students do not self-disclose before an incident occurs. These and other issues challenge the SSAO's ability to govern and guide.

In the past, decision making may have been more of a tried and true process. Many of the problems administrators faced were known; the problem-solving and decision-making processes were generally accepted; the boundary conditions were often known; most of the critical inputs and assumptions could be identified; and the cause-and-effect process would likely lead to one right or optimum solution.

All of this has changed. The problems SSAOs face today are often vague, with many unknown factors, and boundary conditions are porous and dynamic. It is human nature to see every new challenge as similar to those we have encountered before. We also cannot and should not assess every situation as new or we will lose efficiency. However, relying too heavily on former situations or systematic approaches to decisions may not work best in the ever-changing environment in which we now must function. A few examples student affairs professionals at community colleges may face include:

- A state police detective calls to inform the campus that he has received a credible tip that a person is coming to campus to confront a student and shoot her when she leaves class.
- A few notes have been found that indicate a student is going to commit suicide on campus Friday. It will be a "bloody mess." A similar phone message was left on the voice mail of the administrative assistant to the president.
- A student presents a court-issued restraining order to the dean of students that restricts the movement of another student. Both have classes in proximate areas of campus on the same days.

In these examples, how does one react? Who else needs to be involved? How fast must a decision be made or action taken? The administrative practices and legal ramifications of decisions are continuously changing in today's world and on our campuses, and SSAOs must apply new and flexible decision-making processes.

COMPETENCIES IN MANAGING MULTIGENERATIONAL STAFF

Today's workforce is more diverse than ever before, and one component of this diversity is that multiple generations work together or simply interact with each other. In the community college setting, it is possible to have up to four generations working in one office:

- **Traditionalists** were born before 1945—the oldest generation in the workforce.
- **Baby boomers** were born between 1945 and the early 1960s.
- **Generation X** was born from the mid-1960s to 1980.
- **Generation Y/millennials/the echo generation** is the youngest generation in the workforce, born after 1980.

Supervising and leading four generations in one workplace poses a challenge for community college administrators. In addition, competition for competent and skilled staff is intense, and we live in a highly mobile society. In the face of all these factors, how can you find and keep quality staff?

The first step is to get to know your staff. Administrators should strive to understand and appreciate the mind-set of each generation, especially the youngest. However, although the generalizations above may apply, each person is an individual—there is no substitute for working with people, getting to know each other, and sharing opinions. Confirming or debunking generalizations can be a strong first step to effective supervision. Only when you get to know people can you tailor tasks, committee assignments, expectations regarding structure, and other aspects of work to their particular situation.

The most effective administrator is one who knows what people want. For example, some employees glow when identified in public as having done a good job, while others are embarrassed and uncomfortable. Knowing which employees to praise publicly and which to congratulate privately can go a long way toward achieving harmony.

An effective administrator continuously monitors the team and watches for opportunities to help people grow. Sometimes this process involves assigning to a team people who work well together and have similar qualities. At other times—for example, to diversify the team or to help one person grow—staff members who are not similar may be grouped. The latter is trickier—the supervisor must know the strengths of the individuals and be able to predict how they will interact with one another. From the generational perspective, we know that Generation Y and traditionalists share similar conservative views, but the younger generation can be impatient with the older generation's lack of technology skills and the older generation can find the Ys' inability to deal effectively with conflict frustrating.

Learning how the generations interact with each other is an ongoing process, and organizations need to invest in training and development for managers. This includes training in performance management and conflict resolution to help the multigenerational workforce cooperate and produce. And, as with all supervisory training, we must recognize that these characteristics do not exist in a vacuum. Planning and execution must include ongoing analysis of demographics, turnover predictions, retirements, promotions, staffing projections, and many other variables to develop the strongest possible teams, today and tomorrow.

PARTNERSHIPS

Community colleges, more than any other institutional type in higher education, collaborate and partner with agencies, businesses, and groups to fulfill their mission. These partnerships can reduce costs and increase efficiencies, strengthen students' educational experience, and enhance the college's role as a community resource and contributor toward the overall growth of the area.

The community college can save money and promote efficiency by partnering with outside sources to provide services that it is financially unable to develop and maintain on its own such as campus safety and security or campus police. Paying for these services can be much less expensive for a college than attempting to operate its own program and hire its own staff. Or the college might not feel compelled to provide certain services but recognizes that they would benefit students. Examples of these services are recreation and fitness, student health services, personal counseling services, and housing arrangements. The community college might enter into referral arrangements with certain providers in return for special pricing structures for students (and staff) to encourage them to use that provider rather than a competitor. Often, but not always, the college receives a donation from the service provider for its endorsement or referral. Depending on the nature of the arrangement and the services provided, the relationship between the college and the provider can be quite passive (students and staff are informed of the choices if they ask) or more proactive (the institution provides lists of people to the provider for marketing purposes or includes information about the provider in college materials).

Partnerships can also be used to strengthen the educational experience for students. The most common example is transferability, in which students who complete coursework and educational programs at one college or university can transfer the credits to fulfill degree requirements at another. Often, these partnerships are established by higher education governing boards, but sometimes individual institutions work together.

Other examples of partnerships that strengthen the educational experience are intern programs, co-ops, work-study placement, and observation sites, through which students receive educational experiences in businesses and agencies engaged in work that is directly related to their professional interests. The positions are often unpaid, but the student receives on-the-job training and experience, as well as guidance and direction from a supervisor or coordinator who helps ensure that learning is taking place. Common examples of these partnerships are students in health fields working at a clinic or health care facility, business students working in an office, or students completing special projects with local nonprofit agencies.

Partnerships also function as part of the college mission to be a community partner. Many community colleges form partnerships or otherwise work with the local area in much different ways than other types of institutions of higher education. These arrangements can be very loose and informal or more highly structured. Most community colleges offer meeting space for community gatherings and forums; encourage their employees and students to be active in community issues; and provide space for polling places during elections and for various kinds of information centers. Partnerships can be more extensive and formal as well. A college library might join forces with the local library to create a single facility. Arrangements with local art museums and other cultural centers can result in beneficial experiences for all parties involved.

PROFESSIONAL DEVELOPMENT

For state officials, community and business leaders, and the general public, the quality of an institution of higher education relates directly to the economic success of the state and local area. Community colleges contribute to increased student success and degree completion, increased tax revenues, higher real estate values, and overall quality of life for the area. Politicians, community leaders, and parents all agree that they want the most competent instructors and administrators in the community college. Professional development is the most effective strategy to ensure continuous staff and faculty improvement and to make sure educators strengthen their practice throughout their careers and remain knowledgeable about best practices and emerging research. The most effective professional development is presented on various levels and encourages professionals to network and work together for discovery and implementation of lessons learned.

Community college faculty and staff have choices regarding professional development. Through the use of technology, an administrator can obtain solid professional development experiences without leaving the office. However, the exclusive use of online resources can severely limit development. Membership in one or more professional associations is a must for the serious educator. These associations offer literature, a variety of services, standards, important resources, and networking opportunities—all of which should be incorporated into the administrator's self-improvement toolbox.

There are three "absolutes" in the field of student affairs. The first is the set of standards set by the Council for the Advancement of Standards in Higher Education (2006). Developed through a collaboration of more than 30 organizations, these standards provide a framework of benchmarks against which all community colleges can judge themselves. The second is the American College Personnel Association/National Association of Student Personnel Administrators Professional Competency Areas (ACPA & NASPA, Joint Task Force on Professional Competencies and Standards, 2010). These competencies guide you toward required skills and knowledge and provide a framework for assessing yourself within the field, regardless of your position in student affairs. The third is membership in a professional association. Whether it is a specific subject area or a more comprehensive organization, active involvement will ensure that you stay current in your profession.

Active participation in state, regional, national, and international workshops and conferences can enhance your skill set and increase your network of trusted colleagues. You will be able to spot emerging trends, gain valuable insights about strategies, and make contacts and friends you can call upon throughout your career. Professional association memberships cost very little compared with the wealth of information and opportunities they offer.

Community colleges are often very lean organizations, and staff members have multiple roles and duties. Because of these responsibilities, some staff members find it is difficult to take time to attend workshops or conferences. This is understandable but regrettable and short-sighted. All staff and faculty members should be encouraged to participate in professional development activities of various kinds, including those that facilitate peer interaction and networking.

Thomas Snyder, president of Indiana's Ivy Tech Community College, says that investment in people is prudent. Professional development is an important component of growth and an important element for giving people the tools they need to carry out the mission of the college. Growth and development occur through exposure to new ideas and strategies. Conferences, workshops, and seminars will help you discover opportunities and resources that will strengthen your ability to serve others. Snyder says that when time or money is tight, some decision makers suspend or eliminate professional development opportunities. He believes this is a mistake. How else, he asks, does one encourage creativity, collaboration, and discovery, if not by engaging with and learning from others (T. Snyder, personal communication, November 11, 2010).

In conclusion, policymakers, community leaders, and administrators have a responsibility to ensure that all educators engage in professional development and continuous learning to better serve their students and the community. Educators must learn and then apply that learning to create the best environment possible for students. This ongoing process of learning, applying the lessons and techniques, and maintaining a constant state of continuous improvement is the only way to educate our students and prepare for the future.

REFERENCES

American College Personnel Association (ACPA) & National Association of Student Personnel Administrators (NASPA), Joint Task Force on Professional Competencies and Standards. (2010). *ACPA/NASPA professional competency areas for student affairs practitioners.* Retrieved from http://www.naspa.org/programs/prodev/ACPA-NASPA%20Professional%20Competency%20Areas-Preliminary%20Version.pdf

Council for the Advancement of Standards in Higher Education. (2006). *CAS Professional Standards for Higher Education.* Washington, DC: Author.

Galagan, P. (2010, February). Bridging the skills gap: New factors compound the growing skills shortage. *T+D*. Retrieved from http://www.astd.org/TD/Archives/2010/Feb/Free/1002_BridgingSkillsGap.htm

Gallagher, R. P. (2007). *National survey of counseling center directors.* Alexandria, VA: International Association of Counseling Services, Inc.

Sandeen, A. (1991). *The chief student affairs officer: Leader, manager, mediator, educator.* San Francisco, CA: Jossey-Bass.

Traynor, C. (2009, March). Higher enrollments increase safety, privacy concerns. *Community College Times.* Retrieved from http://www.communitycollegetimes.com/article.cfm?ArticleId=1538

U.S. Department of Labor. (1991, June). *What work requires of schools: A SCANS report for America 2000,* pp. xvii–xviii. Washington, DC: Author.

The New Nexus of Transformational Leadership in Various Collegiate Settings

Joanna M. Iwata

AS WE CONSIDER the many different leadership roles and unique management challenges that face senior student affairs officers (SSAOs), we can see that we are not only being required to do more with less (human/fiscal/operational resources) but also to harness new opportunities that will allow us and our teams to reinvent ourselves and our best practices in transformative ways.

Whether we are working in a public state university, community college, or private liberal arts college, the new bottom line is no longer "business as usual" but being able to operate from an entirely different mode of leadership in which we are consistently ahead of the change continuum. Never before have college administrators been required not only to manage change but to lead change.

We can extrapolate this even further within the context of a recent special issue of *Harvard Business Review* on "Managing in the New World." In their article "Leadership in a Permanent Crisis," Heifetz, Grashow, and Linsky (2009) outline several critical leadership tasks in managing change that include:

- **Fostering adaptation:** Helping people develop their "next practices" to enable their organizations to thrive.
- **Embracing disequilibrium:** Keeping people in a state that creates enough discomfort to induce essential changes in the workplace without creating despair, anger, or resignations.
- **Generating leadership:** Giving people at all levels of the organization the opportunity to experiment and lead, to facilitate your organization's capacity to adapt.

Having worked as an SSAO at both public state universities and private liberal arts colleges, I will address what I believe *reconstitutes* our best practices as SSAOs drawing from different leadership and management models provided by Heifetz et al. (2009), Kouzes and Posner (2006), and Kotter and Cohen (2002).

As we begin to *reenvision* our roles as SSAOs, I believe the possibilities associated with our capacity to effectively lead our teams in different collegiate settings will become the new nexus of transformational leadership—moving our institutions beyond surviving to thriving as dynamic learning organizations of the new millennium.

Fostering Adaptation, Embracing Disequilibrium, and Generating Leadership

As student affairs professionals, we have been fortunate to benefit from the visionary national platform *The Student Learning Imperative* (American College Personnel Association, 1996), which redefined the context of our work as both educators and change agents on our campuses. We continue to generate innovative and evolutionary best practices with the help of our professional associations, which individually and collectively publish studies on relevant and timely issues, from learning outcomes, assessment, and diversity to serving traditional and nontraditional students.

During the past decade, I have worked within eight different institutional settings: in private liberal arts colleges and public state universities; with student populations ranging from 1,500 to 33,000; and on the East Coast and West Coast, and in Hawaii, within two denominationally based institutions and an all-women's college. I have been able to draw numerous best practices from these varied higher education settings and from my leadership consulting and nonprofit management work. I will illustrate how the critical tasks of *fostering adaptation*, *embracing disequilibrium*, and *generating leadership* can be incorporated within our best practices as SSAOs.

Fostering Adaptation

> Executives today face two competing demands. They must
> execute in order to meet today's challenges. And they must
> adapt what and how things get done in order to thrive in
> tomorrow's world. They must develop 'next practices' while
> excelling at today's best practices. (Heifetz et al., 2009, p. 65)

In the early 1980s, I worked at Mills College as a new professional. My
return 20 years later (under a different senior administration) as the new
SSAO presents a unique case study in *fostering adaptation*.

One Mills tradition was alive and well: the dynamic nature of student
activism. In the 1990s, students, faculty, and alumni staged sit-ins and
protests, and even took over the college for weeks, to reverse the decision
of the administration and the board of trustees to make the women's
college co-ed. (While the undergraduate program has remained all
female, our graduate programs include both men and women.)

As the new SSAO, I faced several unique leadership and organizational challenges, as well as opportunities in being the third SSAO to step
into this senior leadership role within a two-year time span (following
the departure of a 15-year veteran). We never really know what we are
inheriting with a new job; in this case, it was important for me to quickly
assess and stabilize our division after these recent changes.

The good news was that I arrived at the college after a successful capital
campaign that coincided with a surge in enrollment, so I was allowed to
hire new directors in four key departments: Student Activities, Student
Diversity Programs, Services for Students with Disabilities, and Spiritual
and Religious Life.

While I was fortunate to inherit a fairly seasoned professional staff, I
could not afford to conduct "business as usual," especially as I hired new
staff to fill vacant or frozen positions and promoted other staff members
into more senior roles, which naturally changed the team dynamics. One
of the many advantages of working at a smaller college is that the divi-

sional reporting structure is relatively flat—all the directors could report directly to me, both as a team and in one-on-ones. This structure allowed me to address key issues and new initiatives in a timely manner and to capitalize on best practices.

The Four Phases of Fostering Adaptation

Beginning in the summer and continuing through my first fall semester at Mills, I constantly took the pulse of our different student life teams—addressing their concerns and harnessing their individual and team aspirations and best practices as we worked through various challenges in the division. I initially constructed a series of internal assessments that I carefully orchestrated over the first 120 days, which provided me with a 360-degree view of our organization (by soliciting input from staff, students, and campus partners). The information allowed me to assess our strengths and opportunities for growth within our teams and determine where internal gaps existed. The assessment process was time-consuming on the front end, but it was worth its weight in gold in the long run.

Phase 1. Staff Assessment (the first 30 days)

I designed a three-page self-assessment that included 12 questions on four topics and distributed it to my direct reports, their staffs, and our support staffs. The four topics on which they self-reported were related to their own assessment of their: (1) accomplishments and challenges, (2) teamwork, (3) aspirations, and (4) expectations. This exercise provided them a chance to step back and assess their strengths, challenges, and opportunities individually and as a team. I also met with each staff member to discuss their self-assessment, which gave me more insight into their work and personal lives. I then compiled relevant information from the surveys to bring into the context of several larger divisionwide discussions on our core values and beliefs related to working together as a team.

As a result of reviewing this with my staff, I not only learned more about the organizational history that preceded me, but also the full impact associated with the previous turnover of senior leadership and vacant positions. More importantly, this exercise provided me and my staff with an important context and common language to begin to reframe our mutual expectations in working together as a newly congealed team.

Phase 2. Divisional Teams (within 60 days)

Within the context of our weekly divisionwide meetings, I facilitated different team-building exercises such as communication, listening, and problem-solving skills, and assigned staff to meet with colleagues outside their departments to compare notes on best practices.

In my experience, resistance to change falls into several different categories: those who do not know how to change, those who are not able to change, and those who are not willing to change. Therefore, it was important for me to convene different sets of meetings with seasoned, mid-level, and new professionals, as well as create different opportunities for staff to participate in half- to full-day planning sessions, and even a two-day, off-campus retreat that reinforced our new team matrix.

Utilizing different mind mapping tools and reflective exercises allowed us to examine our division's best practices (past/present/future) and helped us rethink our mission and revitalize our vision and goals. I also periodically revisited the different team exercises we did throughout the course of the semester to assess and reframe our team priorities, which would eventually evolve into our new strategic plan for the division.

Phase 3. Students and Our Campus Community (within 90 days)

I recognized early on that one of the critical parts of my job as the new SSAO was to meet with as many students as possible (in the dining halls, student center, student organization meetings, etc.) and to communicate regularly with all students (through weekly e-mail updates). Some students were skeptical about my role as a senior administrator and others were unaware of what my job entailed as a student advocate. This kind of proactive outreach to students later proved helpful when we had to deal with protests on campus—by then, my staff and I had built a reputation for being fair-minded and effective student advocates, so we were able to facilitate opportunities for civil discourse and transparency between students and the administration. Throughout my tenure, I found that ongoing communication and meetings with students allowed me to keep my finger on the pulse of campus issues, such as those affecting students of color in the residence halls; hate activities toward faith-based groups and students with disabilities; and critical issues facing nontraditional students, especially single parents and commuter students.

As our division also worked in tandem with many other key departments, such as Admissions, Financial Aid, Registrar's Office, Public Safety, Alumni Affairs, Dining Services, Facilities/Grounds/Maintenance, and academic departments, it was important for me as the new SSAO to convert our critics into allies. This presented a special opportunity for me to create another important conceptual and organizational tool: a unique student engagement matrix that mapped the intersections and common denominators that linked campuswide services along with our divisionwide programs and services. This ultimately proved to be a very useful tool in helping identify our institutional resources differently.

Phase 4. Division of Student Life (within 120 days)

After pulling together all the composite assessments related to students, our team, and the campus community, I began to use another organizational tool that allowed me to creatively cluster certain departments and their staffs as smaller cross-functional teams, such as a student wellness team (Health Services/Counseling Services/Residential Life) and a student involvement team (Student Activities/Diversity Programs/ Spiritual Life). This example led to other opportunities for joint programming among departments, in which they could share resources (fiscal/ staffing) and respond to the diverse needs of our campus community. For example, by expanding our alliances and joint initiatives with like-minded campus departments, such as the Institute of Civic Leadership,

Women's Leadership Institute, and Nursing Programs, we created a new hybrid initiative (Women2Women) that increased the level of involvement of not only students but also faculty and staff in campuswide programs from 25% in the first year to 50% in the second year.

To handle at-risk students, our division already had a unique team of directors representing Health Services, Counseling Services, International Students, Services for Students with Disabilities, and Residential Life. This team met with me and our associate deans each week to review cases and determine interventions to address critical student issues in real time.

As the team mobilized triage efforts more effectively, we were able to expand our proactive outreach to include a wider range of student advocates among faculty. As the faculty became more familiar with how the team operated, they were able to quickly report problem behaviors among their students, which helped us intervene and manage the problems.

In some ways, the process of implementing sweeping changes and allowing people time to adapt is like growing bamboo: The root system takes time to become firmly established (initially, all you can see above ground is a small sprig while underground the bamboo is growing a dense internal root system), then "suddenly" you see amazing results (the bamboo will grow to 7 feet in one night) as we did during my tenure as SSAO of Mills College.

Therefore, the early use of a variety of internal assessment tools allowed me and our teams to begin *fostering adaptation* almost immediately. We reenvisioned our mission and goals to focus on three key strategic areas—student development, student success, and social justice—and created an organizational matrix that showed how our various student life services linked together throughout the college. As a result, we also redefined our commitment to diversity, multiculturalism, and social justice while rededicating ourselves to being part of the solution. Our new initiatives in this area were reflected in ongoing staff training on these issues and the transformation of some of our cocurricular programs (such as orientation and resident advisor training).

EMBRACING DISEQUILIBRIUM

> The art of leadership in today's world involves orchestrating the inevitable conflict, chaos, and confusion of change so that the disturbance is productive rather than destructive.... Keeping an organization in a productive zone of disequilibrium is a delicate task; in the practice of leadership, you must keep your hand on the thermostat. (Heifetz et al., 2009, p. 66)

At Chaminade University in Hawaii (CUH), I stepped into a position in the middle of the year. My predecessor had resigned before the fall semester, and the division had been led in the interim by another senior staff member (internal to the division) prior to my arrival. I found that while the faculty was extremely supportive of my role as the SSAO, some of the senior members of the student life team were apprehensive.

I had to address the imbalance (disequilibrium) in our division both mindfully and sensitively while establishing new informal and formal lines of authority as the new SSAO. First, I recognized that it was important for me to symbolically extend the appropriate level of recognition to the former interim director who served in my role (prior to my arrival) and our senior staff; second, I framed our work so we could focus on what was essential for us to do together. As the new SSAO, I tried to set the tone for candor and risk taking in safe and constructive ways with all of my direct reports and their teams.

One of my first assignments from the president was to create a new strategic plan for our division. We had only eight weeks to pull the plan together, which created a sense of urgency for our divisional teams to rally around. I had only two months to assess the strengths and weaknesses of my staff. First, I asked our directors to begin to revise the vision and mission statements in their own departments; then we worked collectively on the bigger picture, in which our separate missions, programs, and services were all linked to one another in a larger divisionwide model.

As I began to articulate our new bottom line during this transitional time, we were able to refocus our individual and collective efforts on critical student life initiatives around which we could all wrap our best practices, especially as they applied to student retention efforts and developing a campuswide enrollment management plan with our university partners.

In reflecting on these experiences, I am reminded of the important steps in effectively navigating certain critical changes in our organizations: pushing urgency up, pulling together a guiding team to create visions and strategies, removing barriers to action, accomplishing short-term wins, and pushing change until the job is done (Kotter & Cohen, 2002). Kotter and Cohen also stressed the importance of changing people's behaviors, attitudes, and perceptions so they work with us rather than against us to embrace important changes. All of these were instrumental to my success at Chaminade as the new SSAO.

GENERATING LEADERSHIP

> It is an illusion to expect that an executive team on its own will find the best way into the future. So you must use leadership to generate more leadership deep in the organization . . . you need to mobilize everyone to generate solutions. . . . (Heifetz et al., 2009, p. 60)

Unlike Mills College or Chaminade, I had been at Guilford College for four years as director of student activities when I was asked to step in as interim SSAO when my boss left. Fortunately, I had a sound track record in working effectively with students, faculty, and staff on various campuswide and divisional initiatives; therefore, as the new SSAO, I knew how to combine the strengths of different teams in a seamless fashion.

Yet this was a unique challenge in being promoted internally, especially in navigating being the boss of my peers. As the interim SSAO, while I kept certain organizational and divisionwide structures in place, I now had the latitude to redistribute leadership responsibility more broadly within the division to "mobilize everyone to generate solutions by increasing the information flow that allows people across the organization to make independent decisions and share the lessons they learned from innovative efforts" (Heifetz et al., 2009, p. 68).

This approach enhanced our capacity to provide more comprehensive crisis management practices to deal with risky behaviors of students in the residence halls, address issues that arose in our advisement of student organizations, and upgrade our leadership programs and service–learning initiatives (by partnering with academic departments and campus ministries). We even redesigned our orientation program and made our baccalaureate program more inclusive by inviting parents to attend our special campuswide events.

This type of adaptive and transformative approach to our work together helped promote a culture of care that allowed us to take our best practices to the next level. Our teams were mutually committed to envisioning a future that we could create by operating not apart from each other but with each other. I believe that SSAOs can collectively develop a greater internal strength or bandwidth that will enable us to make the most of the inevitable changes on our campuses by being proactive in how we anticipate, act, and adapt to these changes together.

A Quaker campus such as Guilford College, which operates from a consensus-seeking, community-building model where everyone is given an opportunity to voice their concerns and share their experience, no matter who they are—student, faculty, staff, or administrator—helps promote a greater sense of shared responsibility or group accountability that also allows us to *generate leadership* deeper within our organizations in various value-added ways.

CONCLUSION

As we all know, there are certain parameters related to how far we can move our teams and our student life initiatives beyond the conventional or traditional practices of our institutions. In addition to fostering adaptation, embracing disequilibrium, and generating leadership, we must attend to another important practice: *taking care of ourselves*.

It is easy to immerse ourselves in the work of leading and managing change, but we risk "being corralled by the forces that generated the crisis in the first place" (Heifetz et al., 2009, p. 69). The authors suggest that as leaders we reflect on five key "balancing points": (1) give yourself permission to be optimistic yet realistic; (2) find sanctuaries that allow you to reflect and regain the balance you need; (3) reach out to confidants; (4) bring more of your emotional self to the workplace; and (5) don't lose yourself in your role.

As long as we are willing to experiment with new ideas—especially in reinventing and fortifying our best practices—no matter how challenging it seems, the rewards will outweigh the risks. While I am not a proponent of orchestrating massive changes simply for the sake of change, there are different ways to approach leading and managing change that entail enlisting the support of the entire campus in an inclusive way.

Therefore, when we consider the complex challenges facing SSAOs on a variety of different collegiate settings, the new nexus of transformational leadership revolves around our capacity to not only continually reinvent ourselves and our best practices, but to consider how we can sustain "a culture of courageous conversations" (Heifetz et al., 2009, pp. 67) and a place where our individual and collective passion, experience, and talents can flourish not because of us, but in spite of us.

I am often reminded of a compelling insight on the significance of the important leadership—if not navigational—roles we play on our campuses as change agents that I believe speaks to the greatest gift we as SSAOs can leave an institution: "When we move on, people do not remember us for what we do for ourselves. They remember what we do for them. A leader's legacy is (therefore) the legacy of many" (Kouzes & Posner, 2006, pp. 10–11). May we all be reminded that there are never any challenges too large or insurmountable for us to overcome as SSAOs. Like the bamboo, we possess the fortitude and capacity to jettison and champion the important changes we seek to transform the norms. Anything is possible in our capacity as SSAOs to not only manage but lead change as we work together to creatively "mobilize the resources of people to thrive in a changing and challenging world" (Heiftez, 2009, p. 69) in the new millennium and beyond within our academies of higher learning.

REFERENCES

American College Personnel Association. (1996). *The student learning imperative: Implications for student affairs.* Washington, DC: Author.

Heifetz, R., Grashow, A., & Linsky, M. (2009, July–August). "Leadership in a permanent crisis." *Harvard Business Review*, 62–69.

Kotter, J. P., & Cohen, D. S. (2002). *The heart of change.* Boston, MA: Harvard Business School Press.

Kouzes, J. M., & Posner, B. Z. (2006). *A leader's legacy.* San Francisco, CA: Jossey-Bass.

From Professional Ownership to Intentional Coproduction: New Competency Demands

BRIAN SULLIVAN

IN MY 24 years as a senior student affairs officer (SSAO) at several research-intensive public North American institutions, the most pronounced and demanding shift I have experienced is the movement from profession-centered program models that address student needs to highly accountable and shared program arrangements directed toward student success and institutional strategic aims. Planning, delivery, and assessment in this emergent model require deep links with the expertise of clients (be they students, faculty, staff, alumni, or the institution itself) and a belief in the wisdom resident in those client groups. This can be a wrenching change and has profound implications for the type of leadership SSAOs are called on to provide and the skill sets they must have. In the following pages, I describe the competency demands I am increasingly experiencing in my role as vice president for students (VPS) at the University of British Columbia, a multicampus research institution with 53,000 students.

STRATEGIC ENROLLMENT MANAGEMENT (BUILDING THE CLASS)

Even if the SSAO does not have formal responsibility for enrollment services, there is no escaping the responsibility and opportunity to help shape the new undergraduate and graduate classes, affect retention as they progress through the institution, and encourage positive affiliation as alumni. Contributing to strategic enrollment management (SEM) means thinking systemically, crossing organizational boundaries effectively, remaining focused on institutional aims, and working very hard to understand the value of each new increment of staff input and each new program initiative. The questions are: "What kind of university do we want to be?" "What do we need to do to get there?" and "What are the costs and benefits of trade-offs?" This is all about matching goals and aspirations with capacity—physical, human, and financial. It is a very different way of thinking from the profession-driven program construct. At UBC, we recently developed a SEM structure that partners faculty and administrative unit staff; created the position of executive coordinator for enrollment management strategy who reports to the VPS and works across the institution at both campuses; and publicly articulated a SEM matrix for the Okanagan and Vancouver campuses that specifies long-term enrollment goals for specific student populations (graduate/undergraduate, domestic, international, in-province/out-of-province, transfer, direct-entry, and aboriginal). We have also added part-time faculty associates to the VPS executive team to keep the SEM and partnership lens firmly in place.

ECONOMIC SUSTAINABILITY (TAKING CARE OF BUSINESS)

It is one thing to demonstrate a stand-alone pro forma for new student housing when seeking approval. It is quite another to answer the question of the overall financial implications for the institution, including tuition revenue capture, of an additional staff member to support the transition of new international students or the return on investment (ROI) for alumni engagement from a proposed expansion in student leadership initiatives and networks. There is a greatly heightened expectation that business practices will be progressive and nimble, and that responses to important new demands and requirements will be met through innovative revenue generation and expense sharing. The reenvisioning of the admissions process getting under way at both campuses is going to be funded through reallocation of existing staff, with a start-up grant from the institution for first-year research and development sourced from year-end reserves. The ROI case takes many things into account, including the ongoing cost of enhancement and repair that would have been required to sustain the existing system.

TRANSFORMATIVE STUDENT LEARNING (DELIVERING ON OUR PROMISES)

To make a difference and be distinctive in the area of student learning at a large research-intensive university, the idea needs to be big and the implementation unflagging. UBC's new Place and Promise strategic plan links three goal areas under the heading of transformative student learning: (1) quality and impact of teaching; (2) enriched (high-impact) educational opportunities for all; and (3) student well-being, personal development, and positive affiliation with the institution. To provide effective leadership, the SSAO needs to think systemically and broadly across student communications, mental health and well-being, customer service, student advising, and a range of student systems and technology platforms. The thinking needs to be holistic, even though many of the detailed negotiations are still one-offs. New approaches must be evidence-based, so there is a premium on when to survey and how to use the results.

SERVICE PARTNERSHIP MODELS (GETTING BY WITH A LITTLE HELP FROM OUR FRIENDS)

At UBC, student learning and development staff are increasingly bilocated: cost-shared with faculties and interacting in those faculties, and simultaneously part of a central VPS portfolio team, which is their home base for professional development and programmatic support. Not only student development officers but career services personnel, international learning staff, and alumni professionals work in this blended manner. Programs with student government and student organizations and student peer programming are similarly partnered. Thirteen separate student peer programs, some based on faculty and academic programs and others based on themes, have come together at the Centre for Student Involvement and operate a shared council involving 400 students. This is creating a very powerful cadre of student leaders who are able to think across degree programs and student-experienced themes.

Surveys and Dashboards (Can't Get No Satisfaction)

"So, Mr. Vice President, how is the portfolio doing and how are students in the institution benefiting from your activity?" It is an appropriate question, and we need to be able to answer it. There is an urgent need at UBC to know how a new grants program intended to support student uptake of enriched educational experiences will affect student behavior. To get that baseline (e.g., the number of students who, by year 4/5, have experienced learning abroad or service–learning or undergraduate research), existing surveys need to be redone to capture student intention at entrance and at year 1 baseline. Something similar is being done with student well-being: A net promoter baseline has been established as a measure of recent alumni affiliation, and one resurvey has shown a slight uptick.

This kind of documentation is increasingly expected at the time of proposal presentation and routinely reported at the level of senior management and the board. To offer the necessary support for unit management means having key performance indicators and data consoles in place that allow people to access timely and relevant management information. As a senior institutional officer, the SSAO is expected to contribute to the dashboard question at the institutional level. If a successful student experience is one in which students are academically satisfied, safe and well, engaged in high-impact experiential education, graduating with a sense of purpose, and positive about the institution, how is this measured and what value is added by various programs?

COMMUNICATION WITH STUDENTS (HELLO, MODERATOR)

In my experience, communication with students is broken almost everywhere, and UBC is no exception. A recent study at UBC of student views on university communication revealed a strong view that e-mail is overused; information is too general and text-heavy; websites are (very) clunky; and there are too few opportunities for students to customize the information they receive. While students want to choose their own channels, institutions find this very difficult to manage. We can sustain it during the prospective student/client relationship management phase but tend to abandon it once students actually show up. There is a tremendous discontinuity between the ways students organize their experience and time now and the ways they did it just 10 years ago. Not just SSAOs but most of our staff members have not caught up with this. A lot of cherished notions must be released if we are to follow the student-driven lead on many aspects of communication and program delivery. SSAOs need to reassure middle management about functioning in this very different world. Junior staff members often have outstanding instincts in this regard and should be given an organizational voice.

Developing and sustaining a narrative about the student experience in the institution is very different now, just as the way student government election campaigns are conducted has changed radically. At UBC, several vice presidents have begun an administration blog; they write a weekly entry that is personal and informal in tone on topics that self-proclaimed student "journalists" who operate channels have indicated are of interest in the student community. At the same time, I find that the information technology competence our students display is matched by a simultaneously high desire for face-to-face communication. Managing and modeling both is very demanding for the SSAO. Having many student peer programs and relying on student-driven initiatives can be freeing, as the partners discover where they can be mutually supportive in the communication undertaking.

TALENT DEVELOPMENT (SHOULD I STAY OR SHOULD I GO?)

With the economic stringencies we are all facing, support for professional development is often near the top of the cut list. Universities do not have proud histories as progressive human resource environments—orientation is often rudimentary, and not enough time is spent specifying skill requirements and performance outcomes. Career paths are not taken seriously; unit managers do not get the coaching and mentoring their skill development deserves; and we lack flexibility about job sharing, job rotation, and secondments to other institutional, private sector, and agency settings. This situation is compounded by the different workplace culture expectations that many younger staff members express. Through a combination of annual professional development forums, P2 (pizza and priority) meetings open to all staff, blogs and videos, intranet newsletters, and identification of talent pools and talent development paths, we are trying to bootstrap into the modern era. It is ironic that just as hospitals are characterized as unhealthy, universities are rarely touted as model learning organizations. This can and must change: It has more to do with managerial will and follow-through than with budgetary sufficiency.

TECHNOLOGY PLATFORMS (SHARING KNOWLEDGE)

Knowledge community—easy to say, very hard to do. Universities and colleges are complicated places with a diverse, detailed, and bewildering range of policies and practices. As students often remark, they are frequently in situations where there is no answer to the questions they ask, yet they are expected to have the right answer before they can take the next step. Nowhere is the need for a robust and shared knowledge platform more apparent than in the many forms of advising that we do with students, including academic, disability, international, well-being, career, residential life, ombuds, and financial.

We are in the midst of a bureaucratic revolution, in which students are insisting that knowledge be organized and presented as they need it to interact with our institutions as learners and clients rather than as our units need it to display and explain themselves to the world. If a student must understand our organizational chart to accomplish something, there is a service lapse. Starting with a commitment to excellence in advising is very different than starting with a commitment to minimizing the risk of rules and procedures being violated. The latter leads to constipation and opacity; the former, to starting with the student's learning plan and supporting that plan through an integrated student system infrastructure. UBC is in the early stages of a complete remake on this, beginning with getting the various advisors across campus to share their common commitment and the critical learning that happens at their intersections with our prospects, students, and alumni. A first step involving radical simplification of existing procedures (many of which cannot be mapped with confidence) will greatly boost knowledge technology performance; SSAOs can do the institution a great service by modeling and encouraging others in this regard.

Conclusion

These competency demands are new and energizing, and often unnerving. What I find affirming and reassuring, however, is that my fundamental goal as an SSAO has remained largely unchanged: safe and well students, academically successful, who are progressing with purpose. As the ways in which our students, institutions, and communities operationalize these commitments change, let us lead through fresh practices infused with curiosity, inclusion, experimentation, and learning. In this shift from professional ownership of programs to intentional coproduction, SSAOs must have the skills to act personally and collectively in ways that are student-driven, evidence-based, academically integrated, and coupled tightly with the institution's aims.

CHAPTER 5

The New, New Senior Student Affairs Officer

SHANNON E. ELLIS

"NEW" MEANS FRESH and unused, sometimes surprising, often mysterious, and typically unknown. "New, new" adds a layer that enhances the difference and heightens the originality, innovation, and creativity of the subject it describes. To be new on the job is one thing, but to be "new, new" means bringing a set of competencies that create the professional edge on which others aspire to perch. "New, new" student affairs administrative leaders are out front in their thinking, vision, strategies, and tactics. The result is a positioning of student affairs work within the institution that creates exciting innovations and alternatives for creating an exemplary collegiate experience.

Being new to any job is a great opportunity to start fresh and redefine your style. In this second decade of the 2000s, you are not only new to the job. You are a new breed of senior student affairs officer (SSAO) with a new set of leadership skills and management practices shaped by technology, inclusiveness, and the global awareness that is characteristic of the post-modern world. Today's new SSAO holds the potential to be the leader whose time has come to help position higher education for future success.

As the SSAO, you are now the leader—the person Tichy says "who decides what needs to be done and the one to make things happen" (1997, p. 25). While it takes the energy and ideas of many people to achieve results, without a leader, things do not get started or, if they do, they quickly die for lack of direction or momentum. This is the most visible and important position you have ever held. It is important because many people depend on you to be a success.

This book is full of excellent insights on key competencies that will lead to effectiveness as a senior administrative leader. This chapter will not repeat that advice. Rather, this chapter is about that once-in-a-lifetime career status of being a *new* SSAO in the *new* world of higher education. While you are not expected to be superhuman, anyone who has taken on the responsibility of new leadership for a student affairs organization should aspire to excel in executing the following six key competencies.

The Competency to be Self-Aware

As a new vice president, dean, or vice provost, you have the rare and wonderful opportunity to start out "right." You do not have any historic rivalries or bad relations, and you do not have to live with past errors or failed partnerships. Even if you have scars from being an internal candidate or inherit problems from the previous administration, you do not have to buy in to any of them, and in fact, you *should not* buy in to them. But this works only if you know *who* you are, *how* you operate, and *where* you are going. The ability to know and understand your own strengths, weaknesses, desires, and capabilities is critical to leading a student affairs organization.

Self-awareness is cultivated in many ways. First, "go sit on a rock." Take on the uncomfortable task of being alone and thinking—honestly—about yourself as a professional and a human being. Consider your frailties and failures as well as your strengths and successes. A helpful tool for this task is *StrengthsQuest* (Clifton & Anderson, 2002), which can lead you "to discover, develop, and apply who you truly are" (p. 10). Watkins (2003) urges new executives to "pinpoint their vulnerabilities by assessing *problem preferences*—the kinds of problems toward which you naturally gravitate" (p. 24). Watkins guesses that your weaknesses lie in the areas you avoid. Another approach is to solicit feedback from people who will give it to you straight. The most useful performance feedback I receive each year is from people with whom I do not see eye to eye. Their honesty always makes me think.

What you affirm or discover about yourself will help you answer the following questions. Is this who you want to be? Are these the competencies of a successful leader in student affairs? Covey (2004) claims that "identity is destiny," and his solution to many issues in the workplace begins with leaders changing themselves "from the inside out" (p. 25). The result is an anchored sense of identity and discovered strengths and talents that you can use to meet needs and produce results. Play up your strengths, shore up your weak spots, and hire team members accordingly.

Confidence and capability can emerge from self-awareness. Do not let anything or anyone hold you back. This clean slate as a new leader does not last forever. Ignore negativism, too much positivism (you are not the savior), naysayers, whispered advice, and "how it's done here" speeches from those around you. Arrive with your strengths and vulnerabilities intact. Then act as though you've done this forever.

Despite the fact that you are "new, new," act as if you're old to the job. When writer Jack Clark gave up journalism to become a cab driver, he was asked how he cultivated a cabby's demeanor. He said, "From day one, I acted like I had done this a long time. I acted like an *old* cab driver" (2010). From day one, act like a veteran vice president for student services. You'll convince others, and yourself, that you know what you're doing.

THE COMPETENCY TO INSPIRE EXCELLENCE

Leadership is the capacity to *influence* others through *inspiration,* motivated by a *passion,* generated by a *vision,* produced by *conviction,* ignited by a *purpose* (Munroe, 2010). In your new role as SSAO, leadership is a vital aspect of your job. New SSAOs accomplish things "by guiding and motivating people. Leaders shape people's opinions and win their enthusiasm, using every available opportunity to send out their message and win supporters" (Tichy, 1997, p. 36).

Effective new SSAOs must take an honest look at the organization and "lead with edge" (Tichy, 1997, p. 166). Such leaders are focused firmly on seeing reality while having respect for their people. Leaders with edge will go to great lengths to explain and help others understand their actions. Collins (2001) calls this facing the brutal facts. "Motivating people with the brutal facts means a new leader must create a climate where the truth is heard and the brutal facts confronted" (p. 74). Collins offers four basic practices for creating such a climate: (1) lead with questions, not answers; (2) engage in dialogue and debate, not coercion; (3) conduct autopsies without blame; and (4) build red flag mechanisms. Collins says, "Red flag mechanisms give you a practical and useful tool for turning information into information that cannot be ignored and for creating a climate where the truth is heard" (p. 80).

All of us inherit an organization with strengths and weaknesses in people, programs, and services. Your job is not to maintain the status quo. Your job is to make it better. Everyone is watching to see what you are going to do. The poor performers (and they know who they are) are worried that they'll be found out. The strong performers are getting ready to show yet another SSAO how good they are at their job. And everyone is wondering if you have the insight and the guts to get rid of the weak programs and people. "Have the unwavering resolve to do what must be done" (Collins, 2001, p. 30). You'll never have a better opportunity to do this than in the new, new period.

As you move through this process, you will gain the respect of those who matter: the effective, committed, and talented professionals under your leadership. They are your most important asset. New, new SSAOs would do well to have a love affair with their staff—really! As he left his post of chief of staff of the army on June 11, 2003, General Eric Shinseki warned in his farewell address against arrogance in leadership. "You must love those you lead before you can be an effective leader," he said. "You can certainly command without that sense of commitment, but you cannot lead without it. And without leadership, command is a hollow experience, a vacuum often filled with mistrust and arrogance."

You can't fall in love with those you lead if you don't get to know them. Spend a lot of time with employees and other constituents to engage in trust building. As Kouzes and Posner (1995) stress, "Leadership is a relationship, founded on trust and confidence. Without trust and confidence, people don't take risks. Without risks, there is not change. Without change, organizations and movements die" (p. 12).

Commit yourself in the first months of your new job to meeting with as many of your staff as possible, in their offices, listening hard and asking important questions. In my first individual meetings with directors, I had them explain their budgets to me. This helped me understand what their priorities were (where the money was spent) and how well they were funded. It also told me whether or not they understood their own budgets—a critical administrative skill. Barbara Krumsiek (2010), chief executive and chairwoman of the investment firm Calvert Group, suggests asking staff members, "Tell me about your job, [then] tell me about what you think you do here that is not in that job description that you think is really critical." Also, "Tell me one thing that's going on at Calvert that you think I don't know that you think I should know."

I ask my staff members what one thing they would change in the workplace if they could. Sometimes it's something I can make happen. Such "quick wins" are particularly important in your new, new leadership role. You will gain a reputation as someone who gets things done, which is how you want your staff to see you. Their leader removes obstacles, secures funding, approves action, and rearranges priorities so the staff can succeed. Isn't that what we do for the people we love?

The Competency to be an Institutional Leader

In creating an effective and cutting-edge student services effort, be sure to reach out and connect your organization's initiatives to the goals of other units in the institution, not just the learning mission. Being new doesn't mean you can't take the lead beyond student affairs. In fact, you are expected to do so, often in collaboration with other senior administrative officers.

In the report on the state of the presidency in American higher education (Association of Governing Boards of Universities and Colleges, 2007), former Virginia Governor Gerald Baliles said that a new style of collaborative but decisive leadership—integral leadership—has emerged. "One exerts a presence that is purposeful and consultative, deliberative yet decisive, and capable of course corrections as new challenges emerge" (p. 33).

An integral leadership style will help you shape every aspect of the collegiate experience. As the "expert on students," you should be infusing every conversation with what you know and with your opinion of whether this decision or that program is in the best interest of students. Other leaders are equally responsible for seeing the broad view, from the vice president overseeing the physical plant to the institutional legal counsel to the athletics director to the faculty senate chair. All are called upon to be institutional leaders and to see issues in the larger context. You must think and act like an institutional leader at all times. Leading a higher education institution is a team effort.

Bensimon and Neumann (1993) say that advocates of collaborative leadership "believe that a team-centered managerial approach enhances the capacity of organizations to master new knowledge and to use it effectively to improve innovation, problem solving, and productivity" (p. ix). Change in administrative and leadership practices makes sense in a changing campus world. Even if your president does not lead through teamwork, identify your senior colleagues and create lines of communication and acts of mutual support that will be the foundation for a teamwork approach to achieving things. As always, it begins with relationships: "when people's interests meet up and are complementary and compatible" (Ellis, 2009, p. 455).

The Competency to Develop and Sustain Relationships

As Larry Roper, vice provost for student affairs at Oregon State University, said, "I would argue that our success as student affairs professionals is more closely tied to our ability to construct and manage essential relationships during our career than any other activity" (Roper, 2002, p. 11). Relationships are essential for SSAOs. They are how we get things done. "The lesson is to develop a multitude of good relationships *with* people and *among* people (Ellis, 2009, p. 448). The new, new SSAO should invest time and energy into relationships from the first day on the job. Never think meetings and conversations are a waste of time. "There is no such thing as an insignificant relationship" (Roper, 2002, p. 12). More than once in the years ahead you will see how this investment helps you be a successful leader of your organization and institution.

Conversations help you understand what is important to others elsewhere in the institution. Reflect on what others say and find ways to support them in what they are trying to achieve. Sometimes that means mustering your resources to assist. At other times it means standing aside and removing obstacles. As you help colleagues succeed, they will often do the same for you. The institution wins in the end. The following four types of relationships will be of greatest benefit to a new SSAO.

Thick Informal Networks

Kotter (1990) points out why a multitude of relationships are important. "These thick networks of informal relationships help coordinate leadership activities in much the same way as formal structure coordinates managerial activities. The key difference is that thick informal networks can deal with the greater coordinating demands associated with non-routine activities and change" (p. 90). Look to cultivate relationships with people who are not typically in your meetings, attending your programs, or involved in decision making. They may be the campus bus drivers or room schedulers, custodians or new faculty. These people see and hear a lot and have much to share.

Coalitions and Alliances

Become influential throughout the institution, not just with people in your direct line of control. Make this a long-term goal, beginning on the first day of your new leadership role. Seek out allies and create meaningful coalitions around your goals. Start right away to identify people with similar agendas who can help you achieve the future you envision for your student affairs organization. Why would they want to help you? Begin by asking for their advice and support. Most will agree to assist. If you encounter resistance or they simply decline, continue the conversation to learn more. The more they talk, the more you will learn, and the more likely you are to gain their support. This information is critical to future conversations and partnerships with these people. You will begin to understand their priorities and their vulnerabilities. Your ability to help them achieve their goals will help both of you and the institution.

Your Team

Watkins (2003) stresses the importance of building your own team. "If you are inheriting a team, you will need to evaluate its members and perhaps restructure it to better meet the demands of the situation. Your willingness to make the tough early personnel calls and your capacity to select the right people for the right positions are among the most important drivers of success during your transition" (p. 14). Collins (2001) emphasizes the importance of your team: "To be clear, the main point is not just about assembling the right team. The main point is to *first* get the right people on the bus (and the wrong people off the bus) *before* you figure out where to drive it. The second key point is the degree of *sheer rigor* needed in people decisions" (p. 44). Be selfish and pick the people you know you will need to move ahead. Be realistic and compensate for your vulnerabilities. Be bold and add contrarians to the familiar and trusted people around the table.

Your Boss

Your most important relationship is with your new boss. "This means carefully planning for a series of critical conversations about the situation, expectations, style, resources, and your own personal development" (Watkins, 2003, p. 13).

No one wants you to be successful more than your new boss. Your boss hired you and wants to be known for making a good decision. Your boss is also depending on you to run a strong student affairs organization that serves the interests of students and moves the institution ahead in its academic mission and other strategic goals.

Get on your boss's calendar on a regular basis. This keeps you aware of the issues your boss is dealing with and gives you face-to-face time. "Take 100% responsibility for making the relationship work. Don't expect your boss to reach out or to offer you the time and support you need" (Watkins, 2003, p. 108).

THE COMPETENCY TO LEAD CHANGE

"In a broad sense, what leaders do is stage revolutions. They are constantly challenging the status quo and looking around to see if they are doing the right things, or if those things can be done better or smarter. And, most important, when they do spot something that needs to be changed, they do something about it" (Tichy, 1997, pp. 28–29). The new, new SSAO sees reality and mobilizes an effective response.

A new SSAO is likely to learn a lot through individual conversations. You can gather more information about what might need to change in meetings and discussions, and through observation. The need to change a process or person may not surface until there is a problem—see this as an opportunity to move decisively to improve things. Be an agent of change who is willing to change yourself throughout your career. Remember, change is never over in your job. Begin your new job with the realization that an SSAO is an agent of change.

Kotter (1990) said that "the most common function of effective leadership in modern complex organizations is to produce change, often dramatic change in some useful direction. Indeed, the promise of major change for the better is at the very heart of what leadership is all about. It always has been" (p. 32).

By embracing this role, you will begin to create a climate within student affairs where change is the norm. "A truly stable system expects the unexpected, is prepared to be disrupted, waits to be transformed" (Robbins, 1976). Your new perspective holds great promise for change. Often, experts and long timers fail to see innovative solutions to novel problems. Past success doesn't make them invulnerable to future failure.

Creating the conditions for change depends, in part, "on your ability to transform the prevailing organizational psychology" (Watkins, 2003, p. 67). If people are panicked, calm them down with face-to-face conversations. If people are in despair, offer hope when possible but, more than that, communicate with them honestly and frequently. To sustain success, you must reinvent the challenge to keep people motivated and energized.

In bringing about change, it is important to match strategy to the situation. An accurate assessment of the culture (heroes, values, rites, and rituals) will help you bring the right set of leadership skills to the organization. "Don't arrive with your spear if you need to be plowing" (Watkins, 2003, p. 69).

THE COMPETENCY TO THINK AND ACT STRATEGICALLY

By applying the much-needed skills of strategic thinking, a new SSAO will find a way to anticipate, respond to, and influence change as it is emerging and before a crisis arises. "Once a strategy has been selected, as the new leader you must decide what actions have to be taken to successfully implement it, and you must take *all* of them. Often it means walking away from the old systems and setting up entirely new ones" (Tichy, 1997, p. 33). Do this with great thought.

"Strategic thinking has insight about the present and foresight about the future" (Sanders, 1998, p. 78). It is all about developing the future you desire for your student affairs organization. It is your role to lead your staff and other stakeholders into making it a reality. "Visualization is the key to insight and foresight—and the next revolution in strategic thinking and planning" (Sanders, 1998, p. 84). Being strategic allows you to re-imagine the fundamental parts of your student affairs operation and the institution itself. To some people, this will be a frightening prospect, but their fear will be lessened if they know what the priorities are (and they have contributed to their establishment) and everyone has the opportunity to commit their efforts toward that end. The relentless eye on the future is more than inspirational. It is achievable.

Being strategic is more than developing a plan. It is about taking control of more than we realize we can control and letting go of things we cannot change, at least for now. That is the heart of what it means to be strategic. A new, new SSAO must think and act in a manner that discovers opportunities for student affairs in any environment. If you start to limit yourself with such factors as budget cuts, incapable staff, or inflexible university policy, you must remind yourself to look for the opportunities these factors present. Budget reductions are opportunities to eliminate expensive programs, programs that do not contribute to retention, and services that are provided elsewhere. A hiring freeze gives existing staff opportunities for job growth as they take on more responsibility and may allow you to create internships for graduate students that enable them to gain experience and produce results on the job.

The essence of strategy is sacrifice. At an April 2, 2010, meeting with student affairs staff, Bourne Morris, marketing faculty member at the University of Nevada, Reno, said, "Be willing to give up something big in order to get where you want to go. This allows you to possess an unshakeable focus on achieving that one priority" (personal communication). For example, pouring everything into retention means organizing people, offices, programs, budget, and time around actions you have researched and found to be contributors to retention (and attrition). Anything that doesn't focus on increasing retention goes away. This is a sure way to get people focused on how their area will be contributing to the goal, especially not-so-obvious areas such as health centers, athletic programs, and transactional offices like cashiers, registrar, and financial aid.

If you have been hired to create a turnaround in the student affairs organization, you will need to move quickly. "The intensity of change, as perceived by people in the organization, will also probably be greater" (Watkins, 2003, p. 85). In situations of realignment or sustaining success, it is wise to take time to learn and plan. This is your opportunity to work with your staff and other stakeholders to develop long-term goals and priorities, along with team-led action plans and measures of accountability.

Once you have decided what to change, you must decide how to bring about the change. Plenty is written to guide a new organizational leader in deciding "how." If people have bought into your compelling vision and the need for change, develop the plan and move forward. If people are in denial about the need for change, find allies, build cross-functional coalitions, and create awareness of the need. This should be done collectively and out in the open. All these reactions to change are normal. As a new, new SSAO, you will encounter them all, so be prepared to address them.

CONCLUSION

"The domain of leaders is the future" (Kouzes & Posner, 1995, p. xxv). As a new leader of student affairs professionals, of students, and of the institution where you now work, it is your role to create the best future for all.

A lot of people, including this author, can tell you "how to be" as a new SSAO. Take it all in, but, ultimately, you must decide who you will be and how you will make your way in the campus world. It is important to be the kind of leader people are proud of—someone the president finds indispensable; who gets things done and helps others get things done; who is principled, empathetic, and courageous.

When I was younger, I attended workshops where the facilitator asked us to write our obituary or the eulogy for our funeral. It was a technique to get 18-year-olds thinking about what they wanted to achieve in life. At middle age, I find it more appealing to imagine overhearing respected colleagues and students talking about me. What would I like to hear them say about my vice presidency? Ultimately, none of us has control over our "brand." It is determined by how others perceive us. What we can control is being clear with ourselves about the leader and administrator our students and staff deserve. Once you have decided what you'd like to hear people saying about you, go at it hammer and tongs. Let no one dissuade you. Trust me—there will be plenty of people around to tell you "you can't be this way" and "no one ever did it this way" or "the last vice president to do that didn't last long!"

Being new at anything is both a curse and a blessing, exciting and nerve-racking; it's a chance to start fresh while sometimes wishing you had a long-timer's familiarity. Grab the opportunities, live with the challenges, and, if all goes well, you'll be a seasoned SSAO someday, offering lessons and advice to those who follow.

At times you may envy the seasoned SSAO for what appears to be an easy confidence and natural capability. But realize that some of us who have been in the role for a while sometimes envy your fresh talents, perspectives, and the opportunity to start anew.

REFERENCES

Association of Governing Boards of Universities and Colleges. (2007). *The leadership imperative.* Washington, DC: Author. Retrieved from http://www.agb.org/system/files/u5/imperative.pdf

Bensimon, E. M., & Neumann, A. (1993). *Redesigning collegiate leadership*. Baltimore, MD: Johns Hopkins University Press.

Clark, J. (2010, August 23). Interview on *Fresh Air*, National Public Radio.

Clifton, D. O., & Anderson, E. (2002). *StrengthsQuest: Discover and develop your strengths in academics, career, and beyond*. Washington, DC: Gallup Press.

Collins, J. (2001). *Good to great: Why some companies make the leap...and others don't*. New York, NY: HarperCollins Publishers.

Covey, S. (2004). *The 8ᵗʰ habit: From effectiveness to greatness*. New York, NY: Free Press.

Ellis, S. (2009). Developing effective relationships on campus and in the community. In G. S. McClellan & J. Stringer (Eds.), *The handbook of student affairs administration* (pp. 447–462). San Francisco, CA: Jossey-Bass.

Kotter, J. P. (1990). *Force for change: How leadership differs from management*. New York, NY: The Free Press.

Kouzes, J. M., & Posner, B. Z. (1995). *The leadership challenge*. San Francisco, CA: Jossey-Bass.

Krumsiek, B. J. (2010, May 23). It's not a career ladder, it's an obstacle course. *The New York Times*. Retrieved from http://www.nytimes.com

Munroe, M. (2010). *Leadership definition*. Retrieved from www.agape-faithworshipcenter.org/files/Leadership_definition.doc

Robbins, T. (1976). *Tom Robbins quotes*. Retrieved from http://www.brainyquote.com/quotes/quotes/t/tomrobbins404093.html

Roper, L. (2002). Relationships: The critical ties that bind professionals. In J. C. Dalton, & M. McClinton (Eds.), *The art and practical wisdom of student affairs leadership* (New Directions for Student Services, no. 98). San Francisco, CA: Jossey-Bass.

Sanders, T. I. (1998). *Strategic thinking and the new science.* New York, NY: Free Press.

Shinseki, E. (2003, June 11). *Farewell address.* Retrieved from http://www.army.mil/features/ShinsekiFarewell/farewellremarks.htm

Tichy, N. M. (1997). *The leadership engine: How winning companies build leaders at every level.* New York, NY: HarperBusiness.

Watkins, M. (2003). *The first 90 days: Critical success strategies for new leaders at all levels.* Boston, MA: Harvard Business School Press.

CHAPTER 6

Competencies for the Seasoned Senior Student Affairs Officer

View From the Top

Ellen T. Heffernan

IN DEFINING LEADERSHIP in higher education, it is noteworthy that what presidents, chancellors, and boards indicate they are seeking across the spectrum of cabinet leadership is consistent regardless of the type of institution or leadership position. A panel of presidents—Bob Kustra, president at Boise State; David Maxwell, president at Drake University; and Ernest Colderón, president of the Arizona Board of Regents—recently articulated what they were seeking in a cabinet-level hire: a vice president or dean appointment. While some of the characteristics could be anticipated, the important message is that the new leadership of higher education is seeking leaders with a complex set of characteristics and experiences.

An obvious characteristic of strong leadership is possessing relevant experience for the position, although having held the position at a similar type of institution is not necessarily sufficient in itself. Possessing a range of professional experience that captures the essence of the responsibilities is far more important than merely having held an identically titled position at another institution. Relevant expertise is equally important. A leader who brings relevant expertise to a position brings a skill set that will expand the way the position is viewed. In essence, the goal of tomorrow's leader is to move the dial in terms of what stakeholders see as possible for the person holding the position to accomplish.

The management versus leadership metric is clear: The strong leader must have the skills to be in charge of his or her part of the institution but must also serve as a member of the senior leadership team. A senior professional must reflect confidence in the president and board, in other members of the senior team, and in the mission and direction of the institution to all constituencies at all times. A successful leader demonstrates leadership capabilities across the college or university, not just in his or her area, and can make decisions that best serve the institution, not just a specific division, school, or cohort. Successful student affairs leaders understand that it is not about "advocating for students"; instead, it is about being able to articulate student issues and concerns and identifying, for the president and board, how a decision will impact the ability of students to successfully graduate.

Leaders possess a breadth of institutional vision, an understanding of the issues and challenges faced by their senior colleagues, and a grasp of key institutional issues and metrics. As an institutional leader, you should be able to converse with key donors, articulate the institution's fundraising priorities, understand your enrollment picture (including enrollment goals), discuss endowment strategies, know what is happening at your benchmark and aspirant institutions, converse with a parent about the academic support services offered by the institution, and generally be able to speak about all aspects of the mission and academic program of your institution as it relates to the national constellation of colleges and universities. An exceptional senior student affairs officer is able to tell the story of his or her institution, express to the board what national best practices are for similar institutions, and move seamlessly among multiple stakeholders with a clear vision for the student affairs division and institution.

Talented leaders are expected to possess the interpersonal skills that allow them to interact with the widest possible set of constituents and the communication skills to craft a narrative that speaks to those constituents. Institutional leaders must be committed to the institutional mission and core values. The most effective leaders know their strengths, build teams that complement those strengths, and are a "fit" with the institution and its culture. Fit is important in the academy, as colleges and universities are built on academic foundations and layered with other nuances—such as religious affiliation, a professional preparation curriculum, a pure liberal arts program of study, or a research focus— that add to the complex weave of an institution's culture. Knowledgeable leaders read the pattern in an institutional weave and carefully consider what they can bring to the institution at this point in its evolution; that is, whether they can see themselves as part of the institutional fabric.

Presidents and boards want leaders who both understand the nature of their institutional culture but who can also make change—two sides of the same coin that are equally important. A strategic senior student affairs administrator does not assume that all large, public, land-grant institutions have the same challenges or strengths. Rather, the SSAO works to identify the opportunities for his or her specific institution. A leader understands that good ideas and solutions can be found across all institutions that comprise the academy, and that an idea to improve student retention that works at a small private liberal arts college may also work at a large research institution.

Finally, leaders in the academy must possess intellectual capacity and demonstrate that they understand what it means to work in an environment that values learning. In short, leaders must be active contributors to the "intellectual caretaking of the academy" (D. Maxwell, personal communication, March 7, 2010). Those leading in student affairs today model the ideal of lifelong learning, value advances of technology, and incubate creativity among staff and students. The professionals who are truly leading in the academy today demonstrate integrity, have the ability to see the future of higher education, and possess the strength to move their institutions strategically forward toward that future.

The Search for Authentic Leadership

Larry D. Roper

EARLY IN MY career, the small private institution at which I was working was going through a particularly difficult time. We were in financial peril, struggling with dwindling enrollment, reeling from years of poor retention, and being led by a fractured senior leadership team— the president and vice president for finance had just resigned. In the midst of this turmoil, the vice president for student affairs convened a meeting of all members of the student affairs organization, with the apparent goal of helping us understand what was happening and, it seemed at the time, to help us feel better about the situation. As I reflect on the dynamics that unfolded at that meeting, much of what was shared among the members of our organization is a blur to me. However, what sticks with me to this day is the point in the meeting at which the vice president paused and said to us in his most earnest tone, "Listen, people. Tough times don't last, but tough people do." While I assume that statement was meant to be inspirational, it provoked confusion in me. At that early stage of my career, armed with aspirations to be a small college dean of students, I was questioning what good leadership looked like in a student affairs professional in general, and specifically in a senior student affairs officer (SSAO). I left the meeting frightened and confused—frightened about the plight of the college and what that might mean for the security of my job and confused about whether I had what it took to be a good dean of students. In a matter of days, I had reached a level of comfort regarding my job security—even if my job went away, I felt confident that I would find employment elsewhere. However, my feelings of confusion about my fitness for student affairs leadership were not as easily resolved. Where I got stuck was in trying to reconcile the vice president's statement about "tough people." Since I had never regarded myself as a tough guy, I wondered whether there was a place for me in the student affairs profession. Did I have what it took to survive and succeed? I spent considerable time fretting over the notion that "tough people last."

Thus, my major preoccupation as I began my professional career was figuring out whether a person with a nonauthoritarian personality could make it in this profession. While I know that I am opinionated and can be strong-willed, I also know that I am not capable of sustaining relationships with others that rely on my asserting power or being tough. To resolve this issue, I took the same approach I had taken with many other issues with which I was confronted while growing up in poverty in the inner city: I reframed the statement to fit the reality in which I wanted to live. I resolved my dilemma by reversing the intended inspirational statement, declaring to myself, "Good times don't last, but good people do." While I had not heard this statement previously and have not heard it echoed by anybody else during my professional journey, it has anchored me over the years. When I formulated this belief, it provided me with the outlook that good times will come and go, but if you are a good person you will succeed. Of course, having very limited experience in higher education, I had no verifiable evidence that this declaration was true. But I did have substantial life experience of acting with confidence in situations where I was not sure that I was, in fact, right. Thus, I started early in my career acting on the hope that if I was a good person (and had some idea of my job responsibilities), I could be successful in student affairs. Of course, time and experience would ultimately reveal that success in student affairs depends on much more than being a nice guy and having half a clue. Certain competencies are required for success in student affairs, especially at the SSAO level.

THE NEED FOR SPECIFIC COMPETENCIES

Throughout my career, I have been fortunate to work at a wide range of institutions, which has given me the chance to observe institutions and leaders under the best and worst conditions. I have been exposed to very successful senior student affairs leaders and I have found myself in situations where senior student affairs leaders were justly or unjustly relieved of their responsibilities. In each of my professional positions, I was able to distill learning from the experience. However, it was not until I was in my first SSAO role that I was able to test whether my assumptions about the competencies needed to be an effective SSAO were accurate. In fact, they proved to be inaccurate. Part of my inaccurate picture was attributable to the stance from which I consciously and unconsciously evaluated the SSAOs to whom I was exposed and my expectation that their worldview was no different than mine as an entry- or midlevel professional; that is, I expected them to demonstrate commitment to students through the same behaviors I displayed. It took time, trial and error, reflection, feedback, and humility to get to a place where my approach to performing as an SSAO felt sustainable, effective, and authentic for me.

The perspective on essential competencies that I have constructed is neither elegant nor complex. My suggestions regarding what is needed for success as an SSAO are based on dominant themes in my career and influential experiences during my 20-plus years as an SSAO. The characteristics (competencies) I believe are essential for success are self-knowledge; leadership integrity; the ability to be multilingual; the ability to demonstrate full citizenship participation; the ability to transform advocacy and mediate personal opinions; the capacity to construct durable relationship networks; and the capacity to demonstrate love for your campus.

SELF-KNOWLEDGE

It may sound trite to say that SSAOs should know who they are, but I believe this still needs to be said and that such knowledge is an essential attribute for success. Self-knowledge, from my perspective, means we have the ability to regularly and rigorously ask ourselves difficult questions, such as Who am I? Why am I here? and What do I hope to get done? Clarity about our identity, our purpose, and our desired legacy can be an important anchor during stable, uncertain, or changing times. All professionals need to have insight into their strengths and weaknesses. No matter how uncomfortable the process, we need to be able to articulate for ourselves what we do well and where we may fall short. When we understand our strengths and weaknesses, we are better positioned to make good decisions about the situations in which we place ourselves, the institutions with which we affiliate, and the expectations we negotiate for our performance. Self-knowledge provides a solid foundation on which we can build strong leadership.

When we know who we are, it makes it easier for us to forgive ourselves when we fall short of what others expect of us and what we expect of ourselves. We learn to appreciate when we have done our best and given what we are capable of giving. When we have self-knowledge, we tend to be more emotionally secure in our work and relationships, which creates space for others to excel and develop.

It is essential for SSAOs (as well as other student affairs professionals) to have guiding beliefs anchoring our leadership. These beliefs, whatever they are based on, should be strong enough to sustain us no matter which institution we work for or what circumstances we encounter in terms of institutional dynamics. Central to those beliefs are our attitudes about who we are, why we are here, and what we hope to get done. Such focus and clarity of purpose provide a strong foundation for successful leadership.

LEADERSHIP INTEGRITY

It may be a stretch to say that integrity is a competency. In fact, I am pretty certain it is not. However, managing one's reputation does require skill. Often, how others perceive us in our institutions is a matter of the reputation we create and an outcome of the stories others tell about their interactions with us. Our reputation is the result of simple dynamics as well as complex interactions. Our integrity can be judged by such straightforward day-to-day incidents as whether we return phone messages or e-mails, show up for meetings on time, or follow through on assignments. We are also judged by how we behave during times that test the character of our campus community; how we position ourselves during intercultural conflicts; how we behave when we are personally attacked; and how we handle delicate personnel situations. Every day we present others with countless instances through which our integrity can be judged. The standards most often used to judge the integrity of SSAOs include whether we keep our word, respect the humanity and reputations of others, tell the truth, care about all members of our community, share, and are good team members. When we lose integrity, we lose the trust of those around us. As SSAOs, our success depends greatly on the trust and faith others have in us. Throughout my career, deans, presidents, provosts, and other colleagues have reminded me in direct and indirect ways that opportunities afforded me and invitations for inclusion in particular experiences are driven by the trust others have in what I will bring to the leadership experience. Surprisingly, I have found that these opportunities and invitations often have little to do with the specific content knowledge I possess—often, student affairs professionals are included in important conversations because of the belief that we will add integrity to the process.

Most SSAOs have tremendous knowledge and skills to bring to bear on the leadership dynamics of a campus; however, if we do not pay attention to cultivating our reputation in a way that allows others to have respect for us and faith in our leadership, our professional impact and the campus will suffer. Building leadership integrity requires manifesting our professional values and core leadership principles in a consistently positive and reliable manner. The integrity we cultivate has a tremendous effect on the breadth of leadership opportunities we are afforded.

BE MULTILINGUAL

When I began my career in student affairs, I felt strongly that the most important aspect of my work was to honor the student voice. As I honed my skills and effectiveness, I placed a heavy emphasis on increasing my ability to effectively communicate students' needs, expectations, and concerns to my superiors. Over time, I became very skilled at speaking in the student voice. This skill allowed me to construct good relationships with students, as I was able to approximate their voice and hear their perspectives with clarity. Unfortunately, the side effect of being so singular in my focus on hearing and speaking for students was that I often missed the importance of hearing and responding to other voices. In hindsight, I wish someone had told me, in terms I could have understood, the importance of being attuned to the needs, expectations, and concerns of other key constituents. It was not until I assumed my first SSAO position that I became acutely aware of the requirement that I be "multilingual."

When I achieved my goal of becoming a small college dean, I assumed that my primary role was no different than I had believed it to be in my previous roles: to represent the student voice. That was not the case. While a core aspect of my job was to represent the student perspective, I was not being asked to echo the student voice—a subtlety that took me some time to comprehend. My supervisor, senior leadership colleagues, and other key constituents wanted me to behave as something other than an overgrown student leader. As I moved into this role, I faced the challenge of learning to speak effectively with others in voices they could comprehend. I discovered that speaking in the student voice did not resonate with all the groups with which I had to interact in my role as an SSAO. I was expected to maintain a day-to-day relationship with the president, vice president for finance, vice president for academic affairs, trustees, parents, and others with whom I had previously had only occasional or episodic interactions.

The SSAO position requires that we hone our voice to construct and sustain effective relationships with a wide range of colleagues. For example, in making a case for resources, it is important to know how our colleagues in the budget and finance arena will best understand us. Being multilingual means we will recognize the unique communication needs of the wide range of audiences with which we must interact. Additionally, having skills as multilingual professionals means that we will hear clearly the many voices that are communicating to us. Often, student affairs professionals focus on hearing the student voice to the detriment of hearing other important voices. The skillful SSAO should be able to hear and speak effectively with a wide range of stakeholders and discern important messages from various constituents. The experienced SSAO will be able to sort through the clamor of multiple perspectives to hear the important voices, and will be able to respond in a way that confirms those voices have been heard.

DEMONSTRATE FULL CITIZENSHIP

Too often, the student affairs organization is seen as occupying space on the margins of the college or university. I strongly believe it is the responsibility of the SSAO to behave in a way that places student affairs at the center of campus life. Our colleges and universities rest on a foundation of three essential activities: teaching, research, and service. It is imperative for SSAOs to model full "citizenship" responsibility and engagement by demonstrating involvement in all three activities. When I assumed the SSAO role, I thought I had a pretty good awareness of the need to engage in teaching, research, and service, as well as a strong desire to engage in those activities. Throughout my postdoctoral career, I have been diligent about producing scholarship, staying involved in teaching, and demonstrating commitment to service to my campus and to the student affairs profession. I have also consciously positioned myself to be successful in the tenure and promotion process. I always had a sense that this was the right thing to do but never truly understood the value of this focus (beyond the peace of mind tenure offers) until a few years ago.

I was stunned when my provost approached me to ask if I would serve as interim dean of the College of Liberal Arts. I responded to his request with tremendous self-doubt. I asked myself, "Can I be effective in that role? Will I be accepted by the faculty in the college? Am I smart enough to lead an academic college?" Although I had worked to position myself as a full citizen, I was still psychologically on the margins of the university. My internal conversation in the face of the provost's request was completely contrary to the conversation I had been having with my student affairs colleagues since my arrival at the university. In that moment, I realized that I had to learn to act and think like a full citizen of the university.

I agreed to serve as interim dean and, in my 18 months in the position, discovered a lot about student affairs leadership. The experience reinforced for me the importance of knowing who I am and what I value. It drove home the significance of relationships and the extent to which the quality of relationships is linked to one's reputation. I was also amazed at the extent to which my academic colleagues were tuned in to the leadership dynamics of student affairs—they were aware of our values, the work to which we are committed, our partnership efforts, and other aspects of our work that they viewed as beneficial for their college. I was most struck by how transferable the leadership approaches used in student affairs are to the academic context. The emphasis student affairs leaders place on inclusion, building community, and nurturing teams is equally important to faculty, especially those who feel isolated in their work.

The fact that I am tenured, maintain a regular teaching schedule, and have stayed involved in scholarship was particularly important when it came time for me to review promotion and tenure dossiers and write letters on behalf of liberal arts faculty, supporting or rejecting the recommendations of the college's committee. In those instances, faculty needed to know that I could recognize high-quality scholarship, good teaching, and acceptable levels of service. Without a background of personal involvement in those areas, I would have had no credibility in the eyes of faculty to make such judgments. Early in my career, I had no idea I would be put in a position to exercise those judgments; I am sure that had I not challenged myself to become a full citizen of the university, I would not have been presented with the opportunity to do so.

My transition to academic administrator has been greatly facilitated by the fact that I report to the provost and work closely with academic deans as a member of the Provost's Council. As a member of that council,

I work regularly with deans and share leadership with them in moving our university forward. This leadership experience reinforced for me the importance of being a good citizen and fully investing in my university and my colleagues. As citizens of the campus, we have rights and responsibilities; the extent to which we embrace both will greatly affect the breadth and depth of our influence. SSAOs have the opportunity to participate in numerous leadership groups; our challenge is to derive the greatest possible benefit from those opportunities. One way to do so is to bring all your knowledge and skills to bear in your contributions and to distill all the learning you can in your quest for ongoing development.

TRANSFORM ADVOCACY AND MEDIATE PERSONAL OPINIONS

One of the most humbling moments of my professional career was when I became aware that I had not been hired because of my personal opinions. Like most people, I think pretty highly of my views on social issues. There have been times during my career when I did not shy away from espousing my perspective and seizing whatever platform was available to champion my cause. I took great pride in proclaiming myself to be a student advocate, which, to me, justified being reckless. This perspective and the leadership style that flows from it are not compatible with success as an SSAO. While working at a small Catholic college, I was confronted with the disconnect between my personal values and the teachings of the Catholic Church on the issue of providing access to contraceptives on campus. My inclination, based on my previous leadership history, was to challenge the priest and advocate for what I believe to be the just response. However, for some reason, I resisted my impulse to speak and instead opted to listen and learn more about the issue. In a subsequent conversation with my president, I shared my dilemma: the conflict between my personal views and those represented by the priest. In a most gentle and supportive way, the president helped me understand that a challenge to the Church would represent my personal opinion and that none of us, including him, had been hired on the basis of our personal opinions. We were hired because it was believed that we could help the college advance its mission. Up to that point, it had never occurred to me that there were times when my personal opinion would not and should not matter. This situation and subsequent conversations challenged me to explore my conception of advocacy.

Before assuming the SSAO role, my practice of advocacy could best be described as "any time is the right time for my issue." This approach allowed for randomness and thoughtlessness in my leadership and interactions with others. As an advocate, I often took sides on issues, which made me an ally to some members of the campus community and put me in antagonistic relationships with others. As SSAOs, we cannot allow our leadership to fragment the community; our role is to find ways to bring the campus together and forge a stronger sense of community. Advocacy, as it is most commonly practiced, requires the advocate to take an extreme position on an issue and to view others with differing views as opponents or adversaries. I believe it is damaging to an SSAO's leadership to construct adversarial relationships. The SSAO's approach to issues should be strategic and thoughtful. I have found it extremely beneficial to transform advocacy into strategic leadership—moving from just talking about issues to finding approaches to achieve success with particular issues.

As SSAOs gain more experience, our awareness of interactive dynamics should become more sophisticated. Our maturity should reflect awareness that we have a responsibility to help our campuses navigate challenging issues, rather than escalate matters by not being able to separate our personal feelings from our professional responsibility. While our role is not that of diplomat, we need to understand diplomacy. We need the humility to accept that there are instances when our personal opinion is dwarfed in comparison with the institution's mission, and we need the skills to elevate our mission when our impulse is to raise our voice. Effective SSAOs will skillfully mediate their personal opinions and transform advocacy into thoughtful, strategic leadership.

CONSTRUCT DURABLE RELATIONSHIP NETWORKS

Most experienced SSAOs will concede that the strength of our relationships with other leaders is often the key variable in determining how much we are able to get done. The quality of our relationships also influences our professional advancement, access to resources, job satisfaction, professional development, and other important aspects of our professional life.

The SSAO needs to build strong relationships with a broad cross-section of constituents, relationships that demonstrate the value we place on the issues that matter significantly to our stakeholders. Success as an SSAO is closely tied to our ability to construct and manage those relationships. We build the necessary network of successful relationships by cultivating a reputation of caring about others and demonstrating a pattern of consistently effective interactions, through which we exhibit our capacity to be engaged in the issues that make a difference to others. Being thoughtful about the quality of our relationships and showing generosity in our dealings with others are essential components of being an effective student affairs leader.

If we construct durable relationships, they can withstand the ups and downs that characterize institutional life at a college or university. Seasoned SSAOs will understand that the senior leadership team on which they serve will experience disagreements, miscommunication, competition, stressful interactions, and other dynamics that can challenge relationships. Those who are able to communicate care for their colleagues, even in the face of challenging interactions, will be best positioned for success. We build strong relationships with our colleagues by communicating to them that we value them and we are on their side, regardless of the challenges before us. If we communicate that our relationships are easily fractured or that we will abandon colleagues when times get tough, we suggest to others that our relationships are conditional or easily discarded.

Mature leaders understand the value of building and sustaining strong relationship networks vertically and horizontally in the organization. We must be attuned to what is needed to create a solid relationship with our supervisor, including how to support the supervisor's success, how to balance challenge with loyalty, and how to build confidence in our leadership. In building a strong relationship with a supervisor, there is no substitute for time and communication. We must invest in creating the kind of relationship we want to enjoy. While it is easy to see the supervisor as the most important person in relationship dynamics, we should not minimize the important roles other colleagues play in how we are perceived and the support we receive. The reputation we forge will greatly influence how colleagues regard us and whether they are willing to work with us. While our supervisors will use their personal interactions with us as a basis to make judgments about our future in the organization, they will also use the quality of our relationships with other leaders as a key piece of data in evaluating our performance. Poor relationships with key institutional leaders can be fatal to the SSAO, while positive relationships can enhance our perceived value.

Relationship maturity is reflected in our ability to balance the need to assert independent leadership with the ability to be supportive of and aligned with those with whom we are in relationship. Successful SSAOs construct relationships that will endure regardless of the situation.

DEMONSTRATE LOVE FOR YOUR CAMPUS

Every college and university faces ups and downs, turmoil and harmony, and success and failure. Regardless of the circumstances facing our campus, as SSAOs we need to be mindful about the feelings we project to others. I can recall times earlier in my career when I experienced a love-hate relationship with my campus. I would vacillate between feeling immense pride about certain institutional decisions and feeling heartbroken in the face of other institutional actions. What I discovered about myself, in hindsight, is that my care for my institution was conditional.

As SSAOs, we have the opportunity to be present when high-stakes decisions are made. We are party to conversations about issues that matter significantly to others; we have access to reasoning for institutional actions that others will never hear; and we get to observe our co-leaders at their best and worst. Sometimes being this close to the action can produce disappointment or disillusionment; at other times, our sense of encouragement or hope is strengthened. There are times when I walk out of a meeting of the President's Cabinet or the Provost's Council feeling frustrated by the failure of those bodies to decide a matter in a way that aligns with the outcome I want. In those moments, I am confronted with an important personal decision: Do I support the team, or do I let it be known that although I was in the meeting, I am not in favor of the final decision? This is a common dilemma faced by SSAOs: We are part of teams that make decisions with which we don't agree.

Before I became an SSAO, it was not uncommon for me to grandstand and make it known that I was not in favor of a decision made by a team to which I belonged. At the time, such behavior felt like a shield of honor that I could hold up to show that I was on the right side of important issues. In fact, the behavior showed disregard for the integrity of my colleagues, and it undermined my integrity as well. I had little concept of what it meant to support a team.

As I gained experience as an SSAO, I learned the importance of supporting the team, regardless of how my perspective differed from the final decision made by groups or individuals. I have come to understand that there will be times when the place we land on some important issue will break my heart; I also know that we will do things that will give me a stronger sense of affection for my campus. The longer I work in student affairs, the more I understand the importance of cultivating love for my campus. The more affection I develop for my institution and what I believe we want to stand for when we are at our best, the better I am able to be understanding when we fall short of my expectations. Successful leaders care deeply about their campus. They invest in being committed to the leadership teams on which they participate and staying true to the institution during the most difficult times.

While it is rare to talk about our relationship with our campus as being characterized by love, it is important to acknowledge that the depth of our affection for the institution and those with whom we work is an important part of leadership. I believe successful senior student affairs leaders must care deeply about their campus and should demonstrate that care on a daily basis and in all their interactions.

CONCLUSION

Clearly, there is no definitive set of competencies for SSAOs. For some people, a list of essential competencies would include things I believe are basic job requirements (e.g., manage budgets, supervise effectively). As I think about success as an SSAO, I consider the things that make a difference beyond my ability to manage the core day-to-day activities of the job.

The SSAO position offers immense opportunities to influence the success of our campus. However, the degree of success we enjoy will likely be influenced by our ability to learn from our experiences and transform that learning into a personal style and professional practices that demonstrate our value and commitment to our institution. Each of us will be at our best when we commit to developing an authentic style that honors who we are and what we value, and reveals the contributions we aspire to make to the lives of those with whom we interact in our work.

It Takes a Village to be Effective

KAREN L. PENNINGTON

Scene:
Monday, Labor Day
9:15 a.m.
My kitchen
The phone rings—

SSAO: "Hello."

Chief of University Police: "Hi, boss. We have a missing student. She's a junior and has been missing since last night. Her cell phone activated our safety tracking system, but the GPS is not telling us where she is. We've called her phone every 15 minutes, and there's no answer. We've also called her home and there's no answer there. I just wanted to fill you in on what we've done and what's happened so far. . . ."

SSAO: "Is she a resident student? No? Okay. Keep me posted."

End of scene.

SO BEGINS THE typical academic year for a senior student affairs officer (SSAO) at a large suburban university. Questions run through my mind about what could have happened and where she might have gone, but the background factors of rules, responsibilities, and political fallout soon take over. Sadly, these factors may even momentarily take center stage over my worry about the student. "Why didn't the tracking system work right? How will we explain that to the press? Has it been more than 24 hours? Have we met the requirements of the Higher Education Reauthorization Act? Have her friends contacted their parents—or hers? What kind of panic is starting on campus, and how will we manage that fallout? Oh—by the way—is she all right?"

Whatever happened to the caring and compassion that used to be the hallmark of our work? Have I lost my raison d'être? I hope not. I choose to believe that it's just the life of an SSAO in a 21st-century technologically advanced and litigiously directed society. In this case, the chief phoned back a few minutes later to inform me that the student had been located and was fine. She didn't recall activating her phone's safety application, and then her phone died, so she couldn't be found by GPS or reached via talk or text.

The skills necessary to be successful as an SSAO go beyond helping students navigate the steps of adolescent development and maturation. An African proverb says, "It takes a village to raise a child." To be effective, today's SSAO needs to *be* the village—to fulfill the roles of several members of the community. An SSAO needs be part lawyer, part information and technology manager, part news junkie, part human resources manager, and part stand-up comedian—and sometimes all at the same time! Let's dissect these roles.

LAWYER

It seems that very few difficult conversations with students and parents these days do not end with a veiled or clear threat to bring legal action against individuals or the institution for whatever wrong they believe has befallen them because of your staff's actions or inactions. There are no accidents or mistakes (unless they are the student's, and then they should be ignored), and there must always be some kind of restitution from the institution.

Did we really do something wrong? Is there a cause of action that this person can bring? Why do I even know terms like "cause of action"? As an SSAO, I have to be on the lookout for what can go wrong and what can trip us up. This is not easy, because I am not with my staff every waking moment and can't be aware of everything that they do or say. Back in graduate school, most of us learned the concepts of foreseeability and a duty to care. It is in this position more than any other that we begin to really recognize how vulnerable we and our institutions are to the actions of others. I became acutely aware of that fact a few years ago when I read a story about a university president who was forced to resign from his position. It wasn't anything that he had done or failed to do but, rather, a poor decision made by his SSAO for which the board of trustees held him accountable. As a former supervisor used to say, "There's less room for error as you move up."

But the president can make mistakes, too, and it's often the SSAO's job to keep him or her from doing things that will hurt the institution. Consider the recent ruling in *Barnes v. Zaccari et al.* (2010). In 2007, Thomas Hayden Barnes was a student at Valdosta State University. During the spring semester of that year, Barnes was involved in a campus campaign to alert the community about the University's Master Plan, particularly a planned parking garage and the environmental impact that building might have on the campus. He distributed flyers that caused concern to President Ronald Zaccari, and others became aware of it. When Barnes was informed by other students of the president's displeasure, he removed the flyers and took down the Facebook page he had created. He also wrote a letter to Zaccari indicating that he had removed the information and did not wish to have an adversarial relationship with the university.

Barnes continued his campaign in other venues, including contacting individual members of the Board of Regents, encouraging them to vote against the proposed parking garage. Zaccari sought information from many staff members about Barnes, including his academic record, medical history, registration with the disability office, as well as other personal details. Zaccari expressed his concerns about Barnes to members of his senior staff, including comments that he feared for his personal safety. Numerous conversations and inquiries by his staff indicated that Barnes was not a threat to himself or to others on the campus, and there was no evidence of a threat to Zaccari.

Despite this information, Zaccari proceeded to administratively withdraw Barnes from the university. He made this decision despite the advice of a number of his staff members. Barnes appealed the withdrawal to the Board of Regents and the Board rescinded his withdrawal without comment. Barnes sued Zaccari and other members of the university administration for violations of free speech rights, retaliation, and breach of due process rights. Following testimony, the judge ruled that Zaccari, not the university and not other administrators, had violated several of Barnes' rights and that he could personally be sued and held liable for his actions.

There are numerous opportunities for things to go wrong in student affairs. It is impossible to keep that from happening. But it is important that we do what we can to keep anyone from getting sued. While it isn't always possible to protect people from themselves, more often than not, a highly competent SSAO can help a president understand why a decision is or is not a good idea. Being vigilant, well-informed, and having a working knowledge of major precedents and legislation is essential to being an exceptional SSAO.

INFORMATION AND TECHNOLOGY MANAGER

How do you manage the flow of information inside and outside the campus in the case of an emergency? You don't! That realization will help SSAOs better manage their operations and their campuses. The multiple, ubiquitous means of communication methods and their various owners no longer allow us to control the how and where of information dissemination. The best we can do is try to stay on top of things, and catch up and clean up if necessary. According to Facebook statistics (2010):

- Facebook has more than 500 million active users.
- Fifty percent of active users log on to Facebook on any given day.
- The average user has 130 "friends."
- People spend more than 700 billion minutes per month on Facebook.

As for Twitter (tweettwins, 2010):

- Twitter has 105,779,710 registered users.
- New users are signing up at the rate of 300,000 a day.

- More than 180 million unique visitors come to the site every month.
- Seventy-five percent of Twitter traffic comes from outside Twitter.com (i.e., via third party applications).
- Twitter gets a total of 3 billion requests a day via its application programming interface.
- Twitter users are tweeting an average total of 55 million tweets a day.
- Twitter's search engine receives around 600 million search queries a day.
- Of Twitter's active users, 37% use their phone to tweet.
- Over half of all tweets (60%) come from third party applications.

How can you and your public relations department compete with that? Getting the right information to the right people at the right time takes skill, dedication, and a lot of patience. SSAOs need to develop a close relationship with their colleagues in the media and communications department. Make sure they know how and when to contact you for the right information and, perhaps more important, make sure you contact them before the media start breaking down the door with questions.

It is also critical for senior officers to have media training. It is not unusual for SSAOs to have to speak to the media after a major event. Many news outlets don't want to hear from the university spokesperson—they want to hear from someone close to the situation and close to students. Knowing what to say and how to say it (and, more important, knowing what *not* to say and how *not* to say it) is a significant skill that will benefit your president, your board, and your institution. If your public relations person doesn't have this skill, many local TV stations and newspapers have people who will teach you the ropes. You may not be able to control what's out there, but you will be able to help determine how the public receives it.

Technology also comes in the form of administrative functions— software to manage student records in areas such as counseling, health, recreation, and enrollment. And SSAOs must be familiar with hardware, too, such as door lock mechanisms and ID card systems. It is impossible to know everything, so it is important to surround yourself with people who know the things you don't. Remaining informed about the things that will affect your students and their ability to navigate the campus is an important part of meeting the needs of the entire campus.

A third component of technology is the ability it provides for an SSAO to see the big picture. In fact, it helps to see the "bigger" picture—the world beyond the campus and the community.

News Junkie

A 21st-century SSAO needs to be a bit of a news junkie. You can use many different media methods to remain abreast of issues that affect, for example, students, staff, budgets, accreditation, and enrollment. Reviewing daily news feeds, newspapers and journals, and various websites should become a regular routine. It is naïve to think that only issues that directly affect or pertain to students are important to an SSAO. Obviously, everything that happens on a campus or at the university has an effect on students and our relationship with them.

While gaining knowledge is important, it is even more critical to analyze, synthesize, and apply your knowledge to the SSAO role. How does it relate to the current aspects of your institution? What are the pertinent relationships with faculty, programs, and the functions of your vice presidential colleagues? How do you make it all work for you?

Staying current is easier said than done. Most of us don't have two spare minutes to rub together in the course of a day. Time to read papers and analyze and apply the information often has to be scheduled. This realization sometimes comes slowly to the 21st-century SSAO. Day-to-day operations take longer than expected; emergencies are normal, not rare; and downtime has to be planned. It's difficult, but it's an important part of being an effective manager.

Human Resources Manager

Management in student affairs has to be hands-on. We have to know our staff and stay aware of what they are doing. Our accountability quotient is high and gets higher each year, as families, boards, and legislators look for a positive return on investment for students and the nation. Federal and state initiatives by departments of education call for institutions to measure and report results. Accreditation agencies more and more seek to measure and assess our objectives and outcomes.

SSAOs need to invest not only in programs but in their employees. Meeting with young professionals recently, I was dismayed to learn that a staff member who started a few years ago did not receive a positive welcome to the university and to her department. The director who hired her resigned about a week before she started, and the interim director was unprepared to provide the welcome this new staff member should have received. She spent her first few weeks thinking her supervisor was someone else in the department before her reporting line was finally made clear! Since that time, each hiring manager gets a clear set of written instructions and a checklist of responsibilities for hiring and welcoming a new employee.

The generational differences among baby boomers, Generation Xers, and millennials often show up when employment matters arise. While most people clearly understand and know how to set personal and professional boundaries, some individuals are less able to do so without assistance. While we may not normally think it would be necessary, supervisors often have to teach about these issues to millennials, who have a less long-range view of the workplace and its parameters as they are less experienced in professional settings.

Start new employee orientation with discussions about Facebook, Twitter, and other social media networks and their position in the workplace. You don't want to end up in a meeting with the president explaining why your coordinator of intramurals' vacation trip to Cancun was the topic of discussion at the last Greek Council social!

Newer professionals often need help seeing the big picture. Recently, a very energetic and enthusiastic staff member wrote me about an idea he wanted me to endorse: "I have a fun idea. Let's have a Food Fight for Charity! You pay to enter, you eat some food (spaghetti and cheap stuff), and then we fight. All proceeds go to the homeless and hungry at Thanksgiving. Our students, while wasting cheap food, get a better sense and appreciation for what they have . . . plus they have fun and we donate money."

I thought he was joking, but he wasn't. He just didn't consider the potential implications of encouraging students to waste food in the name of people who need food to eat. What would the local food banks think about this idea? What about local politicians who sponsor bills for the needy? What about families, either locally or of students, who are struggling to put food on their tables while the "privileged" college students waste food?

The possible ramifications of an idea like this go beyond the immediate situation and even the campus. The staff member obviously didn't see the big picture. He cared very much about student activities as well as about those who need help. He was just very young and very green, and didn't put all of the pieces together on his own. You have to admire the initiative, though. It's instances like this one that provide the opportunity for education and training. Aside from programs that your human resources department might offer for all employees, SSAOs have a captive audience of many new professionals in entry-level positions and the ability to have an impact on their professional growth and maturity. Develop and plan a series of in-service programs that will provide the training they need to see beyond their current positions and recognize the effect of their actions on other areas of the institution. The following are examples of programs:

- Use of Facebook and other social media by professionals
- Professional writing
- What to wear to work
- Learning the campus culture

- Understanding the Family Educational Rights and Privacy Act
- Establishing yourself as a professional
- How to work effectively with faculty
- How to handle disruptive students
- Effective supervision of students and professionals
- Overview of the world of higher education
- Professional etiquette

STAND-UP COMEDIAN

The 21st-century SSAO needs to be able to relate to an ever-changing audience—one minute it's staff, then faculty, then students, the president, the community, and on and on. A good stand-up comedian can maintain a sense of positive energy for all. Even when there is a heckler (e.g., the student newspaper or an angry parent), the effective SSAO must remain calm and collected. Nothing will undermine an SSAO's credibility faster than appearing frazzled during a problem situation.

Through good times and bad, the SSAO needs to maintain a sense of humor. Knowing how to sift through the many layers of a situation and keep everyone calm requires an ability to relate to all members of the audience and keep the community from panicking. That doesn't mean the SSAO needs to turn every situation into a joke, but it helps if you can use a light tone to convince others that you are in control and have everything well in hand.

A good sense of humor is also necessary to keep everything in perspective. The stress and urgency that come with being an SSAO can be overwhelming if you allow the problems that arise to "rent space in your head." When all is said and done, most matters will be remembered as annoyances and inconveniences. Fortunately, very few problems will be consequential or have long-lasting ramifications, and it helps to keep that in mind. When someone says, "Everyone is up in arms and the phone hasn't stopped ringing," remember to ask, "How many calls? Is it 5 or 50?" Establishing perspective on the situation will help you determine your response and decide who needs to be involved in preparing it. It will also allow you to help your staff manage the current and future circumstances surrounding the situation.

Finally, when the time is right, remember to laugh. We in student affairs give care to those who are in medical, physical, emotional, or psychological need. We deal with many emergencies where the caregiving response is our activity. As such, the stress that is produced in staff is often the same as those who are on the front line of illness or health care treatment. Laugh at the day, the responses, yourself—whatever is appropriate and relieves the stress of the situation. Of course, you need to make sure the location and the people you share this tension release with are appropriate. Remember that people will look to you for guidance and direction. How you respond and the "game face" you display will become the face of the division and the institution. Your president and board will be reassured by your effectiveness as their representative and your ability to serve the campus community.

It may take a village to raise a child, but it takes an SSAO to be the village. Welcome to the neighborhood!

References

Barnes v. Zaccari et al., No. 1:08-cv-00077-CAP (N.D. Ga. Sep. 3, 2010).

Facebook statistics. (2010). Retrieved from http://www.facebook.com/press/info.php?statistics

tweettwins. (2010, April 30). Twitter statistics 2010. Retrieved from http://tweettwins.wordpress.com/2010/06/01/twitter-statistics-2010

A Commitment to Serving
Our Changing Communities

JESUS CARREON

PERHAPS THE BEST place to start is by making it very clear that this section is not set at 30,000 feet or anchored by the typical academic rhetoric. My goal is to challenge, inform, and encourage senior student affairs officers (SSAOs) to understand and accept the reality that ongoing change must be factored into how we do business today and well into the future.

My comments will focus on: (a) perceptions and attitudes I have experienced over nearly four decades in higher education; (b) how experienced SSAOs can use internal and external "homework" to understand what has been, what is, and what may be; (c) suggestions for how SSAOs can set the tone in their area and institution by establishing and maintaining a culture of trust; and (d) a description of what I believe is the legacy SSAOs should keep in mind in their day-to-day professional and personal activities.

From my years of interaction and experience with colleagues in colleges and universities and with the general public, I have become very aware that higher education is perceived in some communities as an island, isolated within the real world. This perception is even more of an issue in communities that have been consistently underserved by their local colleges. My direct experience during the past 37 years has allowed me, in real time and real-life settings, to experience what many are not willing to acknowledge: the ongoing separation of higher education institutions from the communities they serve because of leaders who do not understand that the college is the community. An SSAO in today's college environment must understand and deal with the multitude of changes that have taken place in society over the past four decades. Demographic shifts, technological innovations, and changes in the workplace, the workforce, and the economy have had a tremendous impact on all aspects of the academic, economic, and social fabric of our communities locally, statewide, and nationally.

THE LUNCH PAIL MENTALITY

The way we have always functioned in relation to the populations and communities we have served over the past 10, 20, or 30 years is a dysfunctional way to think, act, and do business in today's (and tomorrow's) higher education community. I often hear comments such as these: "We've always done it this way," "This is what we always do," and "We've been very comfortable working this way for many years." The status quo perspective still rules in many institutions. As SSAOs and administrators at institutions of higher education, we must accept the fact that clinging to a "lunch pail mentality" (e.g., the routine of an 8 a.m. to 5 p.m. job) will make us much less effective and efficient in our ability to address the changing environment and the needs and demands of students and communities. The pace and context of change have increased so dramatically that what used to be, what is, and what will be have shaken many people and institutions to the core. We have to constantly rethink and often redo how we conduct our business each day.

Innovation, change, and creativity in education have always been challenges. Why? Because some leaders have not had the vision, discipline, or courage to focus on meeting the needs and demands of changing student populations and communities. I believe that experienced SSAOs should question themselves on a regular basis regarding how they are or should be functioning as managers and leaders. These questions might include the following:

- Am I setting a positive and professional tone as a leader?
- Am I providing clear and focused leadership?
- Am I addressing the challenges of delivering student-friendly programs and services at my institution?

- Am I working closely with academic affairs to meet the needs and demands of the changing workplace, workforce, and economic trends in our local and regional economy?
- Do I make student affairs decisions on the basis of my formal job description?
- Do I make decisions on the basis of my personal commitment to serving students and changing communities?
- Do I make decisions using a combination of my formal job duties and a commitment to meeting the needs and demands of students and communities?

Many of us get so involved with our daily workloads and the variety of activities that we do not step back and ask ourselves the big-picture questions about who we are and how we should function each day and into the future.

ORGANIZATIONAL STRUCTURES: ACADEMIC AFFAIRS AND STUDENT SERVICES

The standard organizational structure, which has been around for decades, reflects "two sides of the house"—academic affairs and student services. This is still pretty much the framework at colleges and universities across the country, except for some that have combined these two areas in an effort to improve coordination, collaboration, and the efficient use of resources in this era of finite public funding.

Truckee Meadows Community College in Reno, Nevada, has combined academic affairs and student services. Continuous improvement in how programs and services are developed and delivered is a major focus of the combined team. For example, the college recently implemented a new technology to facilitate the way in which students, faculty, staff, and the general public access the college's online system to do things like register for classes. To prepare for this major technology transition, a cross-functional team was created to identify key issues, establish expected outcomes, and develop solutions. The cross-functional team did a great job handling the many issues that resulted from this new technology implementation. As a follow-up approach, the team now meets at the beginning of each semester to ensure that any issues resulting from this new technology are addressed in preparation for the upcoming semester.

THE INTERNAL AND EXTERNAL WORLDS

To stay current, SSAOs should continuously assess the internal and external environmental factors. Anyone in a leadership role cannot ignore or minimize the impact of internal and external changes on the direction, functioning, and success of an institution—as well as the individuals in that institution—in serving students.

SSAOs should take time on a regular basis to accomplish the following tasks related to the internal college environment:

- Assess internal college data and information each year to understand the makeup and functioning of the institution.
- Assess each area of responsibility to make sure all are aligned with the vision, mission, needs, and demands of the students and the communities served by the college.
- Determine whether standard operating procedures have been documented and are regularly updated. If they do not exist, initiate a process to document how functions are accomplished each day and at key times each term;
- Assess how student affairs programs and services are perceived by the larger college community. You cannot assume that everyone truly understands the roles and functions in this area.
- Assess the communication flow between and among areas of responsibility in student affairs and throughout the institution. You can do this by surveying staff on a regular basis and by making communication an agenda item in meetings between the SSAO

and other administrators. The point is never to assume that communication flow is always smooth.

Student affairs leaders also need to monitor the external environment, including factors that are constantly changing and that directly affect the institution, such as demographics, technology, the workplace, the workforce, the economy, and politics. It is very important for SSAOs and their colleagues to assess and interpret what is happening on the local, regional, state, and national scene. An SSAO should make time for the following tasks:

- Review data and information related to demographic, technology, workforce, workplace, and economic trends and shifts.
- Connect with the community—not just the civic and business organizations but also the key community organizations and leaders who can be helpful and supportive of higher education.
- Be an innovator and an entrepreneur. *Really listen* to the needs and demands of the communities served by your institution, then take steps to adjust the way you do business.

BUILDING AND MAINTAINING TRUST

First, we must accept the reality that trust is critical because organizational success depends on everyone (faculty, staff, and management) working together collaboratively and interdependently to achieve the vision and mission of the organization. When we fail to work together because of mutual fear and mistrust, people will be unable to understand and solve problems. They will have a diminished capacity to achieve its vision, mission, and strategic goals. Second, trust is essential to build authentic, effective, and sustainable relationships among faculty, staff, and management. Relationships are critical to individual and organizational success.

From my experience, the following approaches can encourage colleagues to establish and maintain a culture of trust:

- **Give each other credit for great work.** We should openly acknowledge each other's hard work, innovative ideas, and contributions toward team and organizational success.
- **Practice personal accountability and take responsibility for problems.** We should openly admit mistakes so that problems and potential difficulties are identified early, preventing others from making the same mistakes.
- **Share accurate information on a regular basis.** We should make sure that information regarding important decisions, problems, issues, and rumors is frequently and accurately shared in a feedback loop among management and staff.
- **Work in the spirit of collaboration.** We should all commit to working in the spirit of partnership, collaborating to accomplish institutional goals and support new initiatives.
- **Think and speak using the term "we" instead of the "us versus them" dichotomy.** We should realize that, as members of an institution, we will flourish or perish together.
- **Think systemically, guided by shared responsibility.** We should understand that we all have shared responsibility for making things work and for achieving the institution's strategic goals.
- **Keep all commitments.** We should follow through on promises and agreements we make to one another. Once a commitment is made, everything must be done to fulfill it.
- **Give and receive feedback with care and respect.** When we give each other constructive feedback, we help each other identify what works well and where personal and professional change and growth are needed. We should behave respectfully toward one another, even in the face of disrespectful behavior and regardless of position.
- **Avoid distractions and behaviors that make us lose sight of our mission.** We should stay focused on what is most important—

customer service and satisfaction—and avoid behaviors that distract us from our individual and functional responsibilities.

Changing dysfunctional individual behaviors, regardless of rank or position, is critical if we want to change the psychosocial and interpersonal dynamics that prevail in our workplace. When everyone commits to practicing positive new behaviors, a culture of trust and authenticity begins to emerge. As this occurs, our capacity to achieve our organizational vision, mission, values, and strategic goals is greatly enhanced.

CONTINUOUS SSAO IMPROVEMENT

SSAOs need to be lifelong learners and never fall into the trap of thinking they know it all. In my mind, a team is only as strong and functional as the focused and competent individuals who are on that team. The following are some suggestions for ongoing professional improvement:

- Stay up-to-date by reading professional journals, articles, and books recommended by colleagues who are leaders in your field.
- Attend workshops and seminars, and make sure to interact with colleagues from other institutions to get innovative and creative ideas.
- Identify and connect with a mentor or mentors. Success comes from a solid educational background, experience, and in having someone to guide you when you need direct and honest feedback.

In addition to the formal professional opportunities and activities, SSAOs should raise their awareness of the relationship between thought and action. They should continue to refine and enhance their management and leadership skills and abilities by reflecting on how effective and efficient they have been in their role. Just "doing" is only part of the journey; you have to think about it, too.

Our Legacy

Finally, what do SSAOs want to be remembered for when they leave? I believe that the legacy of an SSAO should be determined by his or her passion and commitment to serve students and our changing communities. For the status quo, administrators who see their job as just a job, it will be a rough ride. The real leaders are those who are willing to step up to the proverbial plate, adjust their leadership paradigm, and accept the fact that the world will continue to change. These are the leaders who will make a difference in our communities and, ultimately, in the success of our nation.

Life is not a dress rehearsal. We have one shot at making a positive difference in the lives of those we serve in higher education and those who live, work, and play in our communities. Let's go for it!

CHAPTER 7

The Road to the Presidency:
Competencies for the Senior Student Affairs
Officer Who Will Be President

A Community College Student
Affairs Officer's Perspective

KATHLEEN HETHERINGTON

"Service is what life is all about." —Marian Wright Edelman

FOR A YOUNG woman growing up in Philadelphia in the 1970s, career options were limited. Most women I knew were homemakers, teachers, or nurses. Not many women I knew finished or even attended college. I was encouraged by my high school counselor to attend college, but I was adamantly advised to avoid attending a community college. I was told it was populated by hippies and communists. However, after 12 years of attending a Catholic girls' school, I decided I was ready for a change and signed up the next day to attend the Community College of Philadelphia. In the early 1970s, community colleges were welcoming people from the women's movement and the civil rights movement, veterans from the Vietnam war, and young people who could not afford a four-year education. I experienced culture shock on my first day in college, and a kindly Vietnam veteran (who had probably seen his share of shock victims) looked me in the eye and said, "Pick up your pen and start taking notes." I was on my way!

It's funny to think about it now, but I started my career in education at the very bottom—as a work-study student working for the dean of students. Behind his gruff exterior, the dean was a campus leader who championed enhancing the student experience through planned and professional student services. He laid the groundwork at a newly created community college where numerous services for students would be developed, such as advising, financial aid, counseling, and student activities. Over the two years I worked for the dean, I began to understand that the educational experience for students is formed not only by what happens in the classroom but also by what occurs outside of it. I saw that the student affairs officer helped students achieve their educational dreams through a variety of means.

I graduated with a bachelor's degree in social sciences from Penn State in 1974, right in the midst of one of the worst recessions in U.S. history. After graduation I worked as an office worker, served coffee at Dunkin' Donuts, and held a variety of other temporary jobs until I landed a job in the financial aid office of a proprietary printing school in Philadelphia. Eventually my old boss at the Community College of Philadelphia heard I was working in financial aid and asked me to join the staff there. I loved the nitty-gritty of financial aid—the details, the ever-changing regulations, the esprit de corps among financial aid officers. I really believed we were changing people's lives, and we were. I was living proof of that. It was an exciting time. Imagine late registration, using typewriters, working until almost midnight every night during the month before the semester began, few resources, and lines of students going outside the building into the streets of downtown Philadelphia, and you have an idea of the kind of experiences I had. I had found my calling. I was helping students finance their education and navigate through the enrollment system, and at the end of the process they received perhaps the biggest break of their lives: a college education. Looking back, the reason I loved my work was because I was motivated by something larger than myself, or what has become known today as "purpose-driven" leadership. There's no greater purpose than to help people live a better life through education, and student affairs officers are in key positions to do just that.

I was busy serving students, but not too busy to grow personally and professionally. First, I was open to new and different ways of solving problems. It sounds strange now, but there were no desktop computers, no Internet, and not even telephone registration. I fully embraced the many opportunities to create better systems with emerging technologies. Second, I sought chances to serve on committees with colleagues from academic affairs. Rather than focusing on how different we were, I concentrated on how we could partner to effectively achieve our overall mission of helping students.

Along my student affairs journey to the presidency of a community college, I learned a number of valuable lessons, with the help of many people who cared not only about me but about working together to improve the college to help students succeed.

GAINING LEADERSHIP PERSPECTIVE WITH AN ADVANCED DEGREE

Always continue your education. I received that piece of advice while participating in a national program for women leaders. I had just made the decision to start a doctoral program in higher education, and this advice reinforced my decision. For student affairs officers who aspire to executive leadership, earning a doctorate is critically important. It is becoming increasingly rare to find a senior student affairs officer or college president without one. Just as important, a doctoral program will help you think outside your specialty and understand problems across the organization.

Embracing Opportunities

I was not deliberate about progressing in my career, but I was always deliberate in performing at my highest level. I took on jobs that no one else wanted to take. If there was a new project involving using technology to improve services to students, I would jump at the opportunity to be involved. I never said no to an opportunity offered by a senior leader to be part of a project or to lead a project. I learned early from a mentor that senior managers appreciate someone who is always willing to do more. And I have heard from other presidents that when they ask a person to take on a challenge and the person chooses not to accept the challenge, they are unlikely to approach that person again. Instead, they will reach out to others who are willing to step up. And someone always is.

Although we often talk about our willingness to change, the reality is that most of us like to do things that we do well; as a result, we continue to do the same things the same way. However, in order to get our creative juices flowing, we need to break through our comfort zone and try things that are completely different. After I received my doctorate, I decided that I would like to teach as an adjunct professor. I enjoyed speaking at conferences and seminars on the topic of student affairs, but I really wanted to experience teaching in my academic discipline, the social sciences. The experience was so rewarding that I continued to teach in the evenings and on weekends for years. I always began my classes by quoting a statement the Irish-American author Frank McCourt made to his students at the start of the semester. He told them that he could guarantee that at least one person in the class would learn something by the end of the semester, and that one person would be him. I certainly benefited from the experience of becoming more knowledgeable about my subject matter, but I also learned so much from my students. The point is that no matter what you do, try to do something different from how you spend most of your day—something that will excite you and energize you. You will benefit from the challenges and opportunities you encounter.

For example, as vice president of student affairs, I was asked by the president of the college to take over the college's first capital campaign. I had no direct experience in fundraising, but I had experience in creating partnerships and writing grants. I was willing to learn a new area in higher education and get out of my comfort zone, and I realized that if I ever wanted to be a college president I would need to know something about fundraising. So I took on the challenge while still keeping my "day job." I was exhilarated when we received a donation, and I learned patience when we did not; meanwhile, I increased my "friend-raising" abilities, which were important for laying the groundwork for future gifts and opportunities for the college. The end result was a successful campaign of $14 million—exceeding the original goal of $12 million.

HAVING AN ENTREPRENEURIAL SPIRIT

I meet with students every month during the semester, along with the members of my senior staff, to listen to their issues, concerns, and ideas. Each month, we meet with a different cohort of students. These meetings give me an opportunity to hear firsthand what we are doing well and what we could do better. We recently met with a group of students from the college's entrepreneurial program, and I was struck by their enthusiasm, their willingness to embrace change, and their perspective about finding an innovative solution to a problem through their product. It made me realize how important it was to have an entrepreneurial spirit in approaching work as a student affairs officer. The students had a problem or issue, and they came up with what they hoped would be a workable solution that would result in monetary rewards for them. Their energy level was unflagging. While I didn't recognize it at the time, looking back, I see how I embraced this entrepreneurial spirit during my career as a student affairs officer. Ultimately, the goal was not so much monetary but a way of creating better systems that would improve what we did to positively affect students and help them reach their educational goals.

REFLECTING ON YOUR CHOICES

I recall one holiday party I attended before I made a major career move to leave an organization where I had worked for 22 years. A vice president commented that he thought it was unlikely that I would ever leave the college, because I had risen up through the ranks and seemed happy to be where I was. While part of his comment was true and I was pleased that I had progressed in my career, I also read into his comment that I was stuck in my job. What the vice president didn't know was that I was already planning to move on. It took me about a year to make this major move from a college that was really like a second home to me, but when I finally decided to move on, there was no looking back. Although we are in the midst of the worst recession in our nation's history and moving to a new job is more challenging now than in the past, people still do move and get new jobs, and life goes on. Facing fear and embracing an entrepreneurial approach to one's career is so critical and so often overlooked.

KNOW WHAT YOU DON'T KNOW

As you assume more responsibility in student affairs, you inevitably are overseeing areas in which you have no expertise. While you may have the skills to do the job, your staff often has the years of experience and knowledge, and they know more than you do. It is easy to be intimidated as a new leader of a department, and some staff will not fail to remind you of how much you don't know about the department. The first impulse may be to fire someone you believe is not going to be part of your team, but I suggest instead that you give the situation time until people get accommodated to their changed environment. As long as the staff is willing to share information and give you a chance to learn, being open to experiencing a new area can be exciting and rewarding. There is a point, however, when as a leader you have to make decisions about the "fit" of each member of your team. As Burlington Community College President Robert Messina often says when speaking to current and aspiring presidents, "You ask the person what color is their jersey, and if you find out that it is different from yours, then you need to find a new member for your team." Perhaps the biggest mistake you can make is prolonging the inevitable. It results in poor performance in the person and bad morale among the rest of the staff members, and it holds your organization back from reaching your goals.

It is easy in student affairs to view the world from your own perspective. I know this firsthand as a former financial aid officer. I reveled in being the resident expert at my college in financial aid. There wasn't a question too daunting, a problem too big for me to solve. I thought I knew everything. It was only when I moved from being the expert in financial aid to being a novice dean of student services that I realized I had much to learn. I had to get past the fear of asking the proverbial "dumb question." I began to see things from the perspective of how others viewed the world and how helping students could be done in a variety of ways. Even if you stay in the same job for years, it is important to step out of your "silo" and get the 40,000-foot view of a situation. The easiest way for me has always been through partnerships with other departments in the college and, when appropriate, external organizations. In a culture that values performance excellence, benchmarking is an excellent way to see how effective organizations do things and to learn best practices from them.

EMBRACING SERVANT LEADERSHIP

In an article titled "Lessons from Leaders," John Schuh (2002) noted that in a survey of senior student affairs officers about their style of leadership, most of them classified it as "servant leadership" (p. 204). Student affairs officers typically bring value to an organization with a variety of capabilities, including their listening skills, servant leadership orientation, innovation, and focus on performance excellence—all attributes that create a culture that supports providing the best opportunity for students to succeed. Servant leaders focus on serving others through collaboration and empathy. These attributes prepared me as a student affairs officer to be the "voice of students" and their advocate as my responsibilities increased over the years. Asking the question "How will what we do positively impact students?" helps to quickly focus everyone's attention on our most important charge as servant leaders.

Pursuing Performance Excellence

At Howard Community College (HCC), we strive for performance excellence. I am delighted to receive what appear to be many brilliant ideas for improving what we do at the college. My staff members know that I will always ask two questions: "So what?" (What difference will doing something make?) and "Where are the data?" (What data do you have now that show the need to do something, and what have you done so far that leads you to believe that this change will make a difference?) With limited financial and personnel resources and an innovative faculty and staff, it takes real self- and institutional control not to encourage or execute every good idea. In an institution that values performance excellence, we have to be selective and follow the plan-do-check-act process and have it ingrained in every aspect of what we do. One of Stephen Covey's (2004) seven habits of highly effective people is to "begin with the end in mind" (p. 95). I often use that habit in sorting through many ideas—my own and others'—to assess the potential impact of a decision. HCC's culture is data-influenced rather than data-driven. This practice of looking at the data to make smart decisions about limited resources creates an environment that supports the mission, vision, values, and strategic goals of our organization.

Valuing Mentors

I have been fortunate to have people who have served and continue to serve as mentors to me over my career. Interestingly, some of them have not been college presidents or fellow student affairs practitioners. We can often learn from others whose worldview is completely different from ours. When I was a new dean, one of my mentors was the vice president of information technology. I learned many things about doing my work differently and more effectively.

When someone gives his or her time to mentor you, listen to the advice. If I hadn't listened to my mentors, I don't think I would have become a college president. One of my mentors told me I had the right qualities to advance to a college presidency. I hadn't really thought about it and was more focused on doing the best work I could as dean of student systems. Peggy Delmas (2010), in her review of Susan Madsen's book *On Becoming a Woman Leader: Learning from the Experiences of University Presidents*, notes that "not one of her participants actively sought out leadership positions, but . . . hard work and good work brought them to the attention of others who encouraged them to apply for such positions" (p. 273). That quote mirrors my own experience and emphasizes the importance of being open to the suggestions of others to go beyond what we think we are capable of doing.

Conclusion

The common belief when I was a budding student affairs professional was that only people in academic affairs could rise to a college presidency. The landscape has certainly changed since then, and those in student affairs who are willing to undertake the joys and challenges of a community college presidency will have the requisite skills to prepare them for a career that transforms students' lives in a meaningful way. Attaining academic credentials, embracing opportunities, having an entrepreneurial spirit, reflecting on your choices, knowing what you don't know, embracing servant leadership, pursuing performance excellence, and valuing mentors are methods that student affairs officers can use to progress to a community college presidency.

References

Covey, S. R. (2004). *The 7 habits of highly effective people: Powerful lessons in personal change.* New York, NY: Free Press.

Delmas, P. (2010). On becoming a woman leader: Learning from the experience of university presidents [Review of the book *On becoming a woman leader: Learning from the experiences of university presidents*]. *NASPA Journal About Women in Higher Education, 3*(1), 272–274.

Schuh, J. H. (2002). Lessons from leaders. *NASPA Journal, 39*(3), 204–216.

Advice From a New President

KAREN M. WHITNEY

ONE DAY I was the vice chancellor for student life at a large midwestern research university, and the next day I was president of a large master's comprehensive university. On my first day as president, I woke up at the presidential hour of 4:00 a.m. caught a 6:00 a.m. flight to Cleveland, then took a 10-seat prop plane to Franklin, Pennsylvania. By noon, I had arrived at my new university. I dropped my belongings at the presidential residence and began walking the campus. As I met folks along my walk, I introduced myself as the new president. Most folks gave me a pleasantly skeptical look. One student did not believe I was the president; she thought I was kidding. So much for having a "presidential presence." I finally migrated to the administration building and my new office. With a nervous energy that is expected when a person enters a new space, I went into my office and found documents on my desk waiting for my signature. An hour later, I was at a reception and dinner with trustees and faculty before attending my first trustee meeting, fully engaged in a very full agenda. I went home to the residence, where I was the only person in a four-story, 5,500-square-foot house that looked and felt like a museum. Exhausted, I fell asleep at 10:30 p.m., completing my first day as president.

The most common question I was asked when word got out that I had applied to be a university president was "So, how long have you been wanting to be a president?" I found the question curious in that it seemed to imply that I had for some time—if not from birth—held an interest in becoming a university president. In reality, while my commitment to higher learning, student development, and civic engagement has been lifelong, my intentional journey to the presidency was about 12 months. I have always worked hard at my job and developed skill sets to do my job well, including always looking at ways to keep fresh and current. I pursued all the traditional avenues one would expect, and I took a few strategic and innovative detours as well. For almost 30 years, I belonged to both the American College Personnel Association and the National Association of Student Personnel Administrators, and I regularly taught, consulted, presented, and wrote in my field. I also did things that were unique, in that my research area is higher education finance. I taught in the areas of higher education law and administration. I worked to develop an expertise in areas beyond student affairs, including fundraising, assessment, process improvement, and accreditation.

Over the 11 years that I was a vice chancellor, I took the view that I had specific responsibilities in a specialized area—student development and student affairs—and at the same time had campuswide obligations and loyalties. I was both the chief student affairs officer and a campus executive. This professional view of my work guided me well as a vice chancellor and, in my opinion, made the transition to campus chief executive officer a logical next step in my higher education journey.

The eight months I spent reflecting, researching, and ultimately participating in a presidential search were some of the most intense professional development experiences of my career to date. I spent about five months seriously considering whether there was another chapter in my "professional book." Turning 50 precipitated this reflection—I was well past the beginning of my career but not quite ready to consider retirement. At first I was mulling over what might be the next generation of work at my present institution; then other ideas came to me, such as considering a chief student affairs position at another university. One day the audacious notion began to creep into my consciousness that there could be a presidential chapter in my book. That germ of an idea was not an easy one to cultivate, because for many years I had been told that only colleagues from academic administration would be considered for such a position and others need not apply.

To test the notion of a presidency, I began reading books, articles, and blogs on the topic. I sought out folks from the American Council on Education (ACE) and talked to various mentors and a few folks from professional search firms to kick around the idea and solicit feedback. The reading, conversations, and reflections were rejuvenating and helpful. One representative from a professional search firm suggested that I look at position descriptions, select a university that had a mission and values that were compatible with my own, and submit my credentials to test the waters and learn from the experience. After about two months of looking over announcements in the *Chronicle of Higher Education*, I came across one that I felt had a set of values and a mission that were complementary to my personal values and mission as an educator. From what I could tell, I met all the minimum qualifications and most of the required qualifications, so I decided to talk with a representative of the firm the university had hired to manage the search to further explore the idea of a presidency. The representative was very professional, provided excellent information, and encouraged me to submit my credentials. One airport interview, one campus interview, and one system interview later, I was offered and accepted the position of president.

REVELATIONS OF A NEW PRESIDENT

I am about as new as you can get. At this writing, I have been president for six weeks. So, with this in mind, let me push forward as to the revelations that have hit me squarely in the face.

Revelation #1: The student affairs profession prepares one well for a presidency. That's right—this is my first revelation. Coming from student affairs has been an excellent preparation for me. My profession has afforded me a knowledge base of grounded research, an awareness of current best practices in higher education, and a network of trusted colleagues across the nation. Given the challenges and opportunities ahead for higher education, national associations such as ACE and the American Association of State Colleges and Universities have a growing appreciation of the vital role student affairs professionals play in the academy while contributing to the ongoing success of higher education.

Revelation #2: The energy, drive, and passion it takes to be a great president are the same energy, drive, and passion it took to be a great senior student affairs officer (SSAO). Last year, as an SSAO, I would often walk into a room filled with students I did not know and would immediately work to build trusting, authentic relationships. Now, as a president, I walk into a room filled with elected officials, business leaders, alumni, and reporters I do not know and work to build trusting, authentic relationships. A year ago, I was giving talks and welcomes about the value and importance of higher learning; today, I do the same.

Revelation #3: Fit is everything. Fit is everything between a president, a university, and the communities the university serves. The concept applies to how the institution's mission, vision, values, and goals align with your own, and to the larger context that *creates* mission, vision, values, and goals. I realized that as I explored notions of fit with a university and community, I was really exploring who I was and who I was willing to be as a president. The goal is a match that brings out the best of all involved. Everyone wins when the needs and desires of the university and the community match what the president loves doing every waking hour of every day. The literature often says that the presidency is a "lifestyle"—it is how you live every day. It is beyond a job and even beyond a profession. At this point, I feel extremely lucky, because there is a great deal of synchronicity between what I love to do and what the university and the community appear to be presenting as priority needs.

COMPETENCIES TO TAKE YOU TO THE PRESIDENCY

I am quickly coming to believe that the following three competencies are essential to being a successful president: decision making, facilitating, and communicating.

Decision maker: Every day, I make decisions. In my first six weeks, I have made decisions quickly and thoughtfully regarding personnel, the budget, and facilities, as well as less critical issues such as what food to serve in the president's box at the football games. My point is that you have to be comfortable making decisions. You also have to be comfortable knowing that you will often not have all the information you need and will have to make decisions with limited information and limited time. You will have to be at peace knowing that some of your decisions will be mistakes or missed marks. At the same time, you must be aware that your decisions are final; often, the next step is litigation. Your presidency will be defined not only by your decisions but also by the process you use to arrive at these decisions.

Facilitator: As president, I believe my greatest accomplishments will be recruiting and cultivating a solid leadership team that works with faculty, staff, students, and alumni to move the university to ever greater achievements. To leave the university better than I found it will require the efforts of a multitude of constituents. The key is to know that, as president, you might be responsible for everything but you cannot do everything—nor should you. You have to be able to delegate and empower others and be willing to celebrate the great work of others more than your own work. Leading a university is a team sport.

Communicator: Every day, I am communicating. In six weeks, I have held a press conference; given three major addresses; shaken hands and talked with more than 1,000 people (students, faculty, staff, alumni, and community members); visited every business within a four-block radius of the university; led cheers at a football pep rally; and ridden in a parade. This is in addition to meetings with local clergy, elected officials, businesspeople, and the head of the town library, as well as meeting regularly with students, faculty, staff, and alumni. In every instance, I am communicating. First, I am communicating that I am the new president—the "living logo" of the university. I am also communicating the university's values and aspirations, even when I'm shopping at the local grocery store on a Sunday night. To enjoy being president, you need to really like all kinds of people and be willing to listen and care about others, all day, every day.

SKILLS TO DEVELOP TO BECOME PRESIDENT

As far as specific experiences an SSAO who aspires to be president might consider developing, I offer the following outline of the experiences and skills that prepared me for the job. (I used this list in a PowerPoint presentation I gave at my campus interview.) This is just one set of experiences and skills SSAOs might consider developing on their own journeys:

Experiences

- Administrative: 10 years as a campus executive officer; worked with three large state higher education systems
- Teaching: 25 years of teaching (it's why we exist)
- Scholarship: write and present regularly
- Professional engagement: institutional accreditation; consulting on best practices; a leader in the student affairs profession
- Civic engagement: currently serve on three boards

Skills

- Planning, assessment, and improvement
- Finance and budgeting
- Evidence-based decision making
- Entrepreneurial management
- Fundraising
- Building teams and coalitions
- Leading to advance diversity and social justice
- Transparency
- Communicating—telling the story every day in every way

CONCLUSION

I hope my story provides some insight on how you might construct your own approach to considering whether a presidency could be a chapter in your professional book. I would say that the exercise is a good one no matter what the outcome. Whether you remain in student affairs or become a president, in pursuing excellence in student affairs you are pursuing excellence on the larger plane of higher education. Also, a leader is a leader is a leader—when you lead, remember that the only boundaries that exist are the ones you create or allow others to create for you. Finally, higher education needs well-grounded, hardworking, bright, and dedicated leaders to guide us into the future. Why not you?

It's About Preparation

Dean L. Bresciani

"Forget vice president for student affairs positions; with your breadth of experience and skill, you should focus on a presidency."
—Search firm senior partner to finalist interviewing
for a senior student affairs officer position

SOONER OR LATER when I teach graduate courses, students naturally inquire about my career path. I'm sure there is nothing unique about that, especially for those of us who are practitioner–scholars or, for that matter, any of us who meet and talk with entry-level student affairs staff. But my career path and what it has led to may be somewhat unusual in contrast to some of my colleagues. I anticipate that will increasingly be less the case in the future.

Like many of us, I didn't go to college intending to work in student affairs or the broader area of higher education as a lifelong career goal. In fact, the notion that doing so was a career option couldn't have been further from my mind. Looking back, I'm fairly confident that I never really contemplated the fact that there were people who attended to the out-of-class educational and developmental needs of students or who developed and led the administrative aspects of universities. Without much thought, I assumed that all the activities going on at a university materialized without design or purpose. I was a geology major, focused on my coursework and whatever entertaining distractions my less than academically focused roommates would tempt me with, and largely disengaged from the university outside of my courses. Not exactly a storybook beginning for a higher education career. In truth, I probably spent more of my undergraduate career debating my wavering motivation and fit with the college environment, and hovering on the brink of leaving the university, than realizing the potential it offered. But an odd twist of fate changed all that in the summer before my senior year. (Or was it my "second" senior year? Those roommates were terribly effective when it came to providing distractions.)

In any event, I was sure I didn't want to return home to another summer of backbreaking work for my father. There's no more upside to being the boss's son at a large trucking firm than there is to being on a college varsity sports team that your father coaches. Anything had to be better, so when a friend mentioned that there were summer jobs on campus that included room, board, and a stipend—and all a person had to do was tell new students what classes to take—it was a dream come true. However, something happened that I hadn't anticipated.

I found myself inexplicably engaged by the process of helping new students believe they could succeed in a university setting. Guiding them through the complicated process of course selections to fulfill degree requirements, registration, adding and dropping courses, studying, and choosing activities to become involved with was a role I seemed naturally drawn to and one in which I had something helpful to contribute. For the first time in my life, I felt as though I was doing something important and rewarding.

I'll never forget the day when, merely in passing, I mentioned to the director of orientation how life-changing the orientation peer leader experience had been for me. I offhandedly lamented to her, "It's a shame a person can't do that for a real job." To this day, I'm thankful that she was not an easily insulted or angered person.

Suffice it to say, I soon learned that what students experience in higher education settings does not take place by random chance or divine intervention but rather by purposeful educational design, administration, and delivery. I learned about graduate professional preparation programs in student affairs and higher education administration. Perhaps most important, I found out that you can indeed "do that for a real job"; in fact, as a very rewarding lifelong career.

A Career Imagined and in Retrospect

While that experience mirrors similar stories I've heard from colleagues over the years, a blend of dumb luck, what I'd like to portray as an only slightly obsessive personality, and a very fortunate mentoring experience at the ripe age of 20 led to a vision for and structure of a quite purposeful career path. The combination of those factors provided unusual clarity for me around the notion that if higher education administration was to be my career, I would aspire to do whatever it took to build the experience base and expertise to excel at it.

From that day forward, I studied everything and anyone likely to provide an opinion or insight on what it takes to be a successful higher education leader. I watched and talked with those I admired as well as those I didn't. I read every book I could find on the topic—I still have the first: *Pieces of Eight: The Rites, Roles, and Styles of the Dean, By Eight Who Have Been There* (Appleton, Briggs, & Rhatigan, 1978). It is sitting on my bookshelf next to a copy of the "green book," Ursula Delworth and Gary Hanson's ubiquitous *Student Services: A Handbook for the Profession* (1980). I talked with faculty, student affairs practitioners, and other administrators. I asked them what factors had most contributed to their success and that of those around them, and what skills or attributes they lacked and, without which, felt held back. My aspiration, if higher education was to be my lifelong career, was to set a purposeful rather than coincidence-driven course—one that would prepare me to do the job as well as it could be done. I intended for that course to lead to a senior higher education leadership role where I could have the greatest possible impact on the most students. That was no small aspiration for someone not yet out of college. But I credit those early mentors and revelations as leading to a fortunate and, perhaps as a result, also predictable progression of opportunities throughout my career.

In hindsight, my career path wasn't quite as smooth and predictable as all that. While I was very lucky in the opportunities I encountered, I also made countless mistakes along the way and at times had to make sacrifices that I perhaps should have considered more carefully. But when I look back on the string of fortuitous bends in the road and the learning opportunities that came my way, I've increasingly appreciated the Roman philosopher Seneca's axiom: "Luck is what happens when preparation and opportunity meet." If I were to credit my career to any one broad principle, it would be preparation—seeking to be better prepared, on more topics and issues, than those around me. To be honest, part of what motivated me was my fairly competitive spirit. But while that contributed to the development of a strategic plan of career advancement, I was also fundamentally motivated to do my job as well as possible. In fact, the latter served me as well as the former.

Thinking back on what I learned and how to frame those experiences, several mechanisms stand out as critical to realizing my career goals. It is important to note that while they worked for me, they may not work for everyone. However, I think they are worth consideration.

1. Always seek out new experiences and skills. In particular, and somewhat counterintuitively, seek out the experiences and skills that others find unattractive. Doing so will often mean stepping forward on tasks and initiatives that are no more appealing to you than a punishment, but if the end game is to collect any and all experiences that will help you be a more effective higher education administrator, volunteering for roles that will lead to an uncommon collection and breadth of skills will pay dividends. Through that process, you will also establish a reputation for a spirit of selfless volunteerism and as a go-to person for getting things done. That reputation will have its rewards.

2. Volunteering will often lead to or even require becoming broadly experienced and "multilingual" in the practice of higher education and its administration. Our colleges and universities are a mix of exciting, varied, and often competing contexts and subcultures with their own priorities, values, and even distinct

"languages" that others, even those in higher education, can't easily decipher. Imagine putting a theoretical mathematician, a student development practitioner, a finance administrator, and a legislative analyst in a room and posing one simple question: "What most predicts the success of a university?" The conversation likely to take place will be a contemporary version of the Tower of Babel. Imagine, though, the empowerment granted to the person who can speak several of those languages and reflect on and contribute at least a modestly expert perspective regarding the various viewpoints being shared. That person will likely earn a notable level of immediate respect from those in the room and will probably become the leader of the discussion.

3. Seek out the broadest contextual experience base you can amass in terms of roles, institution types, geographic locations, and campus cultures. In my own career, I've been able to span institutions from the West Coast to the East Coast, with passes through both the upper and lower Midwest. I've worked in small liberal arts institutions of fewer than 2,000 students and large public research settings of up to 48,000—and everything in between. I've held positions in student affairs, academic affairs (both administrative and faculty roles), research institutes, a state university system office, and even state government. While I had little, if any, interest in a long-term role in many of those settings, each environment had unique and interesting aspects, and provided important pieces of perspective and experience that enhanced the skill sets I was able to draw on in later settings.

4. Pursue the academic training that will most empower success in what you imagine to be your ultimate career goal, rather than the common, easy, or most obviously attractive option. For me, as I studied the leadership of higher education institutions, a common theme I observed was that few institutional leaders

had scholarly training preparing them to administer large, complex organizations. This observation led me to broaden my graduate academic preparation from a master's degree in student development to a doctoral major in higher education finance with a minor in economics. I can understand if that doesn't sound appealing. The day I found myself in a doctoral econometrics course and realized that no student development theories would unlock the mysteries of statistical economic modeling formulas for me, I was very tempted to throw in the towel. That said, during a discussion of higher education financing with, for example, congressional delegates, my being able to draw on that preparation is both impressive to them and invaluable in terms of what I can contribute to the conversation.

5. If you, like me, aren't necessarily the smartest person in the room, you will simply have to work longer and harder than those around you. That's not in line with what we all know to be the importance of life–work balance (I'll get to that topic in a minute), but it will position you to often be the most prepared and expert person in the room and will affirm you as the person who always gets the job done. You'll find that those who can most influence your career advancement are drawn to go-to people. That reputation can make you the person who most often, in most settings, finds him- or herself enjoying unsolicited but consistent advancement.

6. Identify a set of scholarly reference points that you can always return to for direction, focus, and answers to the challenges you will face. While I've heard many colleagues reference favorite motivational and inspirational books, that is not what I am suggesting. My suggestion is to find scholarly references that form the basis for how you approach your work and offer specific intellectual frameworks for how to face challenges and successfully execute your responsibilities. For me, one of the most powerful reference points,

and one I often turn to, is political scientist Aaron Wildavsky's *The Politics of the Budgetary Process* (1974). Don't let the title fool you; it is a handbook for negotiating advantage in political situations. However, it is also an indispensable source of approaches to acquiring and protecting resources. Another thought-provoking reference is Fincher's *Budgeting Myths and Fictions* (1983), which debunks seemingly rational assumptions on funding in the public sector and replaces them with more practical interpretations of behavior. DiMaggio and Powell's 1983 article "The Iron Cage Revisited" is a provocative examination of what complex organizations often use as proxy solutions when those solutions are in fact unsure. Howard Bowen's "What Determines the Costs of Higher Education" (1980) is one of the most sobering examinations of public sector and specifically higher education's insatiable proclivity toward resource expenditure. It is a must-read for anyone responsible for developing and administering institutional budgets. Finally, the source I most often return to is Bolman and Deal's 1988 treatise on organizational theory and behavior, *Modern Approaches to Understanding and Managing Organizations*. The authors provide frameworks for looking at organizational situations from a variety of well-established perspectives; their text has become a standard for graduate programs focused on public sector administrative activities.

I credit those six mechanisms with leading me to good fortune at various stages in my career path; however, I offer them with several important caveats. Some of these caveats may be as important to you as the mechanisms I've outlined above, and I would urge you to consider the six mechanisms judiciously and subjectively from your own perspective rather than attempting to consider them in an objective manner or by how they may apply to others. In short, it is critically important to honestly weigh each factor against your personal priorities and needs rather than those of any colleague, friend, or mentor:

1. What does it take to bring balance to your life? That simple notion is the most complex, as it involves everything from your need for downtime, sleep, or simply recovery time when you are exhausted, to meeting your own needs or those of your partner or family. What sacrifices are you willing and able to make on those fronts, and for how long can you make them without substantial negative consequences for yourself or others?

2. How often, how comfortably, and how far can you relocate to pursue new opportunities? I know colleagues who have been fortunate enough to amass a breadth of professional experiences and opportunities without a substantial geographic relocation, but that is the exception, not the rule. In fact, the more flexibility you can offer on that front, the more opportunities are available. Again, you need to weigh the benefits of moving every three to six years against your commitments to family, friends, and others who may not be as willing or able to move.

3. What advantages, quality of life, and image are you willing to sacrifice in the name of skill development, experience, and professional advancement? Much like relocating, moving to a less attractive or less prestigious institutional setting can be an effective means of securing new roles and responsibilities for which there would otherwise be much more competition.

My own career path, for better or worse, reflects all of these mechanisms and considerations. I've followed the collective principles for success, but my career path also illustrates the sacrifices or, perhaps more accurately, the less than attractive consequences of those sacrifices. For me, those consequences were of varying impact, but some have given me increasing pause for thought in recent years. I have little doubt that I would not be in the position I am today, at this age and stage of my life, if I had not followed the path I did. That said, I often wonder whether that path would be considered attractive or worth it to others. On a strictly professional level, my path has been quite productive; but, in looking back, I increasingly consider the friends, family, and related experiences I've sacrificed or bypassed to stay on that path.

Be Careful What You Wish For—Something More Might Come True

I was caught off guard by the comment at the beginning of this chapter, which was made to me by the senior partner of a major national search firm. My purpose, throughout my career, had been to develop the skills and experience needed to effectively lead a student affairs division at a major university, where I could have the most impact on the most students. To achieve this goal required an understanding of student development, campus environmental design and quality, and how to measure and assess those aspects of a higher education experience, as well as ancillary understanding of campus master planning, capital facilities design and construction, and the operation of auxiliary enterprises. It also required skills in enrollment management and matriculation and retention of traditional and nontraditional student populations. To be successful on those fronts required an understanding not only of student experiences outside the classroom but of their experience in the classroom, some of which can be fully gleaned only by serving as faculty member. I also learned that success for any institution requires public enthusiasm and support of higher education and the institution itself. To effectively articulate and build support for an institution requires sophisticated communication, public relations, fundraising, and political acumen. It also requires in-depth understanding and expertise regarding the business and operational aspects of turning the lights on and paying the bills, not to mention securing and protecting the resources needed for the institution to succeed. To juggle and excel in all those competing demands and interests requires more time, energy, and commitment than fit into a 40-, 50-, or even 60-hour workweek. But for most student affairs practitioners, the extensive list of requirements for effectiveness in our roles will not sound foreign. For many of us, it may not even sound daunting. In fact, for some, it will sound familiar and all in a day's work.

Given the increasingly complex, convoluted, and often competitive political environments in which we work, student affairs practitioners have, over recent decades of professional evolution, become the people in a university setting who are most likely to "know at least a little about a lot." Few roles in our institutions—besides that of the president—call for broader skills and expertise. It would be fair to say that few in student affairs set out consciously on that path, but, driven by a profound professional commitment to serving our students and our campuses, many of us slowly but surely (often without realizing it ourselves) become the "utility infielder" senior leaders of our colleges and universities.

What we take as givens for doing our jobs well, though, are not the priorities, traits, or skills common in other senior administrative and leadership roles in higher education settings. In fact, the traditional paths to senior higher education leadership roles have become increasingly divergent from and often far too narrow relative to the broad skill sets and demands inherent in these roles.

In my case, the mechanisms and considerations I described above did ultimately result in my achieving my goal of leading the student affairs division of a major university. In fact, I had this job at not just one but two Association of American Universities research institutions. At the second, I had the opportunity to be in a role and work with a portfolio broader than that of many presidents. Long story short, I was incredibly fortunate and did indeed achieve my career and life dreams.

Epilogue

The comment first made to me by the search firm representative came up again in various forms from various sources as I searched for my next professional challenge over a period of almost two years. The first time I heard the statement, it was unanticipated and alarming, and even a little unwelcome; later, it became oddly comforting. Through purpose and good fortune, my career path had led to the desired results; at this point, the idea that it might lead to even more was provocative. Several search firm consultants told me that my résumé reflected the breadth and depth of experience increasingly called for in executive institutional leadership, and that it was the "résumé of the future" for many such roles. (I still struggle with that idea, and I would stress that it was the assertion of the search firms rather than my own.)

My first foray into a presidential search ended in finalist status. That got my attention. Ultimately, my candidacy for that job caused a split board of trustees vote (although no job offer), but that was encouraging, and the new alternative to my career plans suddenly seemed very real.

Higher education is at a point of transition in terms of the assessment and appreciation of a student affairs background by those we work with and for. Student affairs as a profession, a field of scholarly knowledge and practice, and a path of preparation for executive leadership roles has changed dramatically since the days of dons and deans of students. We are increasingly being recognized as bringing broader skill sets and experiences to our leadership roles, and the increasing demands on our roles reflect our new skills. However, we are still the exception rather than the rule in terms of advancing to a presidency.

In my case, it would take months of study, work, and interviews before I secured a presidential position. But what I heard from search firm representatives throughout that process confirmed my own observations. Traditional paths are certainly still viable and far more common, but they are increasingly less successful at providing the preparation to deal with the complexities of leading modern colleges and universities. An increasingly practical alternative to traditional paths to executive leadership is the profession of student affairs, and the list of those making the transition is growing.

Until recently, higher education institution presidents who came from student affairs backgrounds were limited in number and generally restricted to small liberal arts colleges. Over the past decade, however, there has been a documented and increasing trend of student affairs colleagues assuming leadership of comprehensive and master's-level institutions. Recently, some have even moved into presidencies of larger and even research university settings. That has occurred when a student affairs professional has brought to the table a balanced portfolio of scholarly, administrative, and political experience, with a vision for and commitment to the ideals and potential of higher education and how to achieve that potential. I suspect that few of us in student affairs would not recognize and resonate with those traits, and perceive them as reflecting each of us and our profession.

REFERENCES

Appleton, J. R., Briggs, C. M., & Rhatigan, J. J. (1978). *Pieces of eight: The rites, roles, and styles of the dean, by eight who have been there.* Portland, OR: NASPA Institute of Research and Development.

Bolman, L. G., & Deal, T. E. (1988). *Modern approaches to understanding and managing organizations.* San Francisco, CA: Jossey-Bass.

Bowen, H. R. (1980). What determines the costs of higher education? In H. R. Bowen (Ed.), *The cost of higher education* (pp. 1–26). Washington, DC: Carnegie Foundation for the Advancement of Teaching.

Delworth, U., & Hanson, G. R. (1980). *Student services: A handbook for the profession.* San Francisco, CA: Jossey-Bass.

DiMaggio, P. J., & Powell, W. W. (1983). The iron cage revisited: Institutional isomorphism and collective rationality in organizational fields. *American Sociological Review, 48,* 147–159.

Fincher, C. (1983). Budgeting myths and fictions: The implications for evaluation. In R. A. Wilson (Ed.), *Survival in the 1980's: Quality, mission and financing options* (pp. 259–274). Tucson, AZ: Center for the Study of Higher Education.

Wildavsky, A. (1974). *The politics of the budgetary process* (2nd ed). Boston, MA: Little, Brown.

Just the Facts

WALTER M. KIMBROUGH

I HAVE OFTEN said that student affairs professionals have an inferiority complex. We have heard our academic affairs counterparts question what we do, wondering out loud if we are a profession. This questioning seems to cause us to be unsure of ourselves and our role in the life of the campus. Some of this is because of our reluctance to conduct or share legitimate research on students, often owing to our lack of enthusiasm related to assessment. As we like to say, we are people persons, so we aren't excited about dealing with lots of numbers, formulas, or research studies.

But there is a wealth of data regarding students, and as more and more accrediting bodies, system offices, state higher education organizations, and even boards of trustees want evidence of improved student success, every facet of an institution, including student affairs, must be involved in assessment. Senior student affairs officers (SSAOs) have a great opportunity to provide leadership in assessment. If they develop these skills, the entire institution will benefit from a better understanding of its students. And by developing more of an understanding of assessment and data analysis, an SSAO will possess skills needed for today's college presidency in an era of increased accountability.

I decided as a college junior that I wanted to become a college president one day. So I was very intentional as I worked toward that opportunity. When I began my work at Miami University in the college student personnel program, I learned more about the characteristics of college presidents. I soon became aware that many of them possessed hard science degrees and came from the academic side. I initially made plans to pursue a hard science doctorate, but realized after starting the program that my heart was with student affairs, so I sought an appropriate terminal degree in higher education. Knowing that I was training to become a student affairs practitioner, I would need to do something different, something extra, to give myself a chance at a presidency.

When I began my doctoral studies at Georgia State University, I looked for opportunities to strengthen my academic credentials. I took an additional statistics course so I would become proficient in this area. This helped me develop the confidence that I could handle all the statistical analysis for my dissertation, which I did. I was able to use these skills immediately, developing an article for publication based on the dissertation.

The point was to develop a level of comfort with statistics and data analysis so I would have opportunities to use these skills in my professional career. This might not seem like the mind-set for most of us in this field, but it is imperative that more of us develop some affinity for data. Allow me to share several examples of ways, throughout my career, that I effectively used data to better understand students or to improve programs and services for students.

In my first job—coordinator of Greek life at Emory University—I wanted to find a way to quantify the impact of our chapters. Many news stories and even the report of the Franklin Square Group (an assembly of college presidents, higher education associations, and Greek organization executive directors) chided fraternities and sororities because their rhetoric did not match their reality, and even raised major concerns about the relevance of these organizations.

Most campuses calculate chapter grade point averages and rank the chapters. I wanted to look at overall leadership in these organizations, so I developed a leadership index, with a numerical score for each chapter based on its leadership on campus. I determined how many members of a chapter held major leadership roles on campus, including student government, interfraternity and intersorority council, residence life, presidents of major student organizations, and orientation leaders. I factored in the size of the chapter, so small chapters would not be at a disadvantage. In fact, smaller chapters with a higher number of active members were rated higher. By sharing this index with members and key campus departments, we could show the positive effect of the Greek community in terms of leadership on campus.

My primary responsibility at Georgia State University was orientation. Most orientation programs collect survey data to assess their programs. We did the same. However, I wanted to disaggregate the data so that certain offices could determine their specific effectiveness. At this time, academic advising at Georgia State was handled by professional advisors for each college. I began to disaggregate the surveys by college, so the advisors could get specific feedback about the advising experience from the students they advised. This simple step provided feedback that each advisor could use and, in fact, created a friendly rivalry, as each wanted to offer the best services and earn the highest scores.

I routinely reviewed the data with the students working in our orientation program. We could determine which aspects of the program worked well and which needed improvement. We also disaggregated the data by orientation leader; we could determine which ones were rated highest by the students they served and which received lower scores and needed support to improve their performance. Again, the results of our surveys were shared across the campus so that key leaders knew the kind of assessment we conducted and could understand the strengths of our orientation program. It was easy to get buy-in across the campus for orientation when people realized that we took this program seriously. Assessment shows that your activity is important.

As a chief student affairs officer at Albany State University, I had an opportunity to use my assessment knowledge on an institutionwide level. When I arrived, the University System of Georgia had implemented a policy to greatly reduce the number of students requiring remediation at four-year universities by revising the admissions policy. I was tasked with writing the white paper to describe the impact of the new policy on the institution.

This assignment involved gathering data on the institution and its students. The University System of Georgia does an excellent job of collecting data, and that became a primary source for me. I used national studies as well as some institutional data to craft the report. Although we were not able to significantly affect the policy, this exercise helped to quickly acquaint me with the data available on the campus and the kinds of research we could use to improve the campus environment.

As I said, the process of addressing the new admissions standard led me to a lot of unused data. One data set was an ACT student opinion survey led by the System office. We had participated, but the results were never shared on campus. I was able to present those data at a faculty/staff institute so the entire campus could see what our students said about their experience. This data sharing was critical, because it helped drive some practices that led to improved retention and graduation rates. While I was at Albany State, although we did not have the most stringent admissions requirements, our retention rate was bettered only by two of the top institutions in the nation, the University of Georgia and Georgia Tech.

At every level in my career, I found ways to use data not only to assess the work I did but to provide information that the entire campus could use. Even as an entry-level staff member, I had an opportunity to collect new data that provided a better sense of our students and their activities. As I progressed professionally, I worked with data that not only helped describe the students but contributed to institutional policy decisions.

While I did not know it when I was working to develop my ability with data, this ability has been fortuitous in a climate in which there is greater focus on accountability and in which the use of data is more important than ever. Accrediting bodies are asking institutions to prove that they actually do what they purport to do. My institution is accredited by the North Central Association, which has emphasized the need to create a climate of assessment on campuses. Likewise, specific accreditation organizations for areas such as education, social work, and business place a high priority on data gathering and the use of data to improve operations.

As a president, I pay particular attention to data. At the faculty and staff institute at the beginning of each year, I review our strategic plan, focusing on our measurable objectives and our progress toward those objectives. We routinely participate in the National Survey of Student Engagement, and I comb through those findings to lead discussions with our campus leadership team about adjustments we should make to improve the student experience. I continue to push all areas of campus to find new ways to assess performance, so we can close the loop by making changes as necessary and then assessing our new level of performance.

In the new climate of accountability, college and university presidents must be more engaged in campus assessment and must be familiar with national studies that may provide information that affects that particular campus. Student affairs professionals have access to a tremendous amount of data. This offers a great opportunity for an SSAO with presidential aspirations to master a key skill necessary for leading a higher education institution. While we may have a natural inclination to focus on the mastery of soft skills, if we develop an equal ability to master assessment, I think we can become the total package for the presidency.

The Senior Student Affairs Officer as President

JAMES R. APPLETON

THE CHARGE FROM our editors was to write about "the competencies, skills, and attributes that a senior student affairs officer (SSAO) should cultivate to be an effective president." As the deadline for submission of this chapter drew nearer, a task that seemed quite straightforward at the outset became more complicated and fuzzy, until I finally realized what was troubling me. Why would we be trying to position SSAOs to be presidents when so few of our colleagues will actually assume such positions?

Certainly, one can scan across the country and find successful presidents who have emerged from the trenches of student affairs. Indeed, the competencies, skills, and attributes honed in these positions are transferable, and an SSAO often is more broadly prepared than most other administrators to meet the challenges and complexities of the position of chief executive officer in our colleges and universities.

So why the hesitation? Aha! It is the realization that if becoming president is the career objective of the SSAO, most will be disappointed, because it is a weak political platform to use as a springboard. While boards of trustees take comfort in the acumen of student affairs professionals, they choose presidents, for the most part, from the ranks of academic deans and vice presidents who have traveled a career path as tenured faculty. Some college and university presidents will continue to be elected from positions in government, industry, finance, and student affairs, but in modest numbers compared with those chosen from senior academic ranks.

Most college and university presidents are professionals who begin graduate study in an academic area because of their love of learning and scholarly activity, and join the ranks of assistant professors. They engage in teaching, develop a scholarly agenda, and—through a process of review—become tenured faculty members. Along the way, a few of these colleagues are cajoled or required to get a taste of administrative experience as a program director or a major committee chair, which broadens their view of the academic world. Most will flee back to the classroom and their chosen work, but a few will find enjoyment and success in administrative activities and might move along the winding path as a dean or academic vice president. The majority of college presidents will come from among these experienced academic administrators.

There are many exceptions, of course—professionals who achieve an administrative doctorate and move to the presidency from student affairs. And they have been and are very successful. But the odds do not favor this plan. For the SSAO who aspires to the position of president, I strongly recommend adding a "second suit" to one's résumé and experiences. This is a second suit as in cards, in which games are played with four suits. Four isn't so important in the game of presidential aspiration, but for the SSAO, two may prove to be important.

By way of illustration, in 1982, at the University of Southern California, a crisis of leadership in fund development motivated the president to ask me, the vice president for student affairs, to serve as acting vice president for development, though I did not know the craft. I had worked effectively with the deans, the public, and the trustees, and had managed large budgets and a complex organization. While the title of vice president was the same, the academy viewed the move from student affairs to development as a promotion. Within six months, the appointment was made permanent and—after some time spent learning the essential elements of fund development from good mentors and continued success at the institution in a major campaign—I had established a second suit. I certainly had not originally taken the position with a presidency in mind, but the search firm calls began to come in.

Church-related or niche institutions must not only find talented professionals who can serve as president but must also ensure that the person selected is the right fit with the institution's values or religious orientation. This added requirement tends to narrow the pool of candidates but, in one sense, it also serves as the second suit. If a college chooses to select a president from within the organization, it might be an SSAO, whose deep understanding of the organization and status as a known entity and a competent leader might qualify as the second suit.

Receiving an American Council on Education fellowship and spending a year in the office of a president at a liberal arts college might add the second suit. Planning a short-term sabbatical from a senior position to work with a fund development professional or assuming a major responsibility with a community agency might enable the SSAO to be viewed in a more competitive sense. Serving on boards of organizations and engaging in community leadership positions are also ways to earn the ticket.

There will not be a run on the student affairs profession to fill college presidencies, at least not in the foreseeable future. The view that trustees have of "the good old dean of students" typically will not lead to a presidency. Of course, this hypothetical good old dean does manage large budgets and personnel, knows how to handle crises, can work with parents and publics as well as with students, perhaps has built buildings and certainly manages them, and usually has a handle on the curriculum and the assessment of student learning—but this might not be enough from the platform of student affairs.

Yes, competent senior student affairs professionals will be tapped on occasion, might actually be more broadly qualified by experience than their counterparts, and can be very successful. That is not the point; it is that the move to the presidency is tied to the political processes within the academy and usually will require special circumstances as noted above plus the competencies, skills, and attributes necessary to be successful in any key position of leadership in higher education. So, let's explore what is important for successful leadership at the senior level and let the chips fall where they may with regard to promotion to the presidency.

The list of competencies, skills, and attributes desirable for successful leadership is usually long and tedious, in part because the concept of successful leadership itself is elusive at best. My own All-Time Hit List is limited to five variables that rise far above all others and is drawn from the experience of a career spent thinking about leadership, teaching about organizational behavior, enjoying success, and, on occasion, making bad judgments. In this regard (and just for fun), let me recall the story about the person who noted the organizational success of a new friend and asked, "How did you learn to exercise such good judgment?" The reply: "I have the benefit of lots of experience." "Well, how did you gain this experience?" "Bad judgment, my friend, bad judgment."

So here is the list: (1) creating a vision of the possible; (2) staging; (3) creating success for others; (4) the right use of power; and (5) exercising passion. These five top my list for the making of successful organizational leaders. They are offered as advice and with good wishes.

COMPETENCIES, SKILLS, AND ATTRIBUTES FOR SUCCESSFUL LEADERSHIP

Creating a Vision of the Possible

Successful leaders are a widely diverse group. Warren Bennis and Burt Nanus (1987) note that they "are right-brained, left-brained, tall and short, fat and thin, articulate and inarticulate, assertive and retiring, participative and autocratic" (p. 25). They are also young, old, gay, straight, men and women; they represent the spectrum of ethnicity, culture, and race. Their skills and characteristics vary significantly. So, what is similar among successful leaders? What is the marrow of successful leadership? Those who are successful in leading others marshal the skills of others by the sheer weight of their visions. These may be visions that are developed by the leader or they may be a collective from the dialogue and engagement of others.

This is certainly the most important variable that can be used to distinguish successful leaders. Successful leaders have visions of the possible. They create focus, have an agenda, and have an unparalleled concern for the outcome. Leaders are the most results-oriented individuals. Their visions are compelling, even inspiring, and pull others toward them. Others are attracted to successful leaders because of their extraordinary commitment, not because of certain looks, personality, or even skills or traits. To be effective, the successful leader is a shaper of the world by the weight of the agenda, the visions that are built (Bennis & Nanus, 1987, pp. 25–28).

This reminds me of the old story of the passerby who noticed the bricklayer at work and asked him what he was doing. "I'm laying bricks to earn a living," was the response. He passed a second laborer who seemed to be doing the same thing and asked him the same question. "I'm building a wall," was the response this time. He passed a third worker and asked again. This time the worker exclaimed with enthusiasm, "I'm building a great cathedral!" Bricks must be laid, walls must be built, but one's perspective, attitude, and influence will be changed if such activity is thought to enable great cathedrals to be erected. This in contrast with the wonderful lines from *Alice in Wonderland* (Carroll, 1865, Chapter 6):

"Cheshire puss, would you tell me please, which way I ought to go from here?"

"That depends a good deal on where you want to get to," said the cat.

"I don't care where," said Alice.

"Then it doesn't matter which way you go," said the cat.

Staging

Staging is the act or manner of putting on a play on the stage. For the college or university leader, staging might go something like this: the steps that need to be considered in moving a decision, a policy, a program, or a critical analysis to its success . . . with no surprises to the persons or units affected by the eventual actions. This is not a passive process but an intentional series of planned actions that are used to identify the forces at work for or against the desired action; the ways that such forces can be maximized, neutralized, or mitigated; and the actions necessary to create change.

At the core of this concept is the "force field analysis" developed by

Kurt Lewin (1997), who was a pioneer in the field of social sciences. This technique provides a framework for looking at the forces that are either driving toward or blocking movement toward a goal. It is useful when looking at the variables involved in planning and implementing any organizational change; can assist in determining what will be required to overcome resistance to change or to build support for change; and helps identify the steps the successful leader should take in staging the desired change. It is strongly recommended that this technique be reviewed, that it be used in one or two politically sensitive situations, and that the variables discovered be followed in preparation for the implementation of the substantive action steps.

Just as the steps in successful fund development include, in order, identification, evaluation, cultivation, solicitation, and stewardship of donors, so the steps to successful implementation of a desired action require a clear analysis and prepping of the situation, and deliberate actions to engage those affected in an attempt to build consensus or at least begrudging support . . . and with no surprises. There is an art to this; it takes enormous energy and time, and it must be intentional and structured.

Creating Success for Others

Creating success for others has more typically been described as being a transformational leader. This requires a recognition that continual renewal is required in today's organizations including colleges and universities; that change can occur rapidly; and that the processes of renewal are set in motion by leaders who empower the members of the organization. Transformational leaders "renew and reinterpret values that have become encrusted with hypocrisy, corroded by cynicism, or simply abandoned, and they must generate new values when needed. They need to liberate energies that have been imprisoned by outmoded procedures and habits of thought. They must reenergize forgotten goals or generate new goals for new circumstances. Maybe most important, they must foster the release of human possibilities" (Gardner, 1990, p. 122).

To restate this from my experience and to state it in operational language, the transformational leader will attempt in every transaction to exercise the secondary value of helping others to be successful and to increase their ability to enable the organization to meet agreed-upon objectives. When this is done well, the leader enters every meeting, every task, and every human encounter in an organization with the objective of not only completing the tasks or agenda at hand but also enabling others to be more successful. This kind of leader engages with others in such a way that leaders and followers raise one another to higher levels of motivation and results. Ideally, both leaders and followers, as well as the organization itself, change as the activity of the group develops. In the process of task completion, a setting is developed in which others are empowered—indeed, transformed—by the process, so they become more effective.

An important postscript for student affairs officers: Student affairs officers should think as much about being a resource for faculty as for students. The application of this concept of creating success for others should be focused on relationships and work with faculty at every turn. For further elaboration of an intentional approach to faculty collaboration, see Appleton, Conneely, Stewart, and O'Halloran (2008).

The Right Use of Power

Our colleges and universities have specific and unique functions, and traditional academics do not relish seeing elements and definitions of the corporate world slip into our lexicon. However, we are also bureaucracies and political entities. Stated another way, political behavior is inevitable in every organizational setting and found at every level in the hierarchy, and it intensifies as the decision possibilities are more numerous and more important. Colleges and universities are especially susceptible to political behavior because they are goal-diffuse. This fact introduces the need to understand concepts of power as they apply to organizations and to consider the best use of power.

The acquisition and right use of power is part of the dynamic process of effecting change or meeting personal ambitions and institutional objectives. Power for this purpose is defined as the basic capacity to initiate and sustain action or, to put it another way, the capacity to translate intention into reality and sustain it. Various authors have described several configurations of power in organizations (e.g., Appleton, 1995; Appleton, Briggs, & Rhatigan, 1978, p. 153; Bolman & Deal, 2008, pp. 194–210; Webber, 1979, pp. 163–164).

The kind of power most easily understood might be called *bureaucratic power* or *authority given*. It is the core of a traditional influence system and involves the ability to allocate resources, to reward, to employ, and to control information flow. A second kind of power might be called *professional resources power* or *referent power* and can be described as the influence that accrues from relationships with important constituencies. *Coercion* is a kind of power based on the use of force; for example, it might be used by a labor union or student group, or might be drawn from the threat of bad publicity or an appeal to public opinion. A fourth kind of power, *personal influence power*, extends one's influence by building coalitions or developing informal relationships, or building upon one's reputation through stature. Related to this is a fifth power that is easily overlooked: *expert power*, which is realized through the exercise of sheer competence and leads to influence through respect, not assertion.

It is important for the successful leader to understand the different kinds of power. While all are important, coercion is available in every organization but not likely to be appropriate for the senior leader. The important lesson that justifies including power among the five most important competencies, skills, or attributes of successful leadership is this: Successful leaders, especially in the academy, should depend as much on personal influence and competency power as on the elements of bureaucratic power.

Passion

The use of this word might produce some curious responses and carry with it certain overtones, and might at one level sound like the old Protestant ethic at work, but none of this is intended. One of the attributes that is important to me in defining my own success and that of other leaders is the degree to which there is a driving conviction about the importance of the work, even a devotion to the work and the institution. Passion is an emotion that can exceed reason, so there is some limit to the extent to which the word can be applied in this context. One must not identify one's being and self-worth only on the basis of work. So maybe "enthusiasm" would be easier to swallow; but I prefer passion as I define it here.

To talk about passion for the work and the place, however, forces us to ask why one is in a certain position or why would one want to explore other options. There is always a complex set of reasons why we occupy our roles. These include the importance of income, and a collection of other factors that might include status or prestige of the organization or position, security, working conditions, location, opportunities for professional growth, and recognition. If passion for the work and the place doesn't emerge somewhere on that list, success may come in measured increments.

To be clear, I must be just a bit more personal. Some of the reasons listed above for being in senior college or university positions hold true for me. However, passion for the work and not just the position most certainly is also on the list. After graduating from high school at 15, I went to work in a factory, Columbus McKinnon Chain and Hoist Company (CM). No one in my family had been able to attend college. Toward the end of my two years at CM, I was encouraged by a graduate dean to attend his college. So off I went, then to the military, and graduate school, and professional positions with increasing responsibilities. What a privilege! Now, on any given day, I can squint my eyes and bring to mind the names of students for whom my direct contact or the work I helped organize made some difference. Providing opportunities for others like me to enter the academy and succeed sustains my passion for my work.

I have on my desk one metal chain link, normally a part of a long chain but in this instance sitting alone. It is plated and embossed with the letters 'CM' from the factory where I worked those two years. For awhile, it was just a memento that I picked off the greasy factory floor. But somewhere along the way, it became my symbol of the opportunities I have been afforded. Glancing at it reminds me of the passion I feel for the work and not just the position. My rhetorical question is: "What is your passion, and what 'link' do you have to remind you of this passion? Do you like the work as well as the position?"

CONCLUSION

Creating success in the present by building agendas that are compelling, staging important actions, creating success for others, using influence and competency to accomplish important tasks, and learning to enjoy the passion of the work as well as the perks of a position have emerged over many years to top my list of important variables for successful leadership. There are other factors, of course. We could add the importance of action-oriented planning with its attendant accountability patterns, chronicle the importance of faculty interaction and collaboration, and emphasize the marketing skills required to be consistently successful in dealing with the external world. But these discussions are for another time.

Remember the introductory theme of this chapter. These competencies, skills, and attributes are transferable to other senior positions, including the position of college or university president. But it is important that such ambition, not always realized, does not sour the present.

Oh, yes—one more piece of advice. Don't take yourself too seriously, because you may be the only person who does. My good friend Jim Rhatigan—the standard for excellence in SSAOs and now a major fund developer at his university, not to become a president but maybe to use it as his second suit for credit at the pearly gates—said that whenever he begins to get an exaggerated opinion of his own worth, he remembers that "the number of people attending my funeral may well be determined by the weather" (Appleton et al., 1978, p. 145).

REFERENCES

Appleton, J. R. (1995). Chapter 1. The context. In P. L. Moore (Ed.), *Managing the political dimensions of student affairs* (pp. 5–15). San Francisco, CA: Jossey-Bass.

Appleton, J. R., Briggs, C. M., & Rhatigan, J. J. (1978). *Pieces of eight: The rites, roles, and styles of the dean, by eight who have been there.* Portland, OR: NASPA Institute of Research and Development.

Appleton, J. R., Conneely, J. F., Stewart, G., & O'Halloran, K. C. (2008, Spring). Grow together: Faculty, SSAOs forge new collaborations. *Leadership Exchange, 6*(1), 8–11

Bennis, W., & Nanus, B. (1987). *Leaders: Strategies for taking charge.* New York, NY: Harper & Row.

Bolman, L. G., & Deal, T. E. (2008). *Reframing organizations: Artistry, choice, and leadership.* San Francisco, CA: Jossey-Bass.

Carroll, Lewis. (1865). *Alice's Adventures in Wonderland.* London, England: Macmillan and Co.

Gardner, J. W. (1990). *On leadership.* New York, NY: Macmillan.

Lewin, K. (1997). Defining the field at a given time. *Psychological Review, 50,* 292–310. (Republished in *Resolving social conflicts and field theory in social science,* Washington, DC: American Psychological Association, 1997. Also cited in several texts and research documents that can be accessed through numerous websites.)

Webber, R. A. (1979). *Management: Basic elements of managing organizations.* Homewood, IL: Richard D. Irwin, Inc.

Are You Book and *Street Smart?*

Jesus Carreon

SO YOU WANT to be a president? As an experienced and competent student services leader (and not just based on self-assessment), you must consider a variety of factors as you get ready to apply for a college president position. As a college chief executive officer (CEO) myself, I have had the opportunity to hire vice presidents and college presidents. When I was asked to add my thoughts in this chapter, I reflected back to when I was a vice president of academic affairs in the late 1980s and early 1990s—I remember that my due diligence (chatting with many colleagues and assessing candidates for president) allowed me to find out that most presidents came from the academic side of the house.

Having worked in four states, I have also seen student affairs colleagues and business officers appointed as college presidents. While many higher education colleagues think that the road to the presidency should begin in the academic area, I believe that a candidate from student services has a real opportunity today because of the dramatic changes that have taken place within our student populations as well as in our communities. Today, student services is a critical element in the access, achievement, and success of all our students. Candidates for president can anchor their competencies in how they have helped students enroll in college, stay in college, and successfully complete a college degree or certificate, or receive the essential training to be skilled workers and productive members of the community.

UNDERSTANDING THE ROLE AND PREPARING FOR THE POSITION

Some areas that a candidate needs to assess and understand are related to the formal and informal role the college president plays at the institution to which the candidate may want to apply. As a candidate, you should do the following: (a) review the position description and gather information and feedback to understand how the outgoing person functioned on a daily and annual basis; (b) review documents produced by the college to get a sense of what the president accomplished and his or her areas of passion and commitment; (c) assess the accreditation reports related to that college; (d) review the college's vision, mission, and goals to better understand the direction and focus of the college now and in planning for the future; and (e) take time to interact with members of the college community.

Personally and professionally, you should assess your educational and professional background in relation to the formal job announcement. I suggest that you work with your mentor (if you don't have one, find one!) to make sure there is a match between what the college is looking for and what you have accomplished. An earned doctorate is a basic requirement in most cases. Many position announcements use the term "preferred," but the real deal is that most faculty, staff, and management believe that a college president must have a doctorate. Make sure your résumé is well organized and well written, and addresses the areas stated in the position announcement. Make sure that everything on it can be defended: specifically, actual jobs, duties, and accomplishments. Why? Because committee members may check you out and discover that what you say and what is accurate may be in conflict.

One of the questions I have always asked myself when I was hiring a vice president or president was whether the person seemed to have "street smarts." What do I mean? Frankly, people can have a lot of education, degrees, and experience and yet be completely out of touch with what is really going on around them in the internal or external environment. Just because a you are well educated does not necessarily mean that you are "totally educated." A sense of your students and communities cannot be gained by reading books or articles, or attending multiple workshops. Truly effective and successful candidates for a presidency must be able to relate their experience and style in a way that connects higher education to the communities they will serve.

SKILLS AND ABILITIES

As you get ready to apply for a presidency, be very aware that, in today's world, accountability to our public is the major issue that all CEOs must focus on 24 hours a day, seven days a week. The days of higher education being protected from public and private sector assessment, scrutiny, and opinions are gone. A candidate for a CEO position today should be aware of the critical skills, abilities, and leadership styles that are important to many colleagues, especially those on the screening committee.

On a personal level, you will need to be aware that the following characteristics are very important: courage, determination, discipline, consistency, respect, integrity, honesty, and openness. On a professional level, it is important to have a solid understanding of the current college organizational structure in relation to the vision, mission, and strategic direction of the college; knowledge of how to plan toward integrated and results-oriented change; and a real sense of the internal and external environment related to the college. Also, you should make sure that you present yourself (dress and grooming) as professionally as possible. The college president sets the tone for a lot of things, and one of them is the image of the college/university. The first impression is powerful from the nonverbal perspective. However, the key is to show the screening committee that you have done your homework and learned about the college, its issues, and the community it serves.

I trust that these comments and suggestions will help SSAOs who want to go for a presidency to realize that a successful candidate has a lot to think about before actually applying for the job.

Preparing for a Presidency,
Even if It Isn't Your Goal

Cliff L. Wood

THOUGH I CAME to community college education by accident and necessity, America's public community colleges have been my life and passion for more than four decades. After completing a master's degree in student personnel, I got married and needed a job. I was "place bound," because my new bride and I had to stay in the area while she finished her bachelor's degree. Because I had enjoyed my college life so much, my long-term career goal was to replicate my college life from the other side of the desk, and my immediate goal was a college job in the area.

As a college student, I was in the middle of campus life, serving as an officer in student government, my fraternity, and several clubs and organizations, and as an editor of the college literary magazine. I spent four years in the Delta Tau Delta fraternity and was in "bro" heaven. My dream job was to be dean of men at a large residential university. In 1967, I was in the right spot at the right time. The U.S. contribution to the world's higher education system was becoming a reality: Community colleges were springing up all across America. I landed at Tarrant County Junior College (TCJC) in Fort Worth, Texas. What I learned about program development and education has served me well for more than 40 years.

Lesson 1: If you want to be seen as successful by faculty, you must be knowledgeable about the curricula and programs of the college.

No matter how important your job is (or you think your job is) to the college, the real work of the institution is teaching and learning. A college president must be seen as fostering this concept among all employees. I was hired as director of student activities, but my first real assignment was as an academic advisor/counselor. The district was expecting 2,000 students at its new South Campus, and almost 4,700 students came. My original start date was August 1. In late May, my new boss, the dean of students, called and asked if I could come to work on June 1. Therefore, immediately after my wedding, I moved, without my bride, to Fort Worth. The dean said I was needed early to help register students, and register students we did—from 8:00 a.m. until 9:00 p.m. every day. Each student had an individual session with a "counselor." At this point, almost every staff member in student services advised students. We had two days of extensive training/indoctrination by division chairs, who wanted to make sure we understood the programs they offered, the importance of general education courses, and so on. These division chairs were promoting programs and enrollments, and it was our job to fill their courses. I was the kid in the group, and they educated me.

Lesson 2: Acknowledging who someone is and respecting human differences are essential to open up communication between individuals and among groups.

It was also during my first job that I had a seminal/watershed experience that shaped my life personally and professionally. I grew up in Dallas, Texas, and attended segregated schools. My high school graduating class had more than 700 students, all White. There were only three Jews. My college was segregated when I enrolled. The first students of color enrolled when I was a junior, so I was never in a classroom with a student of color until graduate school. As a graduate teaching assistant, I had my first classroom experience with students of color. Nine freshman football players were in my class, and I was the one who had much to learn.

At TCJC in 1967, several hundred Black students enrolled along with more than 4,000 White students. For almost all of these 4,700 students, it was their first experience in an integrated school. During my second year at TCJC, there began to be some racial tensions on the campus. Our student services staff decided we needed to structure dialogue/communication among Black and White students. Several of us agreed to host a supper and conversation in our homes for a racially integrated group of students. On a Sunday evening in October, I sat on the living room floor of my small two-bedroom apartment, talking and having a meal with five Black students and five White students. This evening's conversation helped me understand how young and naïve I was, and I began to understand the importance of open dialogue and candor with groups of students. This is key if there is to be progress in fostering mutual respect.

Lesson 3: Faculty knowledge, engagement, and support are key to the success of student development programs, whatever the program.

What I didn't know the first two months, as I advised students, was that I was building the foundation of a student activities program that would be cited as a model program three years later. As I spent time learning about academic programs, I was fostering relationships with persons who would be advisors to clubs and organizations and who would give time to activities outside their classrooms. James Luck, humanities chair and music professor, said we could build a model lyceum program, and Tarrant County's South Campus could be a center of culture in a town ready to spruce itself up. Freda Powell, who was recruited from Odessa College (an early junior college) because of its outstanding drama program, became a supporter, and there was a real bond between the theater program and student activities. My mantra became "not student activities, but cocurricular activities," which complemented the work in the college's classrooms.

Faculty members from a variety of backgrounds had great suggestions, and notables such as psychologist Dr. Joyce Brothers and film critic Judith Crist spoke at the campus. At every faculty meeting, I was invited to talk about the great opportunities for "your students." At one such meeting, I told them that "there will be the opportunity to hear noted anthropologist Jean Pierre Hallet talk about witchcraft, voodoo, and cannibalism, and other things you do in your classroom." It brought laughs, but it also brought support.

Lesson 4: Professional involvement is essential to be a successful administrator. You must be involved in and contribute to professional associations related to your area of interest.

At TCJC I also had a very ambitious student government that learned about the National Student Association's (NSA) Student Bill of Rights. NSA grew out of the radical student movement of the late 1960s. TCJC's student government decided to develop a similar document and to be the first junior college student government to have its own bill of rights. The conservative board of TCJC was leery about any ties to the national student movement; after much negotiation, the board agreed to adopt the Bill of Student Rights if the group added a Bill of Student Responsibilities. This project brought national attention to the college, and I became involved with both the American College Personnel Association (ACPA) and the National Association of Student Personnel Administrators (NASPA). As a very young administrator, I served with Dick De Cosmo of Delaware County, Pennsylvania, on ACPA's Commission of Community Colleges and was myself appointed to the editorial board of the *NASPA Journal.*

Lesson 5: It is essential that a college president or someone on that path understand the funding and financing of the institution and how to access and expand the source of funds.

The great educator who first taught this lesson to me was William E. Truax, dean of the College of Education at my alma mater. All graduate students in higher education administration did an internship with the dean, who said, "One's first job as a chief student affairs officer is to learn how one's college is funded. If you do not know the funding mechanism at the college, you may never get the appropriate share or your fair share of the resources."

Wet behind the mortarboard, I became dean of institutional and student services at Houston Community College (HCC). The college was three years old, it owned no facilities, its faculty taught mostly in high schools in the evening, and it had an enrollment of more than 30,000 students. HCC had inherited 16 occupational programs (several allied health programs) from the Houston Independent School District (HISD). Because of two key references, I was offered the job after a one-hour interview with the president.

For the next three years, I worked 12 hours a day. The health programs—including a very large licensed practical nursing program—had no written admissions standards or procedures, and the large minority community in Houston (Black and Latino) was demanding equal access to these programs. I spent many hours with program coordinators (all nearly twice my age), developing testing/placement and admissions procedures for access to the programs. The president had given me quotas for enrollment, quotas that he chose not to share with the program coordinators. Though I was "charming," I still had my limits. I also knew the value and necessity of program accreditation and the impact accrediting agencies can have on and demand of institutions. At this time, HCC was facing its initial accreditation by the Southern Association of Colleges and Universities. HCC had two instructional deans, one academic and one vocational, both of whom came from the school district and had no community college experience. The president also had no community college experience, was a researcher from the University of Houston, and was hired for a three-year appointment to develop a plan for this fledgling community college without walls or a tax base.

After my first year at the institution, the founding president completed his contract and the deputy superintendent of instruction for the HISD was appointed president. Because I was the only key administrator with actual community college experience, I was appointed to chair the college's initial self-study for accreditation by the Southern Association.

There I was, 50 miles from the Gulf of Mexico, a fish out of water, and I struggled. But then a miracle occurred. The Southern Association appointed Richard J. Ernst, president/chancellor of the Northern Virginia Community College System, as chair of our college accreditation team. HCC was successful with its initial accreditation, and I became involved with the Southern Association. "Accreditation" was a tool in my box that many colleagues with a background in student services did not have.

Lesson 6: The president must foster relationships among his or her vice presidents so they can negotiate and resolve critical issues among themselves—especially as these issues relate to their ability to see that the college's day-to-day operations run effectively—so the president can do his or her real job as a transformational leader.

One of the most unpleasant experiences I had in my career was at a college where the chief financial officer would not talk to me about funding and finances. He told me not to worry about money—that he took care of the budget. Before long, however, I knew I had to heed Dean Truax's advice and demand a full explanation of the college's resources. I did something I have rarely done as a vice president and rarely do as president. It is also something I do not like to do: I asked my boss—the president—to intervene and insist that the vice president of finance explain the finances of the college to me.

Lesson 7: Student development professionals have knowledge and information that can be shared formally and informally.

My beginning in community college education was shaped by my degrees in counseling psychology and student personnel administration. My academic career and the core courses of my curriculum are at the heart of who I am. A general education course in social psychology (Personality Foundations) taught me the worth of every individual in theory, and this has became one of my core values.

Because of my status as dean at HCC, I was able to help our director of counseling affirm the role and importance of student development services to community colleges. I hired the director of counseling, who had been a friend and fellow doctoral student. Melvin Whitehurst was a very gifted counselor/educator; not only did he see the counseling/advising mission of his staff, but he felt that counselors had something to teach. He developed a series of human development courses, including career exploration, values clarification, and college skills. Whitehurst believed that students would benefit from these courses and that he could strengthen and add to his staff if part of their work generated resources for the college. While the academic folks were not happy, we were successful in implementing these courses as electives for students.

Lesson 8: In leading an academic division of a campus or a college, it is important that the leader be actively involved and demonstrate a thorough knowledge of and appreciation for the programs he or she supervises.

Fate stepped in when my wife was offered a job at the *Washington Post* in the District of Columbia. I remembered Ernst's words after the exit interview of our Southern Association accreditation visit. He said, "Cliff, if you ever want to move to the D.C. area, give me a call. I might just have a job for you." I sent a résumé and letter, and was offered the position of chair of a new division called Visual Arts and Engineering, a position that proved to be an excellent path to academic administration. Because of the variety of programs—which ranged from automotive to fine arts—academic background was not a key factor in chairing the division. In addition to the regular duties of a division chair, I was responsible for a facility that was a mile from the main campus (the student body had outgrown the original facilities). My background in student services proved to be very valuable in this position, and for five years I also co-led art/study tours to Europe with a professor of art history.

The automotive program provided me with a special opportunity based on my experience with student organizations. Our automotive program was one of the country's largest, with more than 700 students enrolled. The program head became involved in the creation of a professional organization for college automotive teachers. H. E. McCartney, a very skilled educator, asked if I would help them develop guidelines, constitution bylaws, and a charter to establish the National Association of College Automotive Teachers, and I became the organization's first executive vice president.

Lesson 9: The ability to demonstrate an understanding of teaching and all that teaching entails is crucial if faculty are to have confidence in your leadership.

At Northern Virginia Community College, all administrators were required to teach one or more courses each quarter. It was crucial that I had started my professional experience as a teaching assistant, where I learned to respect the hard work involved in teaching. Because I had taught only as a graduate student, for the first two years I combined my teaching and student services experiences by supervising cooperative education students from several of the programs offered by the division. This allowed me to work directly with students in a teaching/advising situation and taught me the importance of working with business and industry, which are often deeply involved in community college education. Later, I taught in the human services program at the campus, earning the rank of associate professor. I was qualified for these assignments because of my student development background, and I frequently taught Group Processes and Substance Abuse Education.

Lesson 10: The key to being a respected president is to be a transformational leader, and that is best achieved from a student-centered philosophy and an understanding that places teaching and learning at the forefront of the institution.

I learned this lesson from my background in student services. My experiences at three institutions were major stepping stones that allowed me to move from student development services to academic administration, serving as a dean, a vice president, and the president of a comprehensive community college. Today—six years after becoming president of a troubled institution that is now considered by many to be a model institution—I attribute much of my success to my foundation in student affairs and student development.

Leading With Vision and Practicality

CHARLENE M. DUKES

COMMUNITY COLLEGES OCCUPY a unique place in the framework of American higher education, but those who aspire to a community college presidency will find that the qualities that make a successful candidate do not differ significantly from those required of the leader of any major organization or institution. Leadership is always a balancing act. Leaders must demonstrate authority but invite collaboration. They must be visionary but also pragmatic. As the institution's public face, a president will be held responsible for its successes and failures but must not shy away from the hard decisions. For those willing to take on these challenges, the potential to improve lives, create opportunity, and transform communities is tremendous.

In seeking the presidency, a certain level of education is desirable and expected. In the majority of cases, this means a doctorate, most often in some area of education. Some doctoral programs focus specifically on community college leadership, and they are instructive in that they provide context and some sense of what the job entails and how it works. However, no degree can prepare you completely for the job of president. You must identify and develop a set of skills independent of the program, and this will require another, more extended phase of preparation. There are perspectives and skills you can develop on your way to the presidency, but they cannot be developed overnight, nor can they be picked up in the classroom. They are gained and sharpened over time and through experience.

When to pursue the presidency will be a decision only you can make, but remember that the broader and deeper your experiences are, the easier you will find the job of being president. I began my career working in admissions and financial aid at a four-year institution and moved on to be assistant director of admissions at the Community College of

Allegheny County in Pennsylvania. I was later named director of admissions, then director of minority affairs, and then dean of students. I came to Prince George's Community College in 1995 as vice president for student services and was appointed president in 2007. I share this chronology because it exemplifies the kind of career trajectory that is typical of community college presidents. There is no ideal age or career length that makes a person more qualified or suitable; rather, candidates should be able to demonstrate a progressive record of leadership and responsibility. If the presidency is your ultimate goal, extract as much as you can from each of your learning experiences.

If you are approaching the presidency from a student services background, it is especially helpful to have instructional experience. To lead an institution whose core mission is education, it is imperative to understand what goes on in the classroom. Having been a faculty member, even on a part-time or adjunct basis, will not only lend you a measure of credibility with the faculty but will give you insight into what they and their students are experiencing on a daily basis.

Community college presidents with backgrounds in student services are in the minority. A 2006 report by the American Association of Community Colleges revealed that only 8% of community college presidents held positions in student services before their first presidency; more than half were in academic positions (Weisman & Vaughan, 2006, p. 5). Nevertheless, this should not dissuade you. If you are currently a senior student affairs officer (SSAO), there are plenty of ways you can build up your experience and make yourself a stronger presidential prospect. One is to find ways to partner with another area of the college, whether it be academic affairs or workforce development, through programming, strategic planning, community outreach, and other initiatives. Another proactive step would be to sit down with the current president and ask for leadership opportunities. Such opportunities could take the form of serving as the president's representative in the community, liaising with state and local government, business partners, or the nonprofit sector.

Internally, there are task forces and committees to be chaired. Fundraising is an area that will always need committed and energetic leaders.

More than a third of community college presidents ascended to their office at institutions where they were already serving, as I did. Even though internal candidates may seem to possess an advantage, this is not always the case. Having the inside scoop does not mean you are necessarily the best person for the job. If you are considering the presidency at your current institution, you will first need to determine whether you can make a lasting or significant contribution. This may or may not involve major change. In some cases, it will mean continuing on the same path set by a predecessor. Remember that a president's ability to deliver is paramount. Will you be able to deliver? *What* will you be able to deliver? How will you sustain yourself through the rigorous demands of the office? There is always an element of proving oneself as a new president. If you are moving up internally, you will be faced with the task of supervising people who were formerly colleagues, which can be a delicate matter. Yesterday you were one of them; today you're the boss.

Individuals coming from the student services side will usually bring an empathy and sensitivity to the role of president, both of which are useful qualities in a leader but which some can mistake for weakness. Carving out a place for yourself and establishing your authority will be among your first priorities. I favor a collegial style and welcome the suggestions and feedback of the entire campus community, but I also have to be aware of when the time for collaboration has ended and I need to make that executive decision. The president is the only person who reports directly to the board of trustees, and the board expects a president to lead.

As you move through the community college hierarchy, remember that transparency and collaboration should be characteristics of institutional leadership. Decision-making and planning processes ought to involve as many people as possible. The board, senior administrators, donors, alumni, students, faculty and staff, and the community's formal and informal leaders can all make valuable contributions in different areas. People who are participants feel more invested in their work.

Working together fosters an atmosphere of collegiality. Identifying and developing talent are essential functions of leadership. Hiring good people will make the job easier, but if it doesn't work out, it will be the president's responsibility to help those individuals move on.

Difficult decisions are part and parcel of the job. As chief executive, the president can be a lightning rod for criticism. There is no way to deflect all criticism, nor should you try. But it is always easier to defend controversial decisions if they have been made on the basis of sound research, with fairness, and in a collaborative manner. At my own institution, we made changes to health and retirement benefits that resulted in much-needed cost savings. Changes to the status quo will always face a certain level of resistance, and many consider benefits to be sacrosanct. I knew that it would be a sensitive issue, so I invited suggestions and engaged in dialogue with faculty and staff. I wanted to be as inclusive as possible, even though the decision would ultimately be mine to make. Having the hard data to support my decision was immensely helpful.

Extensive research is a crucial but often overlooked component of decision making and planning. The college's office of institutional research can provide you with detailed profiles of the student body and the community. These reports guide efforts in many areas, including advocacy, outreach, curriculum development, recruitment, marketing, and budgeting. This is valuable information, and it helps tremendously in allocating resources for the future. Reading the reports will give you great insight into the demographics, concerns, achievements, and activities of the college community. Research can illuminate areas that need improvement and serve as a catalyst for new programs.

Presidents are expected to be well versed in the issues facing higher education and knowledgeable about the trends and events affecting their institutions and students. Reading about and understanding what's happening in the community college sector and across higher education, as well as in the world in general, is invaluable. As an institutional leader, you will be showered with requests from media, associations, schools, civic organizations, businesses, and other groups to speak, offer comment, participate in panels, and write. A strong grasp of the topics of the day will prepare you to respond articulately to these requests.

Beyond the skills already mentioned, there are specific functions of community college leadership that you must understand and for which you can lay the groundwork.

The office to which you aspire requires more political savvy now than ever before. Do you have, or can you develop, deft business negotiating skills and the ability to build and maintain strong relationships with other leaders in the community? The growth of community colleges, their increasing popularity as engines of workforce development, rising community college enrollments, state and local budget cuts—these challenges are placing new demands on community college leaders and call for new leadership skills. Very far from being ivory towers, community colleges are central components of the communities they serve, not only as educational providers but as contributors to policymaking, economic development, and civic engagement. Your preparation ought to include an analysis of the issues and concerns facing the community. A community college is a microcosm of the local community, so the community's issues will become your issues. Understanding context is critical to creating effective solutions and planning strategically.

Whatever the individual style or philosophy, no president can be successful without a guiding vision. A vision can be a powerful force, but in order for it to take hold, the institution must be able to see in your vision reflections of its best self. It is through your voice that the institution's aspirations and goals will be defined.

Developing a vision is one thing; implementing it is another. Planning and research, while not glamorous, are indispensable components of leadership. If you are already working at a community college, become involved in its strategic planning process. Strategic planning is of the utmost importance in determining an institution's direction. Planning also includes financial planning and fundraising goals, so if you have opportunities to become involved in development activities, take them.

A president should be at the forefront of the college's fundraising campaigns.

Because the success of community colleges depends in many ways on the relationships they forge with local constituents—both individuals and organizations—community college presidents must be effective champions for their institutions. Advocacy is an integral part of leadership, particularly in light of the budget constraints with which many colleges are struggling. Community college presidents are being asked to serve more students with fewer resources. The increase in the number of students applying to college has created greater competition and exclusivity in the four-year admissions process. Community colleges are increasingly seen as low-cost, high-quality alternatives to four-year schools. While this is good news in many ways, unfortunately this trend has coincided with state and local budget cuts that make it difficult for community colleges to meet the growing demand. This is a not a temporary problem.

Community colleges, as public institutions, are required to continue serving the community regardless of fiscal pressures. They need to seek greater self-reliance and support from nongovernment sources. This means reaching out to the community and developing closer ties with business. The lead role in this effort necessarily belongs to the president. If you know your community, you will know who can help you and what relationships can benefit the institution most.

What makes for successful advocacy? To advocate effectively, you must network aggressively. This is not unique to the presidency, so you will have ample opportunities to perfect your networking abilities before you reach the highest levels of leadership. Social interaction is a valuable and necessary means of promoting the college's agenda and taking the message out into the community. Networking goes beyond business interactions. Elected officials, community leaders, K–12 and higher education administrators, representatives of faith-based and other affinity groups—all should be included in your networking circle. Make yourself visible and accessible in the community. For presidents, networking also provides opportunities to identify and cultivate potential donors to the college. If you have already established relationships in the community in which you will be working, you will have a head start on your development efforts.

It is easy to fill your calendar, but you will need to determine which events, projects, and committees are most worthwhile and apportion your time carefully. It is also necessary to be proactive in creating networking opportunities—not only to be responsive but to initiate contact. Networking on the road to the presidency can, of course, provide visibility. It is also an avenue for you to demonstrate your talents. If you show yourself to be capable, people will remember.

Take note of the ways in which the college responds to the needs of the community. You may be in a position to invite community leaders to the college to serve as keynote speakers for campus events or to participate in discussions. Let them see firsthand the opportunities the college provides. Local businesspeople need to understand how the college keeps their workforces competitive. Elected officials want to see the return on their investment. Even if you end up moving to another institution or another part of the country, the experience you gain from these activities will stand you in good stead.

It is important to understand that the presidency is a 24/7 position with almost no downtime and very little anonymity. Individuals often approach me in public with a question or comment about the college. I recently had someone ask me about employment. People will expect you to be on duty at all times, even when you're running to the store for a carton of milk. They will think you have all the answers. This nonstop accessibility and visibility is not something you can prepare for, and you may never get completely used to it, but be aware that it comes with the territory.

If you take the time to prepare yourself well, establish relationships, and learn from experience, you may find yourself in the office of the president. If you do, do not be disheartened if success is not immediate. Setting priorities, assembling support, and achieving goals cannot be done overnight. New presidents often encounter resistance from entrenched interests. Not everyone is receptive to change. It takes time to establish working relationships and build trust with principal stakeholders. *Being* president, just like *becoming* president, involves taking the long-term view. Your responsibility as president will be to develop a vision for the college that will continue after you are gone.

In many ways, the advice we give our students applies here as well. If your ambition is to be president, you will need to make a long-term commitment. You will need to set goals, develop a plan, and acquire the skills to attain your goals. It may be frustrating at times. However, if you use good judgment, are resilient, and persevere, you will succeed. Certainly, you will face many obstacles along the way, but remember that in the final analysis you are an educator, and education transforms lives. Leading with humility, humor, and heart will result in a better future for your institution, for its students, and for the community. In that sense, the rewards far exceed the effort.

REFERENCE

Weisman, I. M., & Vaughan, G. B. (2006). *The community college presidency: 2006.* Retrieved from http://www.aacc.nche.edu/Publications/Briefs/Documents/09142007presidentbrief.pdf

CHAPTER 8

The Student Affairs
Innovation Imperative

LAURENCE N. SMITH

CROSSING THE FINISH LINE: Completing College at America's Public Universities (Bowen, 2009) challenges our nation's public university leaders to design new approaches to solve a very old problem: their institutions' high attrition rates and the resultant loss of human capital desperately needed for our nation to remain competitive.

Crossing the Finish Line focuses on "patterns of educational attainment at public universities [and colleges], which educate more than two-thirds of all full-time students seeking bachelor's degrees" (Bowen, 2009, p. xiii). However, its challenge applies to all colleges and universities that have high attrition rates institutionally or within specific segments of their student body.

The Obama administration recently announced its American Graduation Initiative, calling for 5 million more college graduates by 2020. This initiative is even more important in view of the fact that the

United States, which for years led the world in the number of 25- to 34-year-olds with a college degree, now ranks 12th among 36 developed nations (Lewin, 2010).

The Bill and Melinda Gates Foundation and the Lumina Foundation for Education, along with a growing number of government agencies, public and private agencies, national and state legislators, labor economists, and employers, also urge significant reform in higher education graduation rates.

Jamie P. Merisotis, president and chief executive officer of the Lumina Foundation, clearly states the challenge to higher education in his president's message in the foundation's *Focus* magazine:

> In some ways college completion is a numbers game, one in which students seems to succeed more by chance than by design. Those who are fortunate enough to be born to the right zip code, to supportive families earning comfortable incomes— these are the ones for whom college success is all but assured.
>
> But for others—tens of millions of others in today's increasingly diverse student population—success is a real gamble. Low-income students, first-generation students, working adults, students of color . . . all face daunting odds as they pursue postsecondary education.
>
> At the Lumina Foundation, we are absolutely convinced that the nation must increase its level of educational attainment. That's why we have committed ourselves to a "Big Goal" for college completion: By the year 2025, we want 60 percent of Americans to hold high-quality degrees or credentials—a significant increase over the current college-completion rate of 40 percent. (Merisotis, 2010, p. 1)

Gaston Caperton, president of the College Board, broadens the challenge when he notes that "[to] improve our college completion rates, we must think 'P–16' and improve education from preschool through higher education" (Lewin, 2010, p. 11).

Research for *Breakthrough! A Blueprint for Mobilizing America's Campuses to Increase Graduation Rates* (2011), a book that Albert Blixt and I are writing, is giving us the opportunity to interview numerous presidents and senior administrators at public universities and colleges that have high attrition rates. In most interviews, campus administrators tell us that the higher education experience works very well for most students: They are recruited, admitted, advised, enrolled, receive financial aid and housing assignments, attend orientation, begin classes, are taught and graded, are exposed to the college experience, and eventually graduate, if not in four years, then most by six years. The system works, we are informed, but obviously cannot work for everyone.

When we confront them with the fact that the "not for everyone" group consists of 50% to 60% of their students, we are told that it is not their institution's fault that so many students drop out, or that many who graduate need several additional years to do so. We are told that these students are victims of forces beyond the institution's control. We hear about the many interventions, programs, processes, and procedures that are in place to help students. We are told, time and time again, that the institution is doing all it can, that it is trying to do more, but there is real doubt that whatever it does will make an impact on these dropout-prone students, who arrive underprepared, unfocused, unmotivated, overwhelmed by their transition to independence and a new learning environment, unwilling to seek help, underfinanced, and working long hours that detract from their study time. There is widespread agreement that these students are victims of socioeconomic conditions and inadequate high school preparation.

We are told that campus frustration runs deep over so many students' lack of success. But we are also quickly informed that the statistical information about attrition and graduation rates being reported to prospective students does not tell an accurate story about how hard the institution tries to be responsive to the needs of all students.

There is also considerable agreement that the many programs designed to reduce attrition—such as the first-year experience, freshman interest groups, residence hall clustering of students by academic or special interest, and early warning systems—may be working but not as intended, since the bottom line on retention has not shifted. If those programs do anything, we are informed, they enrich the college experience of students who are on the fast track to success by virtue of their past academic achievement and test scores. And then we are reminded that unless the institution did what it has been doing, the attrition number might be even higher.

Feelings and frustrations run deep, but ownership of the problems does not, as the following quotes convey (Blixt & Smith, 2011):

"Elite universities do not have to confront these problems, since they only accept students who will be successful no matter where they study," said a university president.

"Public universities in our state are forced to admit at-risk students and then are criticized for high attrition rates, while the elite public universities create satellite campuses to which they funnel their at-risk students instead of having them on their main campus. This keeps their graduation scores inflated for their flagship campus," said another president.

"We may not be able to graduate all of our at-risk students," noted a university president, "but we give all who attend a chance at the American dream. They have a chance to succeed and can, if they try hard and take advantage of the many services we provide that will help them do so. For those who do not achieve their goal, we are assured their lives have been enriched by the exposure to the college experience."

However, when we examine the actual practices on campus and talk with administrators who have direct responsibility for student retention and its many interrelated functions, we quickly realize how fragile the administrative processes are and how tenuous the commitments are to collaborate for continuous improvement.

What we are told sounds like a systemic approach. What we find when we examine it is, at best, a loosely cobbled, fragile set of working agreements and efforts based more on the needs of the service provider units than those of the end users.

We need to face the fact that our public universities and colleges are failing miserably in addressing their high attrition rate and how long it takes to graduate. This record would be totally unacceptable to the stakeholders of any other profession or business. We take solace in the fact that we are among a large group of institutions that have similar results. We are embarrassed that our institutional attrition and graduation results are reported automatically online to students who select us when filling out their financial aid forms and that these rates are also finding their way into many of the college guides students purchase. For the more enterprising students, and especially the parents of prospective freshmen, the National Center for Education Statistics/Institute of Education Science online data paint a painful picture of how well students thrive in detail that includes both general attrition and retention data and data for racial groups.

The big question is whether or not the public universities and colleges that are experiencing high attrition rates and are under pressure to be assertive and innovative in addressing this issue will respond—and when. And if they do respond, what should be the role of the senior student affairs officer in leading an innovative response?

Having spent 40 years in higher education in student affairs at three major universities—31 of them as a vice president of student affairs—I have long recognized our inadequacy at addressing the challenges presented by high attrition and prolonged time to graduate.

In 1982, I was the lead author of a book published by ACT titled *Mobilizing the Campus for Retention: An Innovative Quality of Life Model.* In consulting at a number of universities and colleges, as well as presenting at many national conferences and workshops, I became highly sensitized to the fact that on campus there was wide agreement over what institutional innovation and change was important, but that no one seemed willing to make the personal changes in their performance or work environment to make it happen.

What is remarkable to me is that almost 30 years have gone by since then, and nothing has changed with respect to attrition. This underscores the fact that universities and colleges are institutions, and institutions are value-infused and self-perpetuating. Their traditions and structures insulate them from outside pressures.

It is also apparent that when pressure to change comes from within the institution, it is quickly dampened by keepers of the status quo. Its advocates are exhausted by restraining forces cloaked in institutional traditions, silo thinking, turf protection, and administrator and faculty indifference, and by retention task forces or committees that are politically constituted and encumbered to make sure that by the time they report out, the advocates for change are completely neutralized. And if they are not, the winning argument will be that there are not enough funds to meet current needs, let alone fund a new initiative that has broad financial implications.

Although it sounds as though change is impossible and higher educational institutions are communities of curmudgeons, this is not the case I am making. Rather, it is that resistance to change is embedded in the culture of institutions. It is how they have survived over the centuries. The university was originally designed to be aloof from mundane society and was protected from the intrusions of those who wanted to restrict its teaching and pursuit of truth.

Today, however, the university is an integral part of society. The opportunity to receive a college education is no longer seen as a privilege but as an American birthright and passport to the good life. Many forms of employment that were once open to high school graduates now require a college degree. The transition from an industrial to a knowledge-based economy demands special preparation, and the university is the place to obtain it. The more public funds are spent (and the more the need for qualified graduates grows), the more pressure there will be on public universities and colleges to produce sufficient numbers of qualified graduates.

When major changes have occurred in higher education, they usually have come from outside forces. Universities and colleges that depend on (and are addicted to) federal and state funding, financial aid to students, and foundation research grants have long recognized that they must adapt to accommodate legislation as well as rules and regulations tied to funding allocations. Changes are made. The bromide "money talks" is an operant factor on just about every campus.

The educational franchise has changed as well. For-profit universities, online courses, and cheaper tuition and fees at community colleges have attracted large numbers of traditional as well as adult learners.

Just as many forces are gathering to reshape higher education, significant forces are reshaping our nation and our world. Venerable companies have gone out of business, replaced by new companies selling the same products more successfully. We see major demographic shifts and changes; a move from the melting pot concept to the idea of a diverse societal mosaic. Great changes are occurring in the workplace as the baby boomers are replaced by generation X-ers and millennials, bringing new expectations and attitudes. Other nations are competing for international students whom we have taken for granted and attracting their highly educated citizens back home for employment opportunities in their growing economies.

Change is, in fact, the only constant in our lives. However, when we look at institutions of higher education and how they are organized and administered, and the results they achieve, this may not appear to be true. I believe this is about to change, as the forces of change gain momentum and more attention is focused on accountability and outcomes related to the student experience: attrition, length of time to graduation, and quality of preparation.

Looking to the past for solutions or trying to preserve the present will not work. We need to recognize that outside interests will demand new approaches to what we do, how we do it, and how we change to make it happen.

If you do not believe this can happen, just examine how a change in reimbursement funding by the health insurance industry altered the medical profession's model of health care delivery from an inpatient to an outpatient modality. The success of these ventures relied on rethinking the patient experience and making sure that meeting the patient's needs was the central focus of service delivery.

And if this is not persuasive, think about students who believe that the odds are stacked against their success. When they reach a critical mass, disappointed over their lack of success and the indebtedness they incurred without obtaining a degree, their connectivity to interactive social media will become a force of seismic proportions.

We must change from working harder to working smarter by doing different things differently. Changing times bring challenges, but even greater opportunities for innovation that will lead to substantive change.

INNOVATION

New Campus Dynamics, LLC, and its National Center for Innovation and Change have as their main focus reducing attrition, shortening the length of time to graduation, and enhancing the quality of preparation. The RTG Dynamics™ innovation provides the foundation for this initiative. The five key dynamics of the RTG (Recruitment-To-Graduation) initiative work together to guide planning, mobilizing the campus for action and creating breakthrough results. The key dynamics are: (1) campus mobilization; (2) a unified student support chain; (3) a performance management system; (4) decision support information; and (5) a graduation-focused culture (RTG Dynamics, 2010).

Innovation is the bridge between creativity and change. Idea generation, which is part of the creative process, is the identification of something new—a concept, a product, or a different solution to a problem. Whether or not the idea is practical at the time it is presented is irrelevant. It opens the door to new ways of thinking and new possibilities, and provides the stimulus for building upon them. It is innovation that gives creativity practicality and utility, providing the foundation for change.

Innovation can be best described as the search for solutions. It is characterized by combining previously disparate ideas to give them utility and value. It builds on the foundation of the creative past, but provides a synergistic process that leads to something new.

Innovation is more than connecting ideas. Other facets include taking risks, trying new approaches, and recognizing that failure is part of experimentation. Knowing that there are no simple solutions or answers is critical to success. So is recognizing that innovation is a learning experience and has many unintended consequences, some useful and others not.

It is unproductive to talk about innovation and innovators without talking about idea generators and change agents. Often the innovator and the agent for change are different people.

Our society has a tradition of expecting someone who comes up with an innovative solution to manage the change process that will transform it into reality. But many persons with innovative solutions do not bring them up for fear of being made responsible for leading the way when they lack the skills to do so. There are great differences among creators, innovators, and change agents.

Very few innovations come to fruition without a high-performance team committed to their implementation and sustainment. Henry Ford did not invent the car or the assembly line. His innovation was combining the building of a car with the assembly line and training his workers to make the process efficient. This increased production and lowered costs, making cars affordable to more buyers. His innovation extended to paying his workers a wage that enabled them to buy the product they made. He changed the face of manufacturing. He did not do it alone, but he was the innovator and its champion.

Much of Sam Walton's success came from his understanding of supply chain management and how the new information technologies could improve its impact on the financial aspects of retailing. His innovation provided Wal-Mart with key critical competitive advantages in operations and price savings that he could pass on to his customers. He changed the face of retailing. He did not do it alone, but he was the innovator and its champion.

Less famous is Ed Catmull, who combined making feature films with computers. He did not invent animation or the computer, but if you have heard of Pixar or watched *Toy Story*, you know of his innovation. He changed the face of movie making. He did not do it alone, but he was the innovator and its champion.

Innovators are explorers and pioneers; they know how to give utility and value to ideas. They seek to understand what is going on in other institutions and industries; they scan beyond borders as they search for ideas for their ventures.

There are great differences between an innovative person and an innovative organization. The two are not mutually exclusive, but they reinforce each other. When you have an innovative person in a noninnovative organization, part of the innovative effort involves determining how the individual can thrive in that environment as well as how to change the organization.

I mentioned earlier that universities and colleges are designed to resist change. That does not mean that change cannot take place—it means that implementing change requires people who know how to navigate the system, build support for the innovation, mobilize that support, and diffuse the innovation throughout the campus.

Implementing the Innovation Imperative

In our interviews with campus executives, we have been asked several times what the role of student affairs should be in solving the attrition problem and the time it takes students to graduate. I believe that reducing student attrition is a core function of student affairs and that the senior student affairs officer (SSAO) should be the champion for the innovation.

Several presidents we interviewed also asked why student affairs professionals continue to define their roles as educators, when so much work they should be doing goes undone. A composite statement from them would read as follows: "It confuses the roles they should play"; "annoys the faculty," who see student affairs as intruding on their turf; and gives rise to the provost (or vice president of academic affairs) pressing for student affairs to be moved under academic affairs "to ensure greater coordination and better use of resources." Said one president, "Student affairs vice presidents should pursue their roles as change agents in the life of students and in the events that touch them on campus."

What roles would presidents like to see their student affairs leaders play in the attrition/retention cycle? To be more imaginative institutional leaders, to take greater risks, to focus on the entire student body, to bring solutions, to be artful agents of change, and to hire staff who embody these traits and allow them the freedom to do what needs to be done. As one campus chief executive said, "The student affairs people need to unhitch their organization from the past and focus on the real work that needs to be done." We learned from a number of presidents and executive administrators that, even though they viewed attrition and retention as campuswide issues, they thought the mission of student affairs empowered the SSAO to play a more decisive role in stimulating success on campus by leading the efforts of innovation and change.

We have not determined how representative these sentiments are. We have, however, learned that since everyone is responsible for student retention, no one is truly responsible. Someone at the senior executive level has to be the point person, be the guardian of the student experience, represent the student voice when policy and programs are being designed, keep the moral compass of the university pointed in the right direction, and own what happens to the students. As far as I can determine, the vice president for student affairs should assume this mantle.

If you already have the campus leadership role for retention, or are newly inspired to play this role, you might want to consider the following. The external pressures for change are gathering strength; they will be significant driving forces for addressing the attrition/retention issue and the time to graduation. Your campus probably has individuals already dealing with attrition/retention issues who are deeply committed to their work and frustrated by the lack of results, even though they can point to some successes. Their efforts should not be minimized, but they have not resulted in significant improvements. Remember, for your institution to make a significant difference, it has to embrace a new approach to how it deals with its attrition/retention issues by doing different things differently.

Your job is to inspire the campus so that innovation and change can make a difference in the lives of countless students. Donning this mantle means changing the way you and the division of student affairs work. This may be the biggest obstacle you will encounter. Use the five dynamics to provide the framework for what you do, but organize your efforts around decisions, not structures, as suggested in the following steps (Blenko, 2010):

1. Be clear about which decisions are most important.
2. Figure out where in the organization those decisions need to be made.
3. Organize your structure around sources of value.
4. Figure out the level of authority your decision makers need, and give it to them.
5. Adjust other parts of your organizational system to support decision making and execution.
6. Equip your managers to make decisions quickly and well.

Invite everyone you can from throughout the campus to embrace your division's efforts to dramatically affect student retention. Remember that people support what they help create! Helping you to be innovative and change-oriented will expand the horizons of those who are involved, and they will carry the experience back to their work areas.

Taking risks will be good for you—it will invigorate you as a professional and stimulate others to take risks as well. Keep in mind that at least a half-century of activities have not moved the needle on retention or graduation. What is going to matter in this century is not activity but outcomes. Those who focus on outcomes and measuring the right things are the ones who will be able to lead and have others follow.

Finally, if you are looking to be a key player in the strategic development of your institution and be on the pathway to a presidency, successfully pursuing the innovation imperative will help you attain both objectives.

References

Blenko, M. W. (2010, June). The decision-driven organization. *Harvard Business Review*, pp. 54–62.

Blixt, A. B., & Smith, L. N. (2011). *Breakthrough! A blueprint for mobilizing America's campuses to increase graduation rates.* Manuscript submitted for publication.

Bowen, W. G. (2009). *Crossing the finish line: Completing college at America's public universities.* Princeton, NJ: Princeton University Press.

Lewin, T. (2010, July 23). Once a leader, U.S. lags in college degrees. *The New York Times*. Retrieved from http://www.nytimes.com

Merisotis, J. P. (2010, Spring). President's message. *Focus*. Retrieved from http://www.luminafoundation.org/publications/focus_archive/Focus-Spring_2010.pdf

RTG Dynamics. (2010). *New Campus Dynamics.* Retrieved from http://www.newcampusdynamics.com

CHAPTER 9

The Senior Student Affairs Officer as Leader in the Global Context

JAMES M. MONTOYA AND MARC WAIS

ONE OF THE major shifts taking place in American higher education that will surely endure is the expansion of the global education experience for students and scholars of all descriptions. This expansion of global education will provide the senior student affairs officer (SSAO) and the department of student affairs with a myriad of opportunities to assume a leadership role in shaping the destiny of their institution.

Global higher education reflects the increasing ability of students and scholars to seek a college education beyond their own country's borders and the increasing competition among colleges to recruit the best of these students. Increased mobility and recruitment pressure also occur among faculty. As a result of this movement of talented students and faculty, global higher education is helping create, shape, and reconfigure the world's epicenters of talent and individual thought. SSAOs should place themselves in the midst of this movement as engaged contributors.

This phenomenon has gained momentum in the past 10 years. There are now more than 150 branch campuses around the world, up from about 100 in 2005, as reported by the London-based Observatory on Borderless Higher Education (Becker, 2010). Branch campuses can range from full-service campuses to storefront operations containing classrooms and offices to market the institution (McBurnie & Ziguras, 2007). Like so many other new developments, most of these campuses are in Asia and the Middle East. Moreover, many schools are considering adding more branch campuses—even though some campuses in the Middle East have recently closed.

Global education can take many forms:

- **Global or satellite campus:** a campus operated by a student's host institution, with its own faculty, course offerings, staff, and facilities (rented or leased).
- **Study abroad:** an opportunity to study in other countries through other institutions, covering a wide range of academic offerings, among them summer study abroad, internships abroad, volunteering abroad, and intensive language programs.
- **Independent study or research:** sponsored by the host institution, sometimes in cooperation with another institution.
- **Alternative breaks abroad:** often in January or during spring breaks, focusing on service opportunities.
- **Coursework on global issues:** taken anywhere.
- **Online courses:** taken anywhere.

Global Higher Education Influenced by Many Sources

That we live in an ever-smaller, interconnected global village is beyond dispute. Educating students to become global citizens can no longer be left to individual initiative, chance, or the movements of history. There is a clear need to educate students to become global citizens so they can take on leadership roles in the 21st century. Students who master cross-cultural competencies will be at an advantage in both their personal and professional lives, and it is incumbent upon student affairs to help shape and contribute to this part of their college experience. To do this, SSAOs themselves must become global citizens and master global competencies.

Changing demographics also drive home this emphasis on global education. Many students we now serve—including students who immigrated as young people, students who carry dual citizenship, and students who spent all or part of their precollege years in other countries because of family circumstances—embark on the college admissions process already knowing that they will seek a global education experience.

Internationally, more students are interested in pursuing educational opportunities in the United States and may consider either exchange programs (for a semester or for an academic year) or full-time enrollment. Many academically gifted students are attracted to the United States, whose higher education system is still considered the crown jewel. In fact, U.S. schools dominate the top 20 rankings of all of the international surveys of colleges and universities, placing anywhere between 14th and 17th.

This desire to participate in U.S. higher education programs persists in spite of significant challenges related to immigration and national security initiatives. Student affairs must actively connect prospective and current international students with resources on campus and in government agencies to help them navigate these issues. International students enrolled in full-time programs at satellite campuses may face comparable immigration issues in other host countries.

THE BENEFITS OF GLOBAL HIGHER EDUCATION

Students increasingly value the benefits of studying abroad and experiencing other cultures. Study abroad enhances insights and understanding in areas such as history, literature, art history, politics, law, education, public policy, and languages. The global experience may create a foundation for lifelong involvement in these areas, as well as giving students the opportunity to create and maintain a network of friendships in their study abroad programs.

The benefits of student talent and experiences flowing into and out of college campuses will enhance the overall experience of all students. An effective SSAO will create a campus environment where this is encouraged. By sharing the skills, languages, and cultural knowledge they have acquired during their study away, returning students will become resources and mentors for fellow students, especially those preparing to study abroad. With the strategic assistance of student affairs professionals, students anticipating or returning from study abroad can establish meaningful connections with foreign students at the home campus. This can be achieved through structured programming activities such as welcome back receptions, programs at which returning students share their stories about studying abroad, and events in which returning students are matched with foreign students from the countries where they studied. Shorter term experiences, including service–learning alternative break programs, can also equip students with new insights and motivation to continue their involvement with cultural exploration and to share this enthusiasm with their peers.

An increased global education profile will help diversify many aspects of the campus community, including race, country of origin, ethnic heritage, socioeconomic status, religion, language competencies, academic field of study, and career interests. This mix of students from different backgrounds enhances learning in and out of the classroom.

An SSAO with a world view understands that an increased global presence potentially opens up new student markets and new sources of revenue for schools. Institutional study abroad sites and programs may be opened to visiting students, and might also be used for continuing education. An awareness of the institution in the regions where the home institution is represented can be increased, especially if faculty, staff, and students can engage local citizens in community outreach programs such as lectures, films, or presentations. Such programs allow the institution to be seen as a good neighbor, as well as sparking interest in the home campus. Programs open to local undergraduate (or equivalent) students may encourage them to consider the home campus for graduate and professional study.

A robust global education agenda may enhance the school's reputation in international forums. Partnerships with corporations and foundations in the regions where the university maintains a strong presence can provide students with access to part-time jobs and internships, and recent graduates with placement opportunities. Student affairs staff, especially career services professionals, must be prepared to advise students about the host nation's work and visa regulations. Career services staff (working with staff from alumni relations) may be able to refer students to alumni working in the area who might help them secure an internship or a job.

With an increased international presence, institutions can expand their admissions pool (at both the undergraduate and graduate levels) and enhance selectivity. Through intentional relationships with local secondary/preparatory schools, institutions can identify competitive candidates for admission and contribute to an increased awareness of the American admissions process among international instructors and guidance counselors. As American students continue to participate in international high school academic programs such as Advanced Placement (AP) and International Baccalaureate, service-based international volunteer programs, and high school international exchange programs, they will likely place more importance on evaluating the global opportunities at the colleges to which they apply.

A strong international presence can lead to new opportunities for alumni development and parent engagement in the locations where the home institution maintains a strong presence. Increased familiarity with the region can reveal ways alumni and parents living in the area might increase their engagement with the institution. Student affairs and other staff at the global location can expand their professional skill set by receiving training and experience with this type of outreach to alumni and parents.

The Opportunity for Leadership

Student affairs leaders have an important role in how this global thinking is played out on our campuses. During his campaign for president, Barack Obama (2008) said, "[T]his world is becoming more interdependent, and part of the process of America's continued leadership in the world is going to be our capacity to communicate across boundaries and across borders" (p. 9). This is exactly what student affairs leaders do—encourage and facilitate communication across boundaries and borders, though mostly those on our campuses and closer to home. Globalism asks that we think more deeply about the world and more boldly about our work.

A second premise is that "university globalism is here to stay" (Wildavsky, 2010) and that SSAOs are in an ideal position to lead their institutions in this arena. This role will require SSAOs to be especially thoughtful and articulate on the subject; be as global as their students; be well informed on trends related to international student admission and global academic programs; and facilitate the crossing of boundaries and borders on and off campus in new and meaningful ways.

The SSAO needs to be viewed as proactive and as an expert on the multifaceted aspects of global education. Global education offers the SSAO a unique opportunity to collaborate with partners in the academy and the university's central administration to create a climate that supports the preparation, experience, and reacclimation of globally competent students, as well as student affairs staff.

While some institutions have been in the business of global higher education for decades, most are fairly new at it, setting up operations within the past 10 years or currently in the planning stages. There is almost a start-up mentality in many spheres of the higher education community regarding global education. What better environment for SSAOs to assert their leadership, expertise, and influence in shaping how their schools approach global higher education?

SSAOs may have the opportunity to play a key role in the strategic planning and development of the global enterprise on their campus. They should view this as an opportunity to influence how learning takes place in and out of the classroom when students go abroad. As an educator, the SSAO should advocate for the holistic development of global students, taking into account their academic, personal, vocational, and social needs.

THE GLOBAL EDUCATION CONCERNS OF THE SENIOR STUDENT AFFAIRS OFFICER

The SSAO will need to be sensitive to a variety of issues as each campus or study away site focuses on the global enterprise. The SSAO should work with colleagues throughout the institution to achieve the following objectives:

- Ensure that students and their parents are aware of the many advantages, challenges, and opportunities the institution affords for a global experience. Conversely, focus attention on barriers and impediments to a successful global experience.
- Train central office staff (i.e., bursar, registrar, financial aid) and student affairs staff to assist parents with questions and concerns related to their student's living abroad.
- Encourage students to consider and help them prepare for a global experience.
- Establish guiding principles for programs, services, facilities, and policies on student life for students who study abroad and decide which of the global site policies will be consistent with those of the home campus and which must be different to accommodate local custom or practice. Consider how the home campus student affairs officers will collaborate with their counterparts overseas. For instance, how will they work together to help a student who develops medical or behavioral issues while abroad?
- Create experiences that respect, value, and celebrate the host country's values, beliefs, traditions, and principles, while adhering to the host country's laws and regulations.

- Collaborate with the academy to provide appropriate counseling and advising to ensure that each global experience provides the right academic fit for each student, and aligns with his or her curriculum and graduation requirements. Provide guidance to the academy on cocurricular programs and activities at global sites.

- Ensure that students are prepared intellectually, emotionally, and socially for their study abroad through a thoughtful and comprehensive predeparture orientation process.

- Create programs, protocols, and services to ensure students' health and safety. This requires a well-developed communications network and protocol to track students at all times, and a close working relationship with the director of risk management. Student affairs may use its expertise to provide guidance to the institution in developing safety guidelines and protocols for faculty and staff as well.

- Identify or create intentional academic, personal, and professional outcomes for students from the global experience. These could include academic and research accomplishments, cultural enrichment experiences, opportunities for special postgraduate scholarships and study, and even jobs.

- Create assessment tools to evaluate the effectiveness of the overall global experience and all the academic, personal, and professional outcome expectations.

- Manage the diverse student expectations of international travel: the quest for adventure, interest in immersion in a new culture, and need for facilities and services to be commensurate with what students are accustomed.

- Create a welcome back reception and continuing re-acclimation programs to allow students to reflect on their global experience and use it to make a difference in their personal, academic, and professional life, in addition to the life of the home campus.

- Prepare and assist overseas faculty and staff in providing quality services by outlining the needs of some U.S. students that may not be customary (e.g., needs of students with learning disabilities, students on daily prescriptions) in the host country.

BEING A GLOBAL PLAYER

Just as we want our students to learn, grow, and be open to the world, we must do the same in our personal and professional lives. The globalism of higher education gives us this opportunity in a profound way. Student affairs leaders must ask themselves the following questions to be "global players" at their institutions:

- How global am I in my thinking?
- How in tune am I with the global character of students at my college or university?
- How familiar am I with the trends in international admissions?
- How does all this affect how my team allocates its time and resources?

Being global is more about how we think about our connectedness to the world than how much of the world we have seen. It helps to have a well-grounded position on the subject, especially since not everyone immediately embraces the idea of globalism. Some campus critics will be concerned that such a focus may divert funds away from other important programs that serve the needs of American students, especially low-income and minority students. Colleagues in business and legal offices often find working across national borders to be complex, frustrating, costly, and overly time-consuming. Alumni may worry that an increase in the number of international undergraduate students may decrease their own children's chances of gaining admission. Humanities faculty may feel at a disadvantage with many academic partnerships (especially with universities in China and India) focused on science and technology.

First, find your inspiration as a global citizen. Inspiration can come from personal and educational experiences, books, speeches, and, of course, your students. My (James Montoya's) personal and professional commitment acknowledges the special role higher education has played in this country in promoting understanding among people from different cultural backgrounds. It is also grounded in a belief that all students in the 21st century should have the opportunity to see themselves as members of the global community. Without this perspective, they will be at a disadvantage in our ever-increasing global economy.

We should also acknowledge the need for collaboration across borders to develop global solutions to global problems. Rischard (2002) conveyed this sentiment in two sentences: "Education is key to building the sense of global citizenship that global problem-solving requires. And it is a major tool for developing global values that may help spare the next generation unnecessary obsolete tensions between civilizations" (p. 102).

Sir Michael Barber (2009), in a graduation speech at the Moscow School of Social and Economic Sciences, noted the need for a different type of education to ensure a more peaceful and equitable world:

> For this we need a deeper education which develops thought as well as knowledge; character as well as intellect; dialogue as well as reflection; humility as well as leadership; and above all, which has a basis in ethics on which our future depends. We need this education for everyone—the poor, the oppressed and the marginal as well as the wealthy, the powerful and well connected. And we need this education to tackle the complex, difficult reality of human existence; to legitimize and encourage debate about conflicting accounts of the past and divergent views of the future. (p. 5)

You will find your own grounding—your own books and speeches that bring meaning to work in this arena. You may find it helpful to write a statement that captures your grounding and your commitment to the global perspective. It will get you thinking on this deeper level.

Being global also requires staying on top of global initiatives on and off campus, especially those that represent bold thinking in American higher education. All SSAOs should have these three basics in their back pockets (this list will change with time, so be sure to keep it current):

1.   Familiarity with China, India, South Korea, and Japan and their educational systems. The reason will be obvious when you read later in the chapter about undergraduate admission trends.

2.   Familiarity with the American educational experiment in the United Arab Emirates, and a sense of the region's geography. As one former colleague who is now working in Education City in Qatar put it, "I came here to be a part of this great innovation in American higher education" (M. Evans, personal communication, August 30, 2010). For him, this has required developing greater understanding of the Arab culture and Islamic tradition, and learning to manage a staff in a truly international environment.

3.   A comprehensive picture of the global initiatives on your campus, and familiarity with cutting-edge global initiatives at those institutions your president and trustees admire.

Consider making the time to participate in at least one educational exchange program in the next few years. The National Association of Student Personnel Administrator's International Exchange Program has been in existence since the mid-1990s and is definitely worth exploring. Follow the same advice you give your students: Take advantage of the resources you have close at hand and pursue those that may seem out of reach. Here are some questions to ask yourself:

How in tune am I with the global character of students at my institution? Our campuses are becoming more diverse, and more students are bringing to campus a global perspective that is strikingly different than just a decade ago. Advances in technology have brought a global perspective on music, fashion, and the cinema to students throughout the world. More freshmen have had a global academic or extracurricular experience, whether by taking an AP class in comparative world government, being in a class with students in another country via videoconferencing, or participating in a community service project in another country. In addition, their sense of the world is different simply because they were born in the early 1990s. McBride and Nief (2010) remind us that for the freshman class entering in 2010, Korean cars have always been on American highways; Czechoslovakia has never existed; American companies have always done business in Vietnam; and the United States, Canada, and Mexico have always agreed to trade freely. Studies show that the concept of globalization is far more popular among youth than among their parents and grandparents. Teens and 20-somethings tend to be a great deal more interested in social responsibility than do their older counterparts, and this definitely affects their wanting to help make the world a better place (Wood, 2010). According to the Pew Research Center's Global Attitudes Project, "Somewhat more Americans than in 2005 (35% vs. 26%) think the U.S. is well-liked around the world. However, fully 60% think the U.S. is generally disliked. As in 2005, only Americans and Turks are more likely to say their country is disliked than to say it is liked" (Pew Research Center, 2010, p. 15). How our students see themselves as Americans must be viewed through the lens of how America is seen by the world.

Pollster John Zogby (2008) explored a group of 18- to 29-year-old Americans he labeled the First Globals. He looked specifically at the 42% of this cohort who possessed passports. Several conclusions related to globalism stood out: About 25% of this group expected to live abroad for a significant period; the majority more closely identified as being citizens of the planet than as U.S. citizens; and, as a group, they were highly sensitized to global issues.

The profile of undergraduate students at the University of California system points to the evolving global character of our colleges and universities: 21% are born outside the United States; 40% of U.S.-born students are from families with at least one parent born outside the United States; and 35% are non-native speakers of English (University of California, 2008). Colleges and universities report only the international students who are enrolled on F-1 visas. However, on many campuses, additional students have an international, if not global, perspective: immigrant students who are U.S. citizens, permanent residents, or undocumented students. Ties to home countries vary, but the cultural perspectives of students who are more recent arrivals to the United States are similar to those of international students.

Erisman and Looney (2007) shared many important statistics that affect higher education:

- Between 1990 and 2000, the foreign-born population increased by 57%. In 2005, about 47% were Hispanic; 24% Asian or Pacific Islander; 21% White, non-Hispanic; and 8% Black.
- In 2003–04, immigrant students made up 12% of undergraduate college students in the United States. (This statistic does not include children of immigrants who were born in the United States, many of whom also maintain a strong cultural identity.)
- In 2005, 27% of California residents and 21% of New York residents were foreign born. In recent years, the Southeast has seen a significant increase in immigrants, with North Carolina and Georgia seeing more than a 200% increase in their foreign-born populations.

In addition to responding to the special needs of immigrant students, there is an opportunity to connect the immigrant experience to the campus global perspective. Westchester Community College in New York has opened an Office of International and Immigrant Student Affairs with the following mission:

The Office of International and Immigrant Student and Affairs (OIISA) is committed to the intellectual, ethical, and social education of a diverse and inclusive community of international and immigrant students. Three primary goals shape the administration of International and Immigrant Student Affairs at Westchester Community College:

- The application of systems to educate and inform the international population; the college community; and the State and County entities of the regulations governing the enrollment of international students;

- The administration of a wide range of client-centered programs and services that meet the needs of international and immigrant students;

- The efficient and effective use of human and financial resources to create ideal conditions for international and immigrant student enrollment, retention, and development. (Westchester Community College, n.d.)

Do you know how many of your enrolling freshmen and transfer students have lived in the United States for five or fewer years? Or speak a different language at home? Or have traveled abroad? Capturing this information provides the SSAO with valuable insights to share with senior staff, faculty, alumni, and students. More important, it allows the student affairs staff to meet student needs more effectively.

How familiar am I with trends in international admission and global higher education initiatives on my campus and other campuses? Undergraduate admission always seems to be on the minds of university leaders and trustees. Given the attention to globalization, it is not surprising that international admission is of increasing interest to university leaders. Admittedly, for some institutions international undergraduate students are a new and needed revenue source. But most institutions are seeking to bring deeper global character to the campus.

In any case, it is important that SSAOs be well informed on international undergraduate admission trends and the countries from which international students are coming. According to Bhandari and Chow (2009), by 2025, 8 million students are projected to study outside their home countries, a dramatic increase from the current 2.5 million. The authors also noted the following:

- The United States is still the first-choice international destination for students, although its share of international undergraduates decreased from 25% in 2003 to 18% in 2008. Other key players in hosting international undergraduate students are the United Kingdom (15%); France (10%); Germany (8%); Australia (8%); and China, Japan, and Canada (4% each).

- In the United States, only 3.5% of total higher education enrollment is international, well below the proportions of other key international student host countries. This suggests greater capacity for international students in the United States.

- India (71,019), China (57,452), South Korea (25,463), Taiwan (15,332), and Canada (13,185) send the United States the largest number of graduate students. South Korea (37,078), China (26,275), Japan (16,770), India (15,600), and Canada (14,261) send the largest number of undergraduate students.

- The five countries with the greatest percentage increase from 2007 to 2008 were Vietnam (46.2%), Nepal (29.6%), Saudi Arabia (28.3%), China (21.1%), and Brazil (15.7%).

- The gap between the percentage of international undergraduate students (40.2%) and graduate students (42.2%) enrolled in U.S. colleges and universities closed significantly in 2008, owing to the increased number of undergraduates from China.

One of this new group of undergraduates from China is a first-year student at a small liberal arts college in the Midwest. He shared some thoughts on his eighth day on campus:

> School stuff goes awesome too. Dorm room is definitely sweet and laundry and cafe can't be more of convenience. There are pre-orientation programs for international students and orientation for all the first year class. I have many chances to make friends with new freshman, upper-class students and faculties. The library and gym are gorgeous. I can get everything I need

and this is a perfect place to study and grow up. (Y. Li, personal communication, September 10, 2010)

A junior at a major university in the Northeast, who will be living off-campus with three other students from China, offered this advice:

> I believe the biggest challenge for international students to get involved into American college is cultural barrier. Cultural barriers often causes misunderstanding to effective communication among students. To overcome and promote interaction between international and American students, universities can set up credit courses to encourage international students to take initiative talking and making friends with local students. The class activity can vary from class discussion, debate to party, so that students will have more choices to integrate into the American college. (C. Wang, personal communication, August 24, 2010)

As the number of students from China, India, and South Korea increases, many campuses find themselves for the first time with a critical mass of undergraduates from these countries. With critical mass comes the challenge of making certain these students have ample opportunity to interact with students other than those from their home country and to feel central to the mission of the institution. As one recent graduate from China put it as she reflected on her experience at a major U.S. public institution:

> Student affairs officers are at the position to foster a sense of belonging and ownership among international students, not to only stress their difference. To have an international student body that do not cast themselves as outsiders, it probably takes a school that truly thinks global, or students come in equipped with the power of suggestion and auto-suggestion. Students

who have made the decision to study abroad are responsible for the challenges while enjoying the benefits. Schools that choose to benefit from a diverse campus climate bear the burden to provide a service in step with the needs of the increasing number of international students they admit each year. After all, what matters is the actual interaction among diverse students, not the enrollment number. (W. Xiang, personal communication, August 27, 2010)

These three student voices set the challenge and make clear the opportunity.

CONCLUSION

Global higher education may present the most exciting new frontier for higher education and our society at large. Student affairs needs to play an important leadership role in ensuring the success of the global higher education initiative for students. It is incumbent upon SSAOs to provide dynamic, thoughtful, and strategic leadership. As any student affairs professional can attest, while a full-time academic load is 15 hours in the classroom, lab, or theater, it is all the other hours in the week that fully educate and prepare the student for the challenges and opportunities of the global community. You may have the opportunity to help your campus connect the dots among existing programs to build a stronger global academic community. If your campus is in the early stages of exploring this arena, you may take the lead and encourage your colleagues to think deeply about the subject. You might propose an all-campus taskforce to explore globalism. Do your best to make certain that your student affairs staff is well positioned to support a generation of students who are more connected to the world and have a strong commitment to making it a better place to live.

REFERENCES

Barber, M. (2009, December 12). *Brief remarks on education and the causes of war.* Retrieved from http://www.eduwonk.com/BarberMosccommDec%2009.pdf

Becker, R. (2010). International Branch Campuses: New Trends and Directions. *International Higher Education, 58,* 3–5.

Bhandari, R., & Chow, P. (2009). *Open doors 2009: Report on international educational exchange.* New York, NY: Institute of International Education.

Erisman, W., & Looney, S. (2007, April). *Opening the door to the American Dream: Increasing higher education and success for immigrants.* Washington, DC: Institute for Higher Education Policy.

McBride, T., & Nief, R. (2010, August). *The Beloit College mindset list for the class of 2014.* Retrieved from http://www.beloit.edu/mindset/2014.php

McBurnie, G., & Ziguras, C. (2007). *Transnational education: Issues and trends in offshore higher education.* New York, NY: Routledge.

Obama, B. (2008, December 2). Transcript: Democratic debate in Austin, Texas. *The New York Times.* Retrieved from http://www.nytimes.com/2008/02/22/world/americas/22iht-21textdemdebate.10292802.html?_r=1&pagewanted=9

Pew Research Center. (2010, June 17). *Obama more popular abroad than at home, global image of U.S. continues to benefit.* Retrieved from http://pewglobal.org/2010/06/17/obama-more-popular-abroad-than-at-home

Rischard, J. F. (2002). *High noon: 20 global issues and 20 years to solve them.* New York, NY: Basic Books.

University of California. (2008). *The University of California undergradu-*

ate experience survey. Retrieved from http://www.universityofcalifornia.edu/studentsurvey

Westchester Community College. (n.d.). *International and immigrant student affairs.* Retrieved from http://www.sunywcc.edu/admissions/international_students/international_students.htm

Wildavsky, B. (2010). *The great brain race: How global universities are reshaping the world.* Princeton, NJ: Princeton University Press.

Wood, M. (2010, August 31). *The TRU presentation: Insights and ideas for connecting with millennials.* Presented at the College Board, New York, NY.

Zogby, J. (2008). *The way we'll be.* New York, NY: Random House.

CHAPTER 10

The Leader as an Agent of Hope

Eileen Hulme

"A leader is a dealer in hope." —Napoleon Bonaparte

GREAT LEADERS ARE individuals who instill hope. Martin Luther King, Jr., had a dream for racial equality. John Fitzgerald Kennedy had a vision to put a man on the moon. Mother Theresa created hope for the poor in the slums of Calcutta. Current political candidates brand themselves as individuals embodying hope and representing change. Rath (2008) discovered through extensive polling by the Gallup Organization that followers have four basic needs: hope, trust, compassion, and stability.

> Hope gives followers something to look forward to, and it helps them see a way through chaos and complexity. Knowing that things can and will be better in the future is a powerful motivator for the future. When hope is absent, people lose confidence, disengage, and often feel helpless. (p. 89)

The Gallup Organization studied the impact of leaders' hope on engagement. Sixty-nine percent of engaged employees believed that the organization's leadership helped them feel more hopeful about the future. Only 1% of engaged employees disagreed (Rath, 2008). The turbulent years that have marked the current decade have threatened to diminish the hope of leaders across the globe.

Most senior student affairs officers (SSAOs) will remember the years between 2008 and 2011 as a difficult period in higher education administration. The financial strains on the U.S. economy led to layoffs, an increased burden on tuition and fees, reduction or elimination of travel and staff development funds, and in some cases, an overall realignment of institutional priorities. Divisional leaders had to accommodate new presidents and negotiate volatile political environments. The rate of technological change demanded new approaches to emerging problems. Against the backdrop of ever-present student tragedies, unrest, and psychological concerns, leaders were expected to maintain dynamic divisions.

As higher education embarks on a new decade of unceasing pressures, SSAOs must adopt or renew a brand of leadership that is marked by unwavering hope and optimism. Staff and students alike will look to the SSAO to provide a vision for a better future, inspire the human spirit, and move their division in a strategic direction. Now more than ever, higher education needs leaders who will rise above the urgency of the day and provide a tough-minded pervasive hope.

WHY HOPE?

It was the "best of times and the worst of times" at Baylor University during my tenure as vice president for student life. In 2002, the university passed an ambitious vision that would ultimately reposition it as a top tier doctoral-granting institution. "Baylor 2012" would ignite imagination, growth, passion, and controversy unmatched in the institution's 158-year history. As both the positive and negative energy surrounding a major change initiative began to emerge, the university was thrust into the national spotlight with the murder of a Baylor basketball player by another athlete. A slow news summer coupled with the nation's obsession with sports led to a month of intense national media focus. Patrick Dennhey's tragic death marked the beginning of a year that would fundamentally change my perspective on the centrality of hope as an essential quality of an effective leader.

During the next 12-month period, the faculty senate gave the president a vote of no-confidence on two separate occasions, a difficult internal investigation of a regent was conducted, the National Collegiate Athletic Association launched a thorough review of the men's basketball program, and our first new residence hall in 40 years was constructed. While we were trying to convince students to live on campus, reversing the trend toward apartment living, I was informed that unbeknownst to me or my staff, the police department had placed an undercover police officer in one of our men's residence halls for four months. A firestorm erupted as the police officer was pulled from the residence hall the week before housing sign-up began for the new hall. I suspended two fraternities, attended student funerals, dealt with grieving parents, and endured a significant retention dip that focused an intense light on the division of student life. And yet, we were thriving. New funding was pouring into the student life division; three new major programs were initiated to re-instill a sense of community on campus; several new positions were approved; the positive buzz around a new residence hall was growing; and the student life division was gaining respect across campus because of its renewed focus on academic integration.

Personally, I endured the death of both parents, made the decision to end life support for a beloved aunt, and battled stage 4 non-Hodgkin's lymphoma for eight long months. I would never wish that year on my worst enemy; however, I would not trade it for the best year of my life. What I learned during those 12 months taught me how to live and lead utilizing the transformative dimension of hope. In the following pages, I will offer thoughts on the role of hope in leadership and utilize Snyder's

(2000) definition of hope from the field of positive psychology to provide a theoretical and practical grounding for the development of hope in our divisions and universities.

WHAT IS HOPE?

Historical Overview

Until the end of the 20th century, hope was considered a theological construct that had little bearing on the psychological or educational disciplines. Menninger (1959), in his presidential address to the American Psychiatric Association, stated, "When it comes to hope, our shelves are bare. The journals are silent" (p. 481). Fifty years later, references to hope proliferate in psychological, medical, and educational journals.

The 1960s saw a significant increase in scholarly and societal interest in hope. The rise of hope-related studies in the medical profession paved the way for an expanded theoretical understanding of the concept. It became "possible to study the role of hope . . . without damage to one's scientific or moral integrity" (Frank, 1968, p. 385). Additionally, a larger societal preoccupation with the future began to emerge as a result of scientific and technological advances (Capps, 1968; Moltmann, 1968).

Hope emerged as central to a diversity of theoretical perspectives over the subsequent decades. Erikson (1959), who is most commonly known for his theory of the eight stages of life, later identified the development of eight virtues (hope, will, purpose, competence, fidelity, love, care, and wisdom) associated with the developmental stages. He wrote, "Hope is both the earliest and the most indispensable virtue inherent in the state of being alive" (p. 115). He postulated an alignment with hope and the trust versus mistrust life cycle stage.

Frankl (1942) integrated hope into his theoretical approach to counseling, logotherapy. His theory emerged from experiences in concentration camps, where he found the pursuit of meaning to be a central predictor of survival. One's level of hope in the face of extreme adversity was crucial for the meaning-making process. The 1970s saw hope being identified as a measureable concept as evidenced by the proliferation of hope measures. The field of medicine took a qualitative approach to understand the complexity of the construct's relationship to health and well-being. By the end of the 1980s, Snyder's hope theory was gaining prominence as the most comprehensive and viable approach in the psychological domain. The following section is devoted to a brief extrapolation of Snyder's work.

Snyder's Hope Theory

Hope theories agree that people are goal-directed and adaptive. Snyder's theorization of hope adds the dimension of hope pursuit. He defines hope as "a positive motivational state that is based on an interactively derived sense of successful (a) agency (goal-directed energy) and (b) pathways (planning to meet goals)" (Snyder, Irving, & Anderson, 1991, p. 287). Hope theory suggests that hope is both a cognitive process and a dispositional characteristic, albeit malleable.

Goal-directed behavior. Snyder's hope theory contains a future orientation or expectancy outcome dimension that is evident in all previous psychological definitions of hope. Central to Snyder's theory is the assertion that goal-directed thinking occupies a significant amount of one's mental processing (Snyder, 1993, 2002; Snyder, Cheavens, & Michael, 1999). However, high-hope individuals set goals that are moderately difficult. If a goal appears to be too difficult or too easy, it can undermine the motivation to achieve that goal (Cheavens, Feldman, Woodward, & Snyder, 2006). What distinguishes Snyder's theory from previous theoretical approaches to hope is its attention to the psychological strength needed to attain goals (agency) and the creation of viable routes to accomplishing goals (pathways).

Pathways thinking. The pathways dimension of Snyder's hope theory relates to a person's ability not only to set meaningful goals but to determine effective means of accomplishing those goals. High-hope individuals can generate multiple pathways for the same goal and are adept at persevering in the face of obstacles (Irving, Snyder, & Crowson Jr., 1998). High-hope persons also tailor their goals more quickly and report greater levels of cognitive flexibility than low-hope persons (Snyder, 2002).

Agency thinking. Agency thinking relates to the motivational aspect of hope theory. It is the engine that fuels the action required to execute the pathways. "Agency is the belief that one can begin and sustain movement along the envisioned pathways toward a given goal" (Snyder, Ilardi, Cheavens, Michael, Yamhure, & Sympson, 2000, p. 749). Included in this aspect of hope theory is the element of self-perceptions and ruminations. Positive self-statements such as "I can accomplish this goal" are frequently found in high-hope individuals (Snyder, 2000). Agency and pathways are interrelated and reinforcing.

Snyder's work has significantly influenced the psychological conceptualization of hope. Through his effort to determine hope's effect on general well-being, academic progress, health, and athletic performance, Snyder provided a vast theoretical grounding to substantiate the central role hope plays in human functioning. Additionally, he has shown that people's level of hope is malleable and influenced by educational interventions, work environment, and leadership.

Becoming a Hope Leader

Developing the attitudes, characteristics, and behaviors of a leader who builds hope takes intentionality. It is more than being positive and encouraging, although those characteristics have a place in hopeful leadership. Hope leaders promote goal-directed behavior by clearing the pathways for new ideas, reframing what appear to be insurmountable obstacles, creating communities whose language promotes personal responsibility, and restoring their own personal level of hopefulness. Below are suggestions for developing these behaviors.

Promote goal-directed behavior. Hope leaders demonstrate a tenacious desire to keep their organizations focused on an inspiring, meaningful vision. That focus requires a significant expenditure of time and effort on their part. The following paragraphs outline three essential actions to help you move your organization toward a positive future.

Don't let the urgent derail the important. Our lives can be governed by the urgent everyday demands of our positions. Dealing with one irate parent can take hours, while the division's strategic vision sits on our desk gathering dust. Our ability to move our divisions in hopeful, inspiring directions is dramatically influenced by the amount of time we give these initiatives. Your staff members are watching how you spend your time and adjusting their priorities accordingly. If you are distracted by endless meetings and e-mails, the message the division receives is that the strategic vision is not critically important. Because hope is grounded in goal-directed behavior, the SSAO must relentlessly pursue future-oriented objectives and refuse to succumb to the tyranny of the urgent.

Nourish hope leadership in your organization. Our divisions are filled with people who are living "lives of quiet desperation" because their dreams and passions are being stifled. Hope leadership requires the courage to find those people and support their dreams. Even if ideas seem unrealistic, impractical, politically charged, time-consuming, or financially improbable, leaders must listen with an open mind. Organization hierarchy, while beneficial to create structure and stability, is an impediment to radical new ideas that are vital to hopeful, innovative organizations. Leaders must mitigate the effects of egos, territorialism, and political obstacles to encourage the creation of thoughtful ideas.

Utilize appreciative inquiry for your strategic planning efforts. Appreciative inquiry is the process of discovering and developing the full potential of a person or organization by focusing on achievements, strengths, and unexplored potential. The threefold process of discover, dream, and design allows participants the opportunity to explore their moments of great success, lived values, and future aspirations (Cooperrider & Whitney, 2005). As positive energy arises from this strategic visioning process, SSAOs will reinvigorate their organizations even in challenging times. By linking the appreciative inquiry process to clear objectives and steps for action, the leader becomes an agent of hope and inspiration.

Practice and teach the daily reframing of challenges. Reframing is seeing a situation or person from a perspective that differs from your own. This sounds easy until you try to reframe a situation even though you are confident that your perspective is correct. Hope leadership is grounded in the ability to reframe negative situations in a more productive and compelling light. Every occurrence can be seen through countless lenses. As leaders, we are challenged to stay mindful of and help others honor different perspectives. Yet some organizations view quick, decisive decision making as a greater leadership virtue than open-mindedness. Steven Sample (2002), president emeritus of the University of Southern California, describes the open-mindedness required of leaders as "thinking gray":

> The essence of thinking gray is this: don't form an opinion about an important matter until you've heard all the relevant facts and arguments, or until circumstances force you to form an opinion without recourse to all the facts (which happens occasionally, but much less frequently than one might imagine). (pp. 7–8)

This does not imply that hope leaders do not make timely decisions. However, their decisions are informed by myriad opinions and perspectives.

Situations that are framed as hopeless engender an attitude of blame or victimization. A hope leader works to help reframe those situations to encourage personal responsibility and commitment. Furloughs, layoffs, budget reductions can all have a long-term effect on a division's morale. Allowing your division to ruminate on difficult circumstances for long periods of time is not productive. Consistently challenging people to reframe those situations into opportunities is at the heart of hopeful leadership.

To reframe difficult situations that are hindering my leadership, I ask myself four questions:

- How would I view this situation if I knew tomorrow was my last day to live?
- What is the absolute worst thing that could come from this situation?
- What is the absolute best thing that could come from this situation?
- How would my (a) dog view this situation?

The last question may seem absurd. However, engaging my imagination reduces fear and negative emotion thus enabling me to generate more creative responses. Taking the time to thoughtfully reflect on these questions has changed my perspective on countless occasions.

The future will continue to provide daunting challenges. As hope leaders, SSAOs must enable their divisions to reframe situations that lead to a sense of hopelessness. Listening carefully to a variety of perceptions of a situation and allowing yourself to be moved from your initial conviction when appropriate are powerful tools to encourage greater hope.

Use words of hope and optimism. Every student life division is a unique language community. Each organization's culture supports or discourages certain forms of speech. This is evident by conversations behind closed doors and in public, between individuals and in groups, with people we trust and those we don't. Kegan and Lahey (2001) suggest that

> ... all leaders are leading language communities. Though every person, in any setting, has some opportunity to influence the nature of the language, leaders have exponentially greater access and opportunity to shape, alter, or ratify the existing language rules. In our view, leaders have no choice in the matter of being language leaders; it just goes with the territory. (p. 8)

All divisional leaders are language leaders. However, the extent to which they embrace this role varies greatly. In difficult times, our words are even more critical to our division.

At the end of the Baylor president's tenure and after all of the emotional turmoil of the preceding 12 months, he was influenced to reorganize the university. Decisions were made with which I strongly disagreed. Another vice president and I were summoned to the president's office, informed of the reorganization plan, and told we had two hours to meet with our staff before the public notice was distributed to the university community.

Before leaving the president's office, I called my assistant and asked her to gather all my direct reports for an emergency meeting. As I walked back to my office, I knew that the next two hours would define my previous five years of leadership. During the 10-minute walk, I considered several approaches. I could discuss the political motivation for this move and the detrimental nature of a lame duck president making a decision like this without the input of the executive cabinet. I could defend my position with evidence of the effectiveness of the student life division and demonstrate the absurdity of the decision. Or I could thank them for their extraordinary service, express my personal gratitude for their support, and ultimately focus on the opportunities that change affords. I chose to focus on the hope that this change could produce positive results for all involved. Taking seriously the notion that leaders create a language culture has made a significant difference in how I approach conversations.

Three assumptions can deter leaders from developing language communities focused on hope in the midst of difficult challenges. The first is that people will perceive the leader is out of touch with their situation. It is important to remember that hope is not synonymous with effusive, unrealistic language. A leader of hope doesn't run onto the street after a tornado has destroyed a town and proclaim, "Great! Those houses and buildings were blocking our view." Rather, the leader acknowledges the current suffering and speaks of a community that will rebuild together.

The second assumption may result from the belief that leaders must be experiencing high levels of positive emotion themselves to express hope. These are difficult times not only for our staffs but for ourselves.

There may be days when you question your call into the profession of student affairs. While enduring chemotherapy, an acquaintance who had survived breast cancer called and offered a piece of advice that left a lasting impression. She said that if on the most difficult days you allow yourself to wallow in self-pity, you will actually feel sicker. If you can pick yourself up and surround yourself with people who believe in a better future, you will feel better sooner. I began to notice that on days when I would not allow visitors and wallowed in self-pity, I felt worse. When I encircled myself with friends who would speak about what we were going to do when I felt better, I was less nauseated and had more energy. SSAOs will inevitably experience negative emotions. However, refusing to give into hopelessness and surrounding yourself with people who can imagine a better future will restore your energy and faith in people.

The third assumption that deters leaders from expressing hope is the belief that if they don't feel hopeful about the current situation, they should not say anything at all. Silence is a powerful force. Martin Luther King, Jr., understood this reality when he said, "In the end, we will remember not the words of our enemies, but the silence of our friends." People in organizations take their mental and emotional cues from the leadership. In turbulent times, silence imparts unintended messages to those most vulnerable to losing their own hope. Leading with hope requires intentional, thoughtful communication that keeps the vision of a better future in the foreground.

Regularly restore your own hope. It is easy to let discouragement seep into your work. The fast-paced world of the SSAO does not lend itself to a deep renewal of hope. In many organizations, the division leader receives student complaints, handles severe disciplinary problems, works with parents grieving the loss of a child, and negotiates difficult employment situations. Each day presents countless issues to address and problems to solve. How can leaders maintain a hopeful mindset in the midst of these demands?

The concept of a day of rest is found in every major religion. The medical profession has demonstrated the detrimental effect of constant, unrelenting stress on the immune system. Psychologists have discovered the relationship of rest and play with an overall sense of well-being. The negative affects resulting from a lack of sleep is at an epidemic proportion in America. During each day, week, month, and year, a time for refreshment must be faithfully protected. Hope leadership is developed in the quiet places of one's life. At a recent staff retreat, I overheard two mid-level professionals discussing a startling discovery both of them had made when they returned to work, one from a major illness and one from maternity leave. To their dismay, they realized that work had gone on without them. Anyone who has left a university and returned a few years later understands that we all can be replaced. A reluctance to rest may be based on the fear of losing a sense of self found in one's work. At some deep level, fear may be at the root of our tendency to work without rest. Leaders of hope face their fears and commit to rest.

CONCLUSION

> *"In all things, it is better to hope than to despair."*
> —Johann Wolfgang von Goethe

Without hope, it is impossible for student affairs divisions to function at their full potential. For decades, people have expressed a desire for visionary leadership. Perhaps their real hunger is for someone who can paint a picture of a more hopeful future in the midst of a discouraging present. To fail to seriously consider the role of hope in leadership is to deny our staff an essential human need. Each SSAO must honestly consider this question: Will my leadership be defined by hope today?

REFERENCES

Capps, W. H. (1968). The hope tendency. *Cross Currents, 18*(3), 257–272.

Cheavens, J. S., Feldman, D. B., Woodward, J. T., & Snyder, C. R. (2006). Hope in cognitive psychotherapies: On working with client strengths. *Journal of Cognitive Psychotherapy: An International Quarterly, 20*(2), 135–145.

Cooperrider, D. L. & Whitney, D. (2005). *Appreciative inquiry: A positive revolution.* San Francisco, CA: Berrett-Koehler.

Erikson, E. (1959). *Identity and life cycle: Psychological issues.* New York, NY: International University Press.

Frank, J. (1968). The role of psychotherapy. *International Journal of Psychiatry, 5*(5), 383–395.

Frankl, V. E. (1962). *Man's search for meaning: An introduction to logotherapy* (Rev. ed.) (I. Lasch, Trans.). Boston, MA: Beacon Press. (Original work published 1942).

Irving, L. M., Snyder, C. R., & Crowson, J. J., Jr. (1998). Hope and the negotiation of cancer facts by college women. *Journal of Personality, 66,* 195–214.

Kegan, R., & Lahey, L. (2001). *How we talk can change the way we work.* San Francisco, CA: Jossey-Bass.

Menninger, K. (1959). *The academic lecture: Hope. The American Journal of Psychiatry, 94,* 481–491.

Moltmann, J. (1968). Hope and planning: Future anticipated through hope and planned future. *Cross Currents, 18*(3), 307–318.

Rath, T. (2008). *Strengths-based leadership.* New York, NY: Gallup Press.

Sample, S. (2002). *The contrarian's guide to leadership.* San Francisco, CA: Jossey-Bass.

Snyder, C. R. (1993). Hope for the journey. In H.S. Friedman (Ed.), *Encyclopedia of mental health* (pp. 421–431). San Diego, CA: Academic Press.

Snyder, C. R. (2000). *Handbook of hope; Theory, measures, and applications.* San Diego, CA: Academic Press.

Snyder, C. R. (2002). Hope theory: Rainbows in the mind. *Psychological Inquiry, 13,* 249–275.

Snyder, C. R., Cheavens, J., & Michael, S. T. (1999). Hoping. In C. R. Snyder (Ed.), *Coping: The psychology of what works* (pp. 205–231). New York, NY: Oxford University Press.

Snyder, C. R., Ilardi, S. S., Cheavens, J., Michael, S. T., Yamhure, L., & Sympson, S. C. (2000). The role of hope in cognitive behavior therapies. *Cognitive Therapy and Research, 24,* 747–762.

Snyder, C. R., Irving, L., & Anderson, J. R. (1991). Hope and health: Measuring the will and the ways. In C. R. Snyder & D. R. Forsyth (Eds.), *Handbook of social and clinical psychology: The health perspective* (pp. 285–305). Elmsford, NY: Pergamon Press.

CHAPTER 11

Tying It All Together

GWENDOLYN JORDAN DUNGY

THE MEN AND women who have contributed to this book have shared their insights on effective leadership as one would share with a friend or colleague who asked, "What do you think I need to be an exceptionally effective senior student affairs administrator?" and "What skills or competencies do I need if my goal is to become president of a college or university?" It is my privilege to summarize some of their insights in this concluding chapter. I will also include comments from others who talked with me about what they see as competencies for exceptional leadership in student affairs. I hope my summary will inspire you to read more and learn more from the leaders who have shared their experience and wisdom in this book.

A FOCUS ON STUDENTS

Jacquelyn Moffi, who has worked at community colleges for more than 30 years and is currently assistant to the vice president and provost

267

at Montgomery College in Rockville, Maryland, shared her perspective based on years of working collaboratively with senior student affairs administrators:

> Senior student affairs administrators have a fluid and fluctuating responsibility when it comes to students—getting them in, keeping them in, and helping them to move on. During my long tenure at community colleges, I have witnessed how this responsibility can be strengthened through the standards of empathy, decisiveness, and integrity.
>
> **Empathy.** I have seen student affairs vice presidents, deans, coordinators, and directors clear precarious paths and cut miles of red tape to facilitate student success. The motivation to do so seemingly went beyond the mere notion of being in charge. They make things better because they truly care about students, and they accept the weight of their responsibilities.
>
> **Decisiveness.** Academic curricula and standards reviews or textbook adoptions happen periodically, but senior student affairs administrators face decisions, large and small, every single day. Unlike the controlled setting of a classroom, students often come to student affairs arenas with urgent expectations, needing help and advice—and wanting it immediately. As Marilyn Moats Kennedy once said, "It's better to be boldly decisive and risk being wrong than to agonize at length and be right too late." I think that this sort of reasoning must guide the hectic lives of outstanding senior administrators in student affairs units throughout the country.
>
> **Integrity.** The 18th-century English novelist Samuel Richardson wrote, "Calamity is the test of integrity." Senior student affairs officers are tested with catastrophes, disasters, and mishaps each and every day. It is imperative that they address these situations by exercising prudent judgment and serving each student who

graces their professional lives with the highest level of integrity. (J. Moffi, personal communication, October 15, 2010)

It is both revealing and rewarding to hear that an observer of professionals in student affairs can discern that students, above all else, matter to student affairs administrators and that the models she has witnessed have been exceptional.

When I began to write this final chapter, I used word cloud technology to highlight the most frequently used words in each chapter (see Appendix). I was not surprised by the results: In almost every chapter, the most frequently used word was "students." In Chapter 2 ("Don't Fence Me In"), Marguerite Culp distinguishes between the skill sets of highly effective and merely competent senior student affairs officers (SSAOs). One of the five distinguishing characteristics she cites for highly effective administrators is their ability to "connect student affairs to learning and the college to its students." Similarly, Deborah Ford, formerly a senior student affairs administrator and now chancellor of the University of Wisconsin–Parkside, says a leader must have a vision for student success and the ability to articulate how student affairs supports the mission of the college or university (personal communication, October 20, 2010). Another former SSAO, Martha Smith, president of Anne Arundel Community College in Maryland, touched my heart when she wrote that to be effective one must "truly care about students. This is not a job or even a career. It is a passion coming from the heart. Helping students succeed is a reflection of one's values and passion" (personal communication, October 28, 2010). As I reiterate some of these leaders' thoughts, it is clear that students always have been and must remain the focus of our efforts.

ENDURING COMPETENCIES

In this book, whether the authors were speaking to new administrators, speaking from the perspective of seasoned professionals, or advising colleagues who want to explore the idea of becoming a college president, they touched on one or more of the following threads of exceptionally effective leadership:

- Responsibility and accountability
- Learning from personal and professional experiences
- The power of knowledge
- Listening and communicating
- Functioning in a large, networked universe
- Collaborations, partnerships, and relationships
- Innovation and creativity

While these threads may be enduring competencies for exceptional leadership, I believe that context makes all the difference. We tend to think of context as our situation in our institution, but the local community in which a college or university is located and the broader context of national and international issues influence what a leader does—when, how, where, to what extent, and to or for whom. For example, in a national and international context, the United States has historically been the leading provider of higher education and the country of choice for international students. Currently (I say "currently" because I'm optimistic that we can turn this situation around), the United States has fallen so precipitously in the international rankings for number of citizens who complete college that the U.S. president and the largest charitable foundations funding education are setting goals for colleges and universities and throwing money at all levels of education to increase higher education's effectiveness and efficiency in helping students complete high-quality degrees, as defined by employability outcomes.

NBC is sponsoring ongoing discussions in a special segment of its programming called "Education Nation." Davis Guggenheim's 2010 documentary, *Waiting for Superman*, excoriates our education system. Some people who have seen it warn their friends and colleagues that the film will make them cry. When you are leading in a context in which people are crying about the condition of education in our country, and every sector of the nation—from businesses to moms—is demanding accountability, responsibility and accountability are priorities in your leadership portfolio.

Responsibility and Accountability

Everyone is responsible for doing the job for which they were hired to the best of their ability. The SSAO—according to the advanced-level leadership competencies approved by the boards of directors of the American College Personnel Association (ACPA) and the National Association of Student Personnel Administrators (NASPA)—is responsible and accountable for facilitating "ongoing development, implementation and assessment of goal attainment at the unit and/or institutional level that is congruent with institutional mission and strategic plans" (ACPA & NASPA, Joint Task Force on Professional Competencies and Standards, 2010, p. 24).

Some suggestions to facilitate the attainment of these goals are shared in *Learning Reconsidered* (Keeling, 2004). Student affairs administrators should be:

- Partners in assessing the student experience and college outcomes.
- Sources of key information about students, students' lives, and student learning.
- Developers of new sources of funding, including gifts, grants, contracts, and research awards.
- Leaders in providing excellent consumer services, in the application of best business practices to those services, and in identifying and publishing best practices for outsourcing specific student services in ways that contribute to student learning. (p. 22)

Taking one example from the list above, we can be more specific about leaders' responsibilities and the outcomes for which they should be held accountable. Responsibility for best business practices is more important than ever, especially with regard to outsourcing student services. As more products are produced by outside vendors, leaders in student affairs have a responsibility to carefully examine the products and assess their impact. "Amid pitches and cost-cutting pushes student affairs officers must decide whether and what to outsource, and to whom" (Lipka, 2010). Outsourcing can be cost-prohibitive, or it can be less expensive but also less effective than an in-house operation. Senior leaders must consider a number of variables in making these decisions.

In Chapter 8 ("The Student Affairs Innovation Imperative"), Laurence Smith explains why we need to accept accountability as the norm, now and into the future. He says leaders in higher education have feelings and frustrations about the problems of attrition and time to degree, but we fall short in owning the problems. He gives higher education an elbow to the ribs when he asserts that the traditions and structures of colleges and universities "insulate them from outside pressures and interference." While these traditions and structures may have protected colleges and universities in the past, Smith warns that a convergence of forces—such as higher education's dependence on public funds and the nation's need for qualified graduates—will increase the demand for accountability for outcomes related to the student experience.

As a president, Walter Kimbrough ("Just the Facts" in Chapter 7) suggests that because of a climate of increased accountability, presidents should be more engaged in campus assessment and should be familiar with national studies for comparative purposes. In other words, anecdotal data alone are unacceptable.

Not only in the United States but abroad, evidence of impact is the new requirement. Brian Sullivan ("From Professional Ownership to Intentional Coproduction: New Competency Demands" in Chapter 4) tells us that at the University of British Columbia "the SSAO is expected to contribute to the dashboard question at the institutional level." By way of explanation, he says that "if a successful student experience is one in which students are academically satisfied, safe and well, engaged in high-impact experiential education, graduating with a sense of purpose, and positive about the institution," then the SSAO should be able to answer the question, "How is this measured and what value is added by various programs?"

Responsibility and accountability are not all about helping others. There are personal and career benefits related to these important leadership characteristics. Cliff Wood ("Preparing for a Presidency" in Chapter 7) writes about executing a task in such a responsible and accountable manner that his efforts were noticed during an accreditation visit, with far-reaching consequences: A few years later, when Wood's circumstances caused him to relocate, the chair of the accreditation team hired him. There is a difference, however, between responsibility and accountability. Responsibility is internally motivated, while accountability is usually externally imposed. The distinction was made in a most elegant manner almost a century ago by Jean-Jacques Rousseau (1923): "Before that time, the Romans were satisfied with the practice of virtue; they were undone when they began to study it" (p. 138).

Learning From Personal and Professional Experiences

"Reflection is a central mechanism for producing new insights through examining experience" (Seibert & Daudelin, 1999, p. 6). Many authors have written with conviction about important skills and competencies that one should acquire to be an exceptional leader. Their conviction is based on real-world experience that they reviewed, savored, and used as lessons to influence their behavior. Some of their lessons suggested that the behavior should be repeated, and some indicated the opposite. I am a firm believer in reflecting on experiences that cause extraordinary pain or joy. However, there is a distinction between reflecting and ruminating. To learn from experience, reflection needs to be intentional; ideally, the learning evolves over time.

In Chapter 4, Barbara Snyder ("A Big Place Requires a Big Picture") reveals, "After 35 years of practice, I still encounter situations that are new and decisions that require a different perspective, but I can rely on the experience and wisdom that I have developed over a lifetime of professional commitment." In the same chapter, when Joanna Iwata ("The New Nexus of Transformational Leadership Within Different Collegiate Settings") reflects on her experiences, she explicitly labels them "lessons from experience." For example, having had positive results with a strategy to assess the strengths of staff members early in her leadership position at one institution, she repeated the strategy at subsequent institutions.

Larry Roper ("The Search for Authentic Leadership" in Chapter 6) says, "In each of my professional positions, I was able to distill learning from the experience." One of the most poignant revelations in Roper's contribution is his description of how he learned through experience that his student advocacy style and tendency to evaluate situations on the basis of his personal opinions were out of place in his role as an SSAO. As a leader, he was responsible for advancing the mission of the college rather than standing up for his personal opinions. This experience helped him "transform advocacy into strategic leadership." In other words, he discovered a way to move from "just talking about issues to finding approaches to achieve success with particular issues."

Typically, when we think of reflecting on experience, we're thinking in the past tense. In the new context of our work and in planning for the future, reflection needs to be in real time as change occurs. Real-time reflection or analysis "involves inquiring into and interpreting elements of an experience while in the midst of acting in that experience" (Seibert & Daudelin, 1999, p. 97). Karen Pennington ("It Takes a Village To Be Effective" in Chapter 6) gives a vivid example of real-time reflection or analysis when she describes receiving a call about a missing student from the chief of police. She shares the questions that ran through her mind in the moment based on her professional experience. She tells us that while caring and compassion are the natural responses, as a senior student affairs administrator, her mind jumps immediately to questions about rules, responsibilities, and political fallout, because *someone* is going to be held responsible.

Learning from experience has been important to these leaders in their personal lives as well as their professional lives. Eileen Hulme (Chapter

10, "The Leader as an Agent of Hope") illustrates the role of hope in leadership when she describes a terrible year in her life. First, there was a murder on campus just as the faculty senate was giving the president a no-confidence vote and the NCAA was reviewing the men's basketball program. In her personal life, Hulme grieved three significant deaths in her family, then discovered that she was seriously ill with a life-threatening disease. Her response to these experiences is truly inspiring: "What I learned about life during those 12 horrific months taught me how to live. If not for 2003, I might have died having never truly understood the transformative dimension of hope, the healing power of the compassion of friends and strangers alike, and the true meaning of life."

What these leaders tell us throughout this book is that they have been their own best teachers, because they have, as Parker Palmer writes, "learned to read their own responses to their own experience." Palmer says they are "writing unconsciously" the texts that guide them as leaders (Palmer, 2000, p. 6). These unconsciously conceived texts are similar to what Marty Smith means when she says leaders should "know how to use your own personal Ouija board" (personal communication, October 28, 2010).

The Power of Knowledge

In Chapter 1 ("The New World of Student Affairs"), Larry Moneta and Michael Jackson speak to "the array of explicit skills needed for the new world of student affairs" and how it has "widened and deepened along with the expanding universe of our areas of responsibility." Most striking about their predictions is that many of the skills needed "have yet to be identified." They tell us that in contrast with traditional models of training, the competent SSAO will "need 'just in time' skill sets to handle the revolutionary changes under way in American and international higher education."

John Laws ("Competencies for the Community College Senior Student Affairs Officer" in Chapter 4) predicts that as increasing numbers of undereducated adults enroll at community colleges, the skills and knowledge required of SSAOs will need to change to meet the demands of this growing demographic. He gives examples of the multiple changes to anticipate in the community college sector and urges SSAOs to "learn to think and act entrepreneurially, instilling the vision and providing the leadership for activities, programs, policies, and services that will enhance student success."

There are many traditional skill sets that the successful SSAO must also have such as understanding the flow of resources. Sarah Westfall ("Success As a Small College Senior Student Affairs Officer" in Chapter 4) urges that in order to be an effective SSAO, you must "engage fully and appropriately in resource-related decisions." To do this, she says you must "invest time in learning and understanding campus financial resources."

James Montoya and Marc Wais (Chapter 9, "The Senior Student Affairs Officer in the Global Context") make it clear that leaders must have a basic understanding of the global forces that affect higher education—and students in particular. They suggest that being informed about the countries from which your international students come is a first step in increasing your knowledge. This kind of knowledge can lead to opportunities in other parts of the world. The authors give an example of a colleague who is working in Education City in Qatar—in order to do his job, he has had to learn about the Arab culture and Islamic tradition as well as how to manage a staff in an international environment.

Walter Kimbrough urges administrators to increase their skills and knowledge about assessment and data analysis. He talks about the practical benefits of this knowledge in improving programs and helping students, as well as the confidence one gains from understanding how to collect, analyze, and use data. In creating his list of lessons learned along the way to the presidency, Cliff Wood emphasizes the value of being familiar with academic programs and knowing faculty members. He says this familiarity is essential if "one is to be seen as successful by faculty."

In describing the various roles a senior student affairs administrator has to play—from lawyer to comedian—Karen Pennington notes that there is "less room for error as you move up." She urges SSAOs to acquire a working knowledge of special areas such as the law and to stay informed about anything that will have an impact on students. She also recommends that leaders keep up-to-date with the media, even becoming "news junkies."

Like Pennington, Jesus Carreon ("A Commitment to Serving Our Changing Communities" in Chapter 6) stresses the need to be aware of what is occurring on the regional, state, and national levels that has the potential to affect higher education, your institution, or students in general. In his list of competencies for the SSAO who aspires to be president ("Are You Book *and* Street Smart?" in Chapter 7), Carreon says that whether you are looking to be successful as a vice president or aiming for a presidency, you'll need to be street smart. You will not become street smart by reading books—this is knowledge acquired by being in tune with your environment and the external forces that might affect you and your situation.

Ellen Heffernan ("View From the Top" in Chapter 6) suggests that aspiring leaders learn all they can about fundraising, enrollment, benchmarking, academic programs, and how your mission and programs relate to the "national constellation of colleges and universities." Few traditional degrees will offer coursework in every skill area in which an exceptional SSAO should be competent. Many successful SSAOs, as Larry Moneta and Michael Jackson write in Chapter 1, have careers that "have been marked by unanticipated, often opportunistic, and occasionally directed role shifts—shifts that have required the immediate development of new skills and competencies." In Chapter 7, "The Road to the Presidency," more than one president talks about knowledge beyond student affairs. James Appleton ("The Senior Student Affairs Officer as President") suggests acquiring a "second suit" of skills in an area outside student affairs. When Walter Kimbrough studied the backgrounds of college presidents, he realized that he would have to broaden his knowledge and experience beyond student affairs to position himself to compete for a presidency. Dean Bresciani ("It's About Preparation") discusses how to achieve a balanced portfolio of scholarly, administrative, and political experience. However, he is sensitive to the fact that a person might have to make sacrifices to acquire the competencies necessary for exceptional student affairs leadership and possibly a presidency. Self-awareness is a crucial factor in determining whether these sacrifices are worth making.

Knowledge is more than the synthesis and understanding of information gained from outside sources. "Know thyself" is as powerful as "knowledge is power." Shannon Ellis (Chapter 5, "The New, New Senior Student Affairs Officer") speaks about self-awareness. She encourages new administrators to examine their strengths and weaknesses, and to pose questions about their identity and what competencies they think they will need to be effective in the roles they assume. Larry Roper describes the dominant themes in his career; his first theme is self-knowledge. He, too, emphasizes the need for insight into one's own strengths and weaknesses. Knowing yourself is an intentional exercise that can begin with the practice of guided reflection, enhanced by keeping a journal in which you record your successes and failures, and analyze what happened, how you feel about what happened, and what lessons you can learn from the experience.

I would be remiss if I ended this section on knowledge without mentioning what Kathleen Hetherington ("A Community College Student Affairs Officer's Perspective" in Chapter 7) calls "knowing what you don't know." For a good part of her career, Hetherington was a financial aid officer, and she admits that she "reveled in being the resident expert on financial aid." She believed that she knew everything there was to know about helping students get financial aid. But her level of confidence declined when she became dean of student services. She had much to learn, and to do that, she had to "get past the fear of asking the proverbial 'dumb question.'" I think we can all agree that there are fewer dumb questions than there are dumb people who never ask the questions that could increase their knowledge and, thus, their power.

Listening and Communicating

Student affairs has much to contribute to the overall mission of the institution. Just knowing that your own unit is addressing its goals and helping a lot of students succeed is not enough. Marguerite Culp writes about the need for the effective senior student affairs administrator to educate the entire college about the skill sets in student affairs and to demonstrate that student affairs can help other areas by sharing research on student success. She warns against the seven deadly sins in student affairs that trouble faculty. The only way to know if you are committing any of these sins is to listen and learn.

Larry Roper discusses the need for "multilingual" communication skills. He says being multilingual is possessing the ability "to hear and speak effectively with a wide range of stakeholders and discern important messages from various constituents." Dean Bresciani uses the same word to describe what he sees as the skills and strategies that helped him realize his goals. He offers this example of the need to be multilingual: "Imagine putting a theoretical mathematician, a student development practitioner, a finance administrator, and a legislative analyst in a room and posing one simple question: 'What most predicts the success of the university?' The conversation likely to take place will be a contemporary version of the Tower of Babel."

Referring to the other side of the coin, Gary Kleemann, senior student affairs administrator (emeritus) at Arizona State University, believes that one thing that makes good leaders stand out is their ability to think and act in multiple paradigms. He says, "Student affairs has had a tradition of using language and paradigms not commonly understood by many leaders in the academy outside of student affairs" (G. Kleemann, personal communication, October 17, 2010). In other words, not only must SSAOs have a grasp of the language of other disciplines to communicate, we must also be sensitive to the fact that our own language to describe our work can be a barrier to those who might want to understand and engage.

Victor Boschini, chancellor and professor of education at Texas Christian University, has an interesting and insightful perspective on communicating based on his experiences as a senior student affairs administrator, an associate provost and president of a state university all before becoming chancellor. He says that he has found that as he interacted more with people at the vice president's and provost's levels, he noticed that they "seemed to listen less and talk more." While he did not state the following as a reason for this occurrence, he said that the "main and overriding skill for any senior student affairs administrator is to 'balance egos'—including and especially your own." One consequence of not keeping the ego in balance is talking more and listening less. Chancellor Boschini went on to say that "it's so easy when you become the chief student affairs officer to start believing too much in yourself and too little in the others around you" (V. Boschini, personal communication, November 3, 2010).

The contributors to this book repeatedly emphasize that listening and communicating with faculty and other stakeholders are extremely important, and these are skills to be embraced. Joanna Iwata says that listening to one's staff is equally important, especially in assessing the skills and attitudes of new staff. She speaks of constantly taking the pulse of her staff, doing internal assessments, and meeting with individual staff members to gain information critical for fostering teamwork and moving forward on common objectives. Sarah Westfall echoes this same idea when she talks about a distinguishing characteristic of a small college: "Ongoing contact with early-career professionals as well as more seasoned colleagues is one of the best and most challenging things about a small college."

"Listening hard and asking important questions" is how Shannon Ellis describes this skill. She emphasizes that leadership is a relationship and, to have a relationship, you need to get to know your staff. This builds the trust needed among team members to take the necessary risks for change. Karen Whitney ("Advice From a New President" in Chapter 7) says that as president you have to be "willing to listen and care about others, all day, every day." This sounds like the life and work of student affairs. She sums it up by describing communicating as "telling the story every day, in every way." I believe that some competencies come naturally and others can be learned from books. Exceptional listening and communication skills come from practice.

Functioning in a Large, Networked Universe

Most of the contributors mention looking and leading beyond the boundaries of student affairs. Cynthia Cherrey and Kathleen Allen tell us that "leadership in a networked world can only be understood through a systemic set of actions, not the actions of a lone individual." In addition to the multiple levels and sources of leadership in a networked world, successful leaders will focus on the "big picture, or *the macro-business landscape*, which reveals how you and your organization relate to society and the world at large" (Cummings & Keen, 2008). Barbara Snyder says that value as a leader will be "directly correlated with your ability to see the big picture." This same expanded frame of reference is recommended for success in business. Like Snyder, who acknowledges the leader's responsibility for day-to-day operations, Cummings and Keen warn that "most leaders falter by concentrating on a single landscape, often the organizational landscape, at the expense of others." The big picture, they say, "creates a context for decision making" (2008).

In Chapter 9, James Montoya and Marc Wais pose questions that student affairs leaders might ask themselves to determine whether or not they are global players. These questions may be the first step in thinking about the connections a leader must make. Because of the diversity and globalization of colleges and universities, leaders in higher education have no choice but to be global players. Montoya and Wais note that 35% of entering undergraduates at the University of California, Los Angeles, are non-native speakers of English (University of California, 2008). The implications of such statistics should be priority areas of study for leaders in preparing for the future demographics of higher education.

The ability to understand the significance of a networked world and to generate a big picture are requisite for making optimal connections beyond the borders of the United States. John Laws ("Competencies for the Community College Senior Student Affairs Officer" in Chapter 4) discusses the challenges created by a "world of volatility, uncertainty, complexity, and ambiguity" when he says that the community college SSAO "must see the big picture and the connections." One step toward acquiring these skills is to "think differently about the language and cultural practices used in student affairs work" (ACPA & NASPA, Task Force on the Future of Student Affairs, 2010, p. 9). Thinking differently about language and cultural practices is what Cynthia Cherrey and Kathleen Allen urge when they tell us that protected boundaries will give way in a networked world to blurred boundaries, clearing the way for the creation of connections that will have an effect on the way we work.

Charlene Dukes ("Leading With Vision and Practicality" in Chapter 7) encourages aggressive networking, especially in the community and with local businesses that are stakeholders for the community college. She says, "The success of community colleges depends in many ways on the relationships [college presidents] forge with local constituents—both individuals and organizations." Local constituents remain a priority. At the same time, all of higher education must be in sync with or just ahead of the curve of global trends because students of the future will have many more options for attaining a college education. In strategies to move a college or university forward, the target location and population will be the world, as well as the local community, region, state, or even the nation.

Collaborations, Partnerships, and Relationships

A thread that runs through the competencies required for the kind of leadership that leads to a presidency is relationships, whether they are partnerships or collaborations. Charlene Dukes encourages building partnerships internally and externally; Karen Whitney talks about relationship building; Kathleen Hetherington addresses partnerships; Dean Bresciani calls this skill public relations; and Cliff Wood notes the importance of fostering relationships among members of the cabinet. This competency area is not to be taken lightly. Ellen Heffernan sums it up when she says, "Talented leaders are expected to possess the interpersonal skills that allow them to interact with the widest possible set of constituents and the communication skills to craft a narrative that speaks to those constituents."

Traditionally, for the senior student affairs administrator, the most important constituent other than students is academic affairs. I spoke with David Schwalm, recently retired vice provost for academic affairs and dean of the college at Arizona State University Polytechnic. He thinks the classic problem in higher education is the divide between academic and student affairs, and he believes that the key to eliminating the divide is to build relationships grounded in knowledge of one another. For example, he thinks faculty should become familiar with student development literature to better understand the training and work of student affairs and what is entailed in developing students. And he thinks student affairs professionals should understand that, while they typically must train to become administrators, academic administrators need not. They come up through their discipline and become administrators without the specific intention to do so.

In Schwalm's opinion, the onus is on student affairs administrators to work at the relationship by understanding faculty and becoming skilled at communicating the student affairs point of view. He acknowledges that SSAOs will have to demonstrate what they bring to the academic enterprise, because faculty do not know and most likely will not make the effort to know. One strategy he suggests is for SSAOs to emphasize the wide variety of professional training they have in areas such as business and assessment, to which faculty can relate. Through joint seminars, SSAOs can help faculty understand the work of student affairs. He believes that building relationships around boundary-spanning areas such as student retention is the most likely route to collaboration, partnerships, and relationships between academic and student affairs (D. Schwalm, personal communication, October 4, 2010).

Jerry Jakubowski, provost at The California Maritime Academy, told me that people who are not in student affairs "do not have a clue about the time commitment and breadth of things for which people in student affairs are responsible." He said, "Academic deans still think that the work is all fun and games." He went on to say that SSAOs "need to do a better job of educating others about what their responsibilities are." Jakubowski believes that the role of a senior student affairs administrator varies, depending on the type of institution. When he was at a large university, the SSAO had to see all the university's functions as parts of a machine and then be responsible for creating the kinds of relationships that would "keep the machine well lubricated and running." He talked about his experience with one of these senior administrators and said that being the SSAO is a tough job—to be effective, he or she has to have a wide range of experiences, be firm and consistent with policies, and show respect for students. He said this tightrope-walking is a skill that does not come easily and should not be taken lightly.

Jakubowski thinks the role of the SSAO at a small college or university is more focused on relationship building—with students, faculty, and administrative colleagues. He said that while SSAOs at a small college or university need the same kinds of skills as those at a large institution (knowledge and experience), they are more likely to be judged on how accessible they are to students and how much of a community the campus is. He considers visibility, accessibility, and being well known as the hallmarks of the effective SSAO at a small school (J. Jakubowski, personal communication, September 22, 2010).

This view is reinforced by Sarah Westfall when she says that relationship skills are a key competency for SSAOs in small colleges. In addition to what she calls "human scale" relationships, she says that the successful SSAO at a small college must have a "well-informed institutional perspective." She describes the institutional perspective as the need for the SSAO to care as much about what happens in other units and divisions of the college as you care about your own area. In other words, she says, "good SSAOs focus on the elements that support and advance the work of the institution as a whole."

Whether the SSAO is at a small college in the United States or at a large multicampus research university such as the University of British Columbia, the idea of an institutional focus holds true. Brian Sullivan notes that regardless of the formal responsibility of the SSAO, "there is no escaping the responsibility and opportunity to help shape the new undergraduate and graduate classes, affect retention as they progress through the institution, and encourage positive affiliation as alumni."

Barbara Snyder sees the senior student affairs administrator as the one to "set an example of reaching out to another area on campus to partner on initiatives." She cites a relationship she initiated with the director of athletics at the University of Utah, which has promoted successes and been enjoyable as well. Shannon Ellis encourages collaborative and team-centered leadership, regardless of whether the president facilitates this approach. As an institutional leader, even a new SSAO can take responsibility for communicating and supporting the work of other senior colleagues.

You might ask how to provide such support. Authors who have written about entrepreneurial leadership suggest that one way to support colleagues is to learn all you can about their work, "even in the most unlikely corners of our campuses and communities." Once we gain this knowledge, we must "determine how we can contribute to their work" (Newman, Olson, Laws, & Whitney, 2010, p. 18). But collaboration is not an end in itself; it should be purposeful and ideally mutually beneficial. Even if there is no immediate or direct payoff for your area, the fact that you have supported a colleague positions you and your area for future beneficial partnerships, as well as credit on your side of the ledger (just in case someone is keeping track).

Marguerite Culp cites examples of what some highly effective SSAOs have done to forge partnerships and foster collaborations. In reading these accounts, one can feel the passion of these leaders as they pursued relationships that directly or indirectly supported the academic success of students.

James Appleton writes almost apologetically about passion. I wonder if he mentions passion last because he was debating whether or not to include it. In fact, he even says that perhaps he should have used the word "enthusiasm." Thank you, Jim, for calling it what it is. His passion for making opportunities for students came from his feelings of gratitude for his own privileges, such as being in the military, going to graduate school, being mentored, and having a career in higher education. It is this passion that motivated him to leave his well-earned retirement to return to the position of president of the University of Redlands in California. Many colleagues will look at his return to university administration and nod in agreement as he describes passion as an "emotion that can exceed reason." How could anyone not want to collaborate with him on his goals for students?

In *High Altitude Leadership* (2008), Chris Warner and Don Schmincke apply mountaineering concepts to executive and leadership training. They describe their experiences on a Himalayan expedition, where they noticed that the team faltered not on the way to the peak but on the way back down. They learned that it was the challenge that energized and sustained the group—on the way up, there was always a leader, pumping the team up with enthusiasm. To test their theory, Warner and Schmincke toured military operations as guests of the secretary of defense. They saw the same concept in action: that people needed something worth fighting for. They concluded that "whether you're commanding an army, summiting a mountain, or leading a team, passion is the critical factor" (p. 38).

Many of the contributors cited being passionate and inspiring as essential competencies. Passion coupled with reason inspires collaborations, partnerships, and relationships.

Innovation and Creativity

"Entrepreneurial ambition, which used to be regarded in academe as a necessary evil, has become a virtue" (Kirp, 2003, p. 4). In NASPA's management magazine, *Leadership Exchange*, student affairs leaders note that whether we call it innovation, creativity, or entrepreneurial leadership, such thinking "must become a part of our language, our being, and our organizational culture" (Newman et al., 2010, p. 17). They define entrepreneurial leadership as the "directed application of innovation" and assert that "this model of leadership can provide much-needed new energy and focus to the SSAO role in the years ahead" (p. 17).

Recognizing the impact of tough economic times and restricted budgets, Larry Moneta and Michael Jackson encourage SSAOs to become entrepreneurs who start or expand "business enterprises that can replace or supplement unrestricted dollars from the college or university." Brian Sullivan endorses this notion when he says, "There is a greatly heightened expectation that business practices will be progressive and nimble, and that responses to important new demands and requirements will be met through innovative revenue generation and expense sharing."

On December 2, 2009, IBM had face-to-face conversations with 1,500 of the most successful CEOs worldwide and some students from their countries. IBM published the findings from these conversations in *Capitalizing on Complexity*. In similar conversations two years earlier, the leaders said that their major challenge was "change." They talked about the "change gap," which is the difference between the change they expected and their ability to handle it. Today, the CEOs feel more confident about dealing with change, but they identified a new dilemma: Their biggest challenge now is a "complexity gap." When they were asked to list the three most important leadership qualities required to deal with the complexity gap, CEOs and students selected creativity more often than any other quality (IBM Corporation, 2010, p. 24).

Shannon Ellis defines "strategic" in a way that emphasizes innovation and creativity, and she warns against limiting oneself because of a lack of resources. She sees these challenges as a way to discover "opportunities for student affairs in any environment."

I like the way Laurence Smith defines "innovation" as the bridge between creativity and change. He describes a phenomenon that many of us have experienced—that of the staff star who does not follow through successfully on his or her brilliant ideas. He explains that the person who has the idea might not be the best person to implement the change. In fact, the expectation that the person with the idea will have to be the change agent may actually keep people from bringing forward their ideas for fear of having to implement the changes.

Yash Gupta, professor and dean of the Carey Business School at Johns Hopkins University, echoes Smith's observation when he says that entrepreneurs "tend to be people with big ideas and big passion; they're not very interested in maintenance. They're seed planters, not bean counters" (2010, para. 10). However, leaders must be careful about the perception that the innovators are a breed apart and that those who are not innovators are "bureaucratic," "robotic," "rigid," "satisfied," "staid," "dull," "decaying," "controlling," and "just plain old." This kind of dynamic on a staff can derail what could be an unstoppable team. The leader's role is to help everyone understand that while the innovation is being brainstormed, pilot-tested, and implemented, other staff members are keeping the shop running. The exceptionally effective SSAO listens and communicates well to foster collaboration among the innovators and those who are "responsible for sustaining excellence in ongoing operations" (Govindarajan & Trimble, 2010, para. 6). Cynthia Cherrey and Kathleen Allen reinforce the notion that innovation is increased through collaboration.

I didn't know what direction the conversation would take when I spoke with David Markee, retired chancellor of the University of Wisconsin–Platteville, about what he saw as the competencies of an exceptionally effective SSAO. He began his career as a director of student life and pursued graduate work to prepare to become a senior student affairs administrator at a community college. As he looked back over his career, he realized that what might have contributed most to his success was that he "did a lot of creative things" (D. Markee, personal communication, October 20, 2010). He said that successful administrators look for initiatives that enhance the areas in which the institution is most proud. He believes in finding niches that can be expanded, such as focusing on enrollment or other areas that bring recognition to the institution. Most institutions care about enrollment, and whether the formal organizational structure makes student affairs responsible for enrollment or not, it is an area that will see drastic changes in the future. Demographic forecasts tell us that the growth area for enrollment will be the adult population, which has traditionally been on the margins of enrollment planning (U.S. Department of Education, Task Force on the Future of Higher Education, 2006). This same realization was cited in *Envisioning the Future of Student Affairs*. "Student affairs professionals must become more skillful in working with diverse learners and more attentive to policies that create barriers for those who may not fit the traditional image of a college student or of how college is experienced" (ACPA & NASPA, Task Force on the Future of Student Affairs, 2010).

If your institution wants to attract its market share of adult students, it will have to make changes in the infrastructure of services and programs for this potential growth population. Larry Moneta and Michael Jackson make a similar point in regard to the "... rapid expansion of online degree programs and virtual universities that provide low cost and increasingly good quality educational programs. . . ." Being on the cutting edge of preparing for these students is one way of creating a niche that adds value for students and for the entire institution.

Students' desire to access their education from remote locations is not new; what is new are the improvements in the technology for online learning and the rapid spread of remote learning. "Enrollment in distance education courses nearly quadrupled between 2000 and 2007" (Van Der Werf & Sabatier, 2009, p. 37). With the increasing demand for online courses across all disciplines, there is a concomitant need for services for these students. If there is an undefended niche to own, it is to create models for exemplary online student services.

Another example of a niche that can be expanded is leadership in global education. James Montoya and Marc Wais see the globalization of the university as a unique opportunity for the senior student affairs administrator to "collaborate with partners in the academy and the university's central administration to create a climate that supports the preparation, experience, and reacclimation of globally competent students, as well as student affairs staff." The authors see this area as wide open for leadership and partnerships throughout the academy.

Reflecting on David Markee's advice to look for innovations that enhance the areas the institution is most proud of, it is obvious that attracting larger numbers of international students has many advantages, especially in a climate where "other countries have become more competitive in attracting international students who would have traditionally studied in the United States" (Van Der Werf & Sabatier, 2009, p. 44).

Attracting international students is not as easy as it might have been in the past, and the "resources required for marketing in new international markets are simply too great for most colleges to be able to afford" (p. 47). As we know, the best and least expensive kind of marketing is word of mouth. What added value can student affairs create that will set your college or university apart as a destination for international students?

Innovation is a skill that can be learned. Dyer, Gregersen, and Christensen (2009) studied the habits of innovative entrepreneurs and surveyed more than 3,000 executives and 500 individuals who created innovative companies. From this work, they identified five "discovery skills" that distinguish the innovators from the rest of the crowd. Not everyone wants to be an innovator, but everyone who wants to can, by practicing these skills:

- **Associating:** Successfully connecting seemingly unrelated questions, problems, or ideas from different fields creates a central backbone upon which innovators tie all the other activities together.
- **Questioning:** Ask "Why?" and "Why not?" and "What if?"
- **Observing:** Act like anthropologists and social scientists in scrutinizing common phenomena.
- **Experimenting:** Construct interactive experiences and try to provoke unorthodox responses to see what insights emerge. (Living and working internationally is a powerful way to experiment.)
- **Networking:** Go out of the way to meet people with different ideas and perspectives. (Dyer et al., 2009)

Applying these discovery skills to student affairs work will be a priority competence for the new generation of SSAOs. No longer can innovation be a once-in-a-while phenomenon or the bailiwick of one person. It must be integrated throughout the college or university to meet the new expectations in higher education.

This approach is recommended by Maria Azua (2010), who refers to the "lighter touch" of leadership in the "social age." She stresses the acceptance of different communication styles as the key to encouraging innovation: "Highly productive innovation teams in this paradigm are guided as much by peer pressure and a desire to showcase each member's contribution as they are by organizational status and financial rewards." These kinds of incentives to innovate cannot be controlled from the top, as Cynthia Cherrey and Kathleen Allen so clearly show in their comparison of a hierarchical world and a networked world.

Innovative leaders are the change we need in higher education, because "to one degree or another, *every* company these days is virtual, horizontal, innovative, and adaptive" (Malone, 2009, p. 21). Though colleges and universities occupy their own niche, they must take some strategies from business as more and more families see themselves as customers who are weighing the costs and benefits of a college degree. Exceptionally effective student affairs administrators will build teams that can respond to students and to the challenging dynamics of a new era.

You might ask for one good reason why you need to be innovative if you are doing your job well already. The most obvious reason to me is that what we do now for our current population of students will not be sufficient for the students of the future. Research on students in the college of the future (i.e., the next decade) concludes that "Higher education will become a more retail-based industry than it ever has been. The students of the future will demand it. Many colleges have a long way to go before they can fulfill that demand" (Van Der Werf & Sabatier, 2009, p. 53). Heifetz, Grashow, and Linsky (2009) capture the idea of adaptation and the future: "Executives today face two competing demands. They must execute in order to meet today's challenges. And they must adapt what and how things get done in order to thrive in tomorrow's world. They must develop 'next practices' while excelling at today's best practices" (para. 13).

Throughout this book, there is general consensus on some specific areas of expertise that future leaders should master. Innovation and creativity is one of these areas. However, while our authors value this skill in an exceptionally effective SSAO, I think it is incumbent on me to caution that innovation and creativity in a vacuum could be a formula for disaster. Our authors all believe that an effective leader is aware of interdependent systems and understands how to think and act strategically within these systems—through relationships, partnerships, and collaborations. Thinking and acting strategically can also be called political savvy, emotional intelligence, street smarts, or creating and retaining trust. In any case, a leader must win the support and engagement of a large percentage of the community to stick with the innovation or change long enough to sustain and institutionalize it. Everyone seems to agree that we need innovation and change in higher education. The debate is generally between those who believe that positive results will win over the naysayers and those who work hard to ensure that everyone who will be affected by the innovation or change feels ownership of the new direction.

Those who ascribe to the *proof is in the pudding* or the *data show* philosophy have often been able to use money as leverage to move people along, because it seems that the new golden rule is "the person with the gold gets to make the rules" (Pfeffer, 2010, p. 87). However, in the current and likely future economic climate, money will not be the only source of leverage. To avoid disillusionment or embarrassing failure when you can't get a brilliantly creative idea off the ground, you must identify some viable points of leverage. Fortunately, by virtue of the role and portfolio of the senior student affairs administrator, you can tap a most significant source of power: "access to information or influential people" (p. 87). To access this power, you will have to be an institutional leader, not just a leader in student affairs. Institutional leaders contribute to issues in significant ways by sharing information and rallying the community to support the direction the college or university should take. Being an institutional leader from student affairs is a powerful position if you understand what James Appleton means by "the right use of power." He brings clarity to the debate on how best to lead change, innovate, and make things happen. Initiating action and sustaining it to meet personal goals and institutional objectives is what the exceptionally effective leader does.

While some people are still debating whether student affairs is a profession and whether professionals in student affairs are educators, innovative leaders will be broadening their portfolios to occupy unattended niches in the institution's new environment.

Integrating our experience with our knowledge is what sets student affairs professionals apart, and addressing problems creatively is second nature to us. Student affairs professionals are known for their flexible, responsive, and creative way of thinking. How many times have you been in a situation where there was a snafu and you or someone else in student affairs piped up, "No problem. We're in student affairs. We can make this work?" Don't lose sight of these important characteristics as you ascend the ladder of leadership.

CONCLUSION

In reflecting on the richness of the advice in this book, I realize that all the contributors have done what is supposedly impossible: They have held two opposing thoughts in mind as they have advised you. They encourage you to strive for the ideal, but, at the same time, they hope that you will excel in your current environment. There is much speculation about what the future holds, but we can all agree on two things: (1) the world will be increasingly more complex, and (2) the decisions we make today will have an effect on how well we do in the unknowable future.

Cynthia Cherrey and Kathleen Allen describe the complexity of a networked system; other authors speak of coming contextual challenges, and it is clear that a new day has dawned regarding the requirement for data. Respecting human differences, standing up for social justice, and doing the best work possible stream through the suggestions contributors make in this book.

If I could take just two ideas to guide me in becoming an exceptionally effective leader, I would try to capitalize on the opportunities of increasing complexity in higher education, and I would keep as a mantra what James Appleton calls "visions of the possible." If you are reading this book, there is a good chance that you are already effective in your current role, are the kind of person who believes in continuous improvement, and work with a purpose larger than personal gratification. You are what businesses call a "standout performer," positioning yourself "to mitigate complexity and even convert it into an opportunity" (IBM Corporation, 2010, p. 20).

References

American College Personnel Association (ACPA) & National Association of Student Personnel Administrators (NASPA), Joint Task Force on Professional Competencies and Standards. (2010). *ACPA/NASPA professional competency areas for student affairs practitioners.* Retrieved from http://www.naspa.org/programs/prodev/ ACPA-NASPA%20Professional%20Competency%20Areas-Preliminary%20Version.pdf

ACPA & NASPA, Task Force on the Future of Student Affairs. (2010). *Envisioning the future of student affairs.* Retrieved from http://www. naspa.org/consolidation/TF_final_narr.pdf

Azua, M. (2010, March–April). The social factor: Innovate, ignite, and win through mass collaboration and social networking. *Wharton Leadership Digest, 14*(5–6). Retrieved from http://leadership. wharton.upenn.edu/digest/03-10.shtml#The_Social_Factor:_ Innovate,_Ignite,_and_Win_Through_Mass_Collaboration_and_ Social_Networking

Cummings, T., & Keen, J. P. (2008, May). The leadership landscape perspective: Reframing leadership. *Wharton Leadership Digest, 12*(7). Retrieved from http://leadership.wharton.upenn.edu/digest/05-

08.shtml#The_Leadership_Landscape_Perspective:_Reframing_Leadership

Dyer, J. H., Gregersen, H. B., & Christensen, C. M. (2009, December). The innovator's DNA. *Harvard Business Review.* Retrieved from http://www.hbr.org

Govindarajan, V., & Trimble, C. (2010, July–August). Stop the innovation wars. *Harvard Business Review.* Retrieved from http://www.hbr.org

Guggenheim, D. (2010). *Waiting for superman.* Hollywood, CA: Paramount Pictures.

Gupta, Y. (2010, June 13). Facebook's leadership: Time for an update? *Washington Post,* Retrieved from http://www.washingtonpost.com

Heifetz, R., Grashow, A., & Linsky, M. (2009, July–August). Leadership in a (permanent) crisis. *Harvard Business Review.* Retrieved from http://www.hbr.org

IBM Corporation. (2010). Capitalizing on complexity: Insights from the global chief executive officer study. Retrieved from http://www-935.ibm.com/services/us/ceo/ceostudy2010/index.html

Keeling, R. P. (Ed.). (2004). *Learning reconsidered: A campus-wide focus on the student experience.* Washington, DC: ACPA & NASPA.

Kirp, D. L. (2003). *Shakespeare, Einstein, and the bottom line: The marketing of higher education.* Cambridge, MA: Harvard University Press.

Lipka, S. (2010, June 13). Student services in outside hands. *Chronicle of Higher Education.* Retrieved from http://www.chronicle.com

Malone, M. S. (2009). *The future arrived yesterday: The rise of the protean corporation and what it means for you.* New York, NY: Crown Business.

Newman, E., Olson, T., Laws, J., & Whitney, K. (2010, Fall). Leadership reconsidered: SSAOs as entrepreneurial leaders of the future. *Leadership Exchange, 8*(3), 16–23.

Palmer, P. J. (2000). *Let your life speak: Listening for the voice of vocation.* San Francisco, CA: Jossey-Bass.

Pfeffer, J. (2010, July–August). Power play. *Harvard Business Review.* Retrieved from http://www.hbr.org

Rousseau, J. J. (1923). *The social contract and discourses* (G. D. H. Cole, Trans.). London, England: J. M. Dent & Sons.

Seibert, K. W., & Daudelin, M. W. (1999). *The role of reflection in managerial learning: Theory, research, and practice.* Westport, CT: Quorom.

University of California. (2008). *The University of California undergraduate experience survey.* Retrieved from http://www.universityof-california.edu/studentsurvey

U.S. Department of Education, Task Force on the Future of Higher Education. (2006). *A test of leadership: Charting the future of U.S. higher education.* Retrieved from http://www2.ed.gov/about/bdscomm/list/hiedfuture/reports.html

Van Der Werf, M., & Sabatier, G. (2009). *The college of 2020: Students.* Washington, DC: Chronicle Research Services.

Warner, C., & Schmincke, D. (2008). *High altitude leadership: What the world's most forbidding peaks teach us about success.* San Francisco, CA: Jossey-Bass.

Appendix

Index

In page references, *f* indicates figures and *t* indicates tables.